Language Creativity

Language Creativity

A Semiotic Perspective

Simone Casini

Foreword by Marcel Danesi

Afterword by Frank Nuessel

LEXINGTON BOOKS
Lanham • Boulder • New York • London

Published by Lexington Books
An imprint of The Rowman & Littlefield Publishing Group, Inc.
4501 Forbes Boulevard, Suite 200, Lanham, Maryland 20706
www.rowman.com

6 Tinworth Street, London SE11 5AL, United Kingdom

Copyright © 2020 The Rowman & Littlefield Publishing Group, Inc.

Lina Riccobene's unpublished poem *Cch'è simpaticu 'stu 'taliese* written in 2020 is printed with permission.

All rights reserved. No part of this book may be reproduced in any form or by any electronic or mechanical means, including information storage and retrieval systems, without written permission from the publisher, except by a reviewer who may quote passages in a review.

British Library Cataloguing in Publication Information Available

Library of Congress Cataloging-in-Publication Data

Names: Casini, Simone, 1982- author. | Danesi, Marcel, 1946- author of foreword. | Nuessel, Frank, author of afterword.
Title: Language creativity : a semiotic perspective / Simone Casini ; foreword by Marcel Danesi ; afterword by Frank Nuessel.
Description: Lanham : Lexington Books, 2020. | Includes bibliographical references and index. | Summary: "This book considers the concept of linguistic creativity in relation to contact languages and language educational. The perspective proposed places semiotic creativity to the rank of first principle, by which languages are defined, function, and interact"—Provided by publisher.
Identifiers: LCCN 2020038377 (print) | LCCN 2020038378 (ebook) | ISBN 9781793634269 (cloth) | ISBN 9781793634276 (epub) ISBN 9781793634283 (pbk)
Subjects: LCSH: Creativity (Linguistics) | Psycholinguistics. | Semiotics.
Classification: LCC P37.5.C74 .C375 2020 (print) | LCC P37.5.C74 (ebook) | DDC 401/.9—dc23
LC record available at https://lccn.loc.gov/2020038377
LC ebook record available at https://lccn.loc.gov/2020038378

Contents

A Note on the Cover	vii
Foreword by Marcel Danesi	ix
Acknowledgments	xvii
Introduction	1
1 A Creative *System?* Of Signs Named Language	15
2 Language and Game Are Typical Creative Activities	29
3 The Language between *Rule-Governed* and *Rule-Changing Creativity*	47
4 Educational Linguistics: From Education to Language Creativity	65
5 Open Questions for Semiotic Creativity	85
Conclusion	123
Afterword by Frank Nuessel	135
References	137
Index	149
About the Author	155

A Note on the Cover

When, in 1512, Michelangelo finally completed the ceiling fresco of the Sistine Chapel, which is considered one of the most famous works in the history of art, the cardinals responsible for the care of the works remained for hours to look at and admire the magnificent fresco. After the analysis, they met with the master of the arts, Michelangelo, and, unashamedly, they fired back: "Do it again!"

The discontent, of course, was not for the whole work, but for a detail, seemingly not important. Michelangelo had drawn the *Creation of Adam* with the fingers of God and Adam touching. The cardinals asked that there be no touch, but that the fingers of both be kept separate and that God's finger be always stretched to the maximum, yet that Adam's finger contract the last phalanx. A simple detail but with a surprising meaning: God is there, but the decision to look for him depends on man. If man wants, he will stretch his finger and reach God; however, not wanting, he can spend a lifetime without looking for Him. The last phalanx of Adam's contracted finger therefore represents free will. It represents human *Creativity*.

Foreword

Linguistic Creativity: Simone Casini's In-Depth Analysis of a Controversial Notion

Marcel Danesi
University of Toronto

Ever since Noam Chomsky put forth his notion of linguistic creativity as a rule-governed and rule-changing ability involved in how we generate well-formed linguistic structures, it has become a key, controversial notion in linguistics. As Simone Casini argues in great detail in this book, the notion is of central importance to any cohesive analysis of language in all its dimensions, from the structural to the conceptual and the aesthetic. It is one of the first comprehensive studies on creativity *per se* within linguistics, semiotics, and cognitive science generally.

However it is defined, *creativity* involves the ability to conjure up something new and valuable in the mind through some preexistent code—language, music, and so on. Among its manifestations are the ability to make analogies, establish associations, to connect elements of experience to each other, to make inferences and hunches, and the like, in order to express or produce something that has perceived value intellectually, socially, and aesthetically. Creativity manifests itself in specific ways in all domains of human activity, from poetry to scientific theories and technological innovations. But pinning down what *creativity* means has turned out to be an impossible task; it crops up in so many forms that it defies explanation, even though it is likely to have an underlying neurological source involving a blend of imagination and logic that is unique among species. All that can be said is that creativity is a universal faculty of mind that allows us to bring something into existence that was not there beforehand, at least *not in the same way or form*. This implies that it is part and parcel of the human brain, either as a specific area within it or, more likely, spread throughout the brain's various modules.

One of the first philosophers to deal with the innatism of certain faculties was Plato, who asked: How it is that children, whose contacts with the world are brief and limited, are able to speak and comprehend linguistic utterances spontaneously, with no training whatsoever? He concluded that the only plausible answer to this question was that language was an innate faculty, and that an actual language, such as Greek, is something that the individual child constructs through the innate faculty. Chomsky referred to Plato's perspective as the "Poverty of the Stimulus" explanation, claiming further that this implies the presence of a language organ, and that the environment in which a child is reared provides only the conditions for activating the organ so that the child can build the specific language grammar required. The environment thus constrains only the ways in which the language faculty is realized physically to produce a specific grammar. In effect, the child comes equipped biologically to deduce the latter from the former.

The innate faculty for language, Chomsky maintained, is characterized by what he called a Universal Grammar (UG), which is the blueprint on which all specific language grammars are built. The presence of the UG in the brain at birth would thus explicate why children learn to speak so naturally without any concrete training. Now, the UG is not a grammar in the normal sense of the word, but a set of rule-making principles that are available to all children, hence the universality and rapidity of language acquisition across cultures. So, when the child learns one fact about a language in some context, the child can easily infer other facts without having to learn them one by one. The latter are specific rule types, called "parameters," that the child creates from the rule-making principles. So, creativity in this theoretical framework implies the ability to deduce the rules of a language grammar on the basis of the principles in the UG. While this is, admittedly, a reductive assessment of UG theory, it is nonetheless true that creativity in this model is seen as a parameter-setting ability based on the brain's pattern-identification capacity; with other forms of creativity, such as poetry, seen from outside of the purview of linguistic competence *per se*.

There are many problems with this model of language that Casini tackles head on, even though they are well known across the cognitive sciences. One of these is that, no matter how we formulate linguistic creativity in grammatical (rule-based) terms, there is an interconnection between the language faculty and the environment in which it is activated that involves other modes of processing language input, such as analogy and metaphor. In the end, the innatist argument of how language is acquired is based on a logical inference. We will never really know what creative processes are involved other than to observe how children create analogical structures in their speech and what these might entail neurologically.

The concept of creativity as such is not found in antiquity. However, there are allusions to this faculty, as Casini discusses in an in-depth fashion. Scholarly interest in creativity as a unique human state of mind became a target of investigation in early psychology only after the Renaissance and then the Enlightenment, both of which assigned great value to human qualities. Since then, the concept has become a central one across various disciplines, from philosophy to cognitive science and education. A major problem that has surfaced from the study of creativity is the following one: What is the difference, if any, among creativity, discovery, and invention? In actual fact, these notions are often blended together and assigned to the operation of an all-embracing faculty—the *imagination*. But, then, what is the imagination? Obviously, a certain dose of circular reasoning is involved, making it very difficult indeed to pin down any differences. Aware of the presence of such ambiguity, Casini looks at the various traditions involved in utilizing the notion of creativity, implicitly or explicitly, from antiquity to today. His main implication is that the only viable way to come to grips with this notion is through illustration—that is, to identify how it has been envisioned historically and what examples of creativity can be utilized to penetrate its operation.

It is relevant to note that *What Is Mathematics?* was the title of a significant book written for the general public by Richard Courant and Herbert Robbins in 1941. Their answer to this question was an indirect one; they illustrated what mathematics looked like and what it does, allowing us to come to our own conclusions as to what creativity in mathematics is. And perhaps this is the only possible way to answer the conundrum of creativity. The same can be said about musical creativity. The best way to answer *What is music?* is to play it, sing it, or listen to it. Casini actually takes the same approach in a key chapter of his book, exemplifying how immigrant Italians living in Ontario, in various generations of immigration, have used their linguistic creativity to come up with their particular koiné—a blend of English, native dialect, and Italian to construct hybrid linguistic models of their new social realities. So, like Courant and Robbins did for mathematics, Casini illustrates a product of linguistic creativity, such as how immigrant speakers adapt their native phonetic and grammatical mechanisms to create new forms via borrowing and nativization. The primary reason why nativized loanwords are so plentiful in immigrant community languages is that people require them in order to refer to the objects and ideas in the new physical and social environment. Lacking an appropriate native word for *mortgage*, for instance, immigrants are forced to adopt the English word and make it their own linguistically— hence, *morgheggio*. The phonetic and grammatical mechanisms of Italian are of course operative here, but the fact that the speakers invented the word literally *ex nihilo* on the basis of these mechanisms is, nonetheless, a clear example of a creative act.

Another aspect that emerges from reading Casini's book, although not stated explicitly, is the following: Are there levels and degrees of creativity within any specific sphere of life? Is Mozart more creative in music than, say, a Broadway composer? Obviously, this is a moot question that can never be resolved in any real psychological sense. The question is more a matter of aesthetics and emotional reactions that cannot be quantified in any real way as the basis for developing a theory of creativity. By and large, creativity is seen within the cognitive sciences as a form of intuitive or imaginative thinking that is guided by the experience of recurring patterns in the world. Psychologist Robert Sternberg conducted empirical research, starting in the 1980s, which suggested that creativity is based on three main processes: (1) the ability to recognize that new information has relevance; (2) the establishment of a nonobvious relationship between the new information and previous experience; and (3) the assemblage of the new pieces of information into novel ideas. Still, this does not explain creativity *per se*, but rather how the mind handles information creatively.

As mentioned, ancient cultures lacked the notion of creativity, seeing art and mathematics, for instance, as a form of discovery, not a result of creativity. There were no terms in ancient languages to refer to creativity, as we now envision it. The Greeks had the expression *poiein* ("to make"), which they applied to *poiesis* ("poetry") and to the *poietes* ("maker of the poem"). However, as Casini documents in rather substantive detail, the same notion was implicit in many other ancient philosophies and, although overlapping with the notion of creativity, was not coincident with it. As Casini cogently argues, the modern concept of creativity starts in the Renaissance (as mentioned above), culminating in the Enlightenment as a unique human quality—possessed in large by original artists, scientists, writers, and thinkers. This idea of creativity as the source of originality in the arts and sciences became a central one in the Enlightenment and Romantic periods, leading to the first scientific studies of creativity by the end of the nineteenth century. It was Wilhelm Wundt (founder of the first "laboratory" of experimental psychology in 1879 in Leipzig) who followed up on Darwin's suggestion that humans and animals are linked by evolution and that consciousness can be studied as an organic principle of life. Wundt's laboratory inspired universities in Europe and America to set up similar programs in psychology. Among his students were Edward Titchener and James Cattell, both of whom are now considered early founders of the discipline alongside Wundt. One of the most important insights put forward by Wundt was that the mind was not only a product of evolution, but also of culture. Wundt also studied how people processed proverbial language, seeing figurative language as a creative force in speech and understanding. By the mid-1950s, the scientific study of creativity became widespread among the cognitive sciences, including linguistics; this was due especially to Noam Chomsky who, in his foundational 1957 work for generativism, *Syntactic Structures*, defined linguistic creativity as syntactic capacity and the ability to generate "all grammatically possible utterances." A decade later, in *Aspects of the Theory of Syntax* (1965), he formally defined linguistic creativity as "the speaker's ability to produce new sentences that are immediately understood by other speakers." Linguistic creativity thus consisted in the ability to control a system of rules and rule-making principles that allow for the generation of an infinite class of symbol combinations and permutations with their formal properties.

Leaving aside the critiques to this theory, and subsequent modifications to it, it is the work in cognitive semantics—spearheaded initially by George Lakoff in the late 1970s—which shows that creativity and syntactic generation are hardly one and the same. Rather, it manifests itself in the unconscious ability to link domains of meaning figuratively, thus creating novel thoughts through metaphor at all times. This view dovetailed with the birth of so-called embodied cognition and the notion of *autopoiesis*, traced initially to the 1973 book by Humberto Maturana and Francisco Varela, *Autopoiesis and Cognition: The Realization of the Living*. This is the view that physical (organic) systems themselves adjust to change beyond any human description of such changes as changes in rule systems. So, in the case of human language, it is insufficient to study linguistic information transfers solely as syntactic structures. It is in the linkages we make instantly between words, meanings, and other interpretive structures that the human brain somehow is capable of gaining a unique form of understanding.

Casini's book is timely, given the ever-growing significance of creativity in all the cognitive sciences. By taking us on a journey into the philosophical origins of the notion, even if it was not conceptualized as such in antiquity, Casini explicates in an erudite fashion how the different approaches to creativity in disparate works are not necessarily incompatible. The crux of the debate revolves around the meaning of *rule* in language: Is it innate or is it created according to need? One aspect that he delves into deeply is the traditional alternative to generativism, namely linguistic relativity, which traces its roots to Wilhelm von Humboldt in the nineteenth century—the century that gave birth to linguistics as a scientific enterprise. In the previous seventeenth and eighteenth centuries, the first surveys of languages were conducted, in order to determine which features of language were universal and which were specific, independent of the cultures that spoke them. Prefiguring Chomsky, a group of French scholars known as the Port Royal Circle put forward the idea of a universal faculty of language that provided every different language with the same set of principles from which they could construct their individual grammars. In contrast to this stance, the German scholar Wilhelm von Humboldt viewed language as springing from the historical needs of its speakers and conditioning how subsequent generations came to view reality. Humboldt summarized his viewpoint in his monumental 1836 book, *On Language: The Diversity of Human Language—Structure and Its Influence on the Mental Development of Mankind* (p. 43):

> The central fact of language is that speakers can make infinite use of the finite resources provided by their language. Though the capacity for language is universal, the individuality of each language is a property of the people who speak it. Every language has its *innere Sprachform*, or internal structure, which determines its outer form and which is a reflection of its speakers' minds. The language and the thought of a people are thus inseparable.

This is the first cogent counter-argument to the Port-Royale paradigm. It maintains (in contemporary terms) that languages may have similar rule types in the construction of their grammars; but, the rules only touched the surface of what the faculty of language was all about. Humboldt argued that, below the surface, the rules of a specific language tell a different story than just the logical selection and combination of forms independently of how they relate to reality (Plato's Truth). They reflect an *innere Sprachform* (internal speech form) which encodes the particular perspectives of the people who speak the language. In the first decades of American linguistic structuralism, Edward Sapir (and later Sapir's own student Benjamin Lee Whorf) elaborated the Humboldtian view, suggesting that specific languages filter reality. As is well known, their approach generally falls under the rubric of *linguistic relativity,* the *Sapir-Whorf Hypothesis,* or simply the *Whorfian Hypothesis* (WH). The WH posits that languages predispose their speakers to attend to certain concepts (rather than others found in different languages) as being necessary, without blocking understanding between speakers of different languages. While this orientation is, and always has been, controversial, it has generated a lot of interesting findings, debates, and applications to the present day.

Now, the question becomes: How is creativity possible within the Humboldtian-Sapirean-Whorfian model of language? Those who dismiss it outright are actually reacting to a "strong version" of the model, or the idea that there is no thought without language, just feelings and instincts. This is a valid critique. The strong version is certainly not the one that Casini envisions in von Humboldt, nor is it the one that most linguists adopt. The so-called weak version is much harder to debunk because, as Humboldt aptly observed, the particular language structures of a group of speakers predisposes them to attend to certain concepts as being necessary, and others as not, even though they may exist and be labeled differentially in other languages. This does not imply, however, that people cannot understand each other. Paraphrases convey the various meanings of culture-specific ideas. Moreover, if the need should arise, then we can easily open up language to new categories. In contemporary technological culture, for example, specialized terms for new devices and media (*iPod, tablet, emoji, Facebook, Snapchat,* etc.) are being devised on a daily basis. The proliferation of such terms bears witness to the growing importance of digital technologies in contemporary culture. Not too long ago, a sophisticated terminology for referring to typewriters existed. Most of the terms have virtually disappeared for the simple reason that we do not need them any longer, unless, for example, one is a collector of typewriters as antiques. In a phrase, creative changes in vocabulary mirror changes in society and culture. A similar situation of creative impulse can be seen, as mentioned, in immigrant koinés, as Casini so brilliantly shows in the case of the Italian used in Ontario and which allows speakers to understand their new environment in truly creative ways.

So, what is creativity in language (and other semiotic codes)? The best way to answer this question is to both revisit comprehensively its various definitions in different models of language and to illustrate it in specific cases-in-point. This is what Casini's book accomplishes. As the Russian psychologist Lev S. Vygotsky pointed out in his relevant work on language acquisition, children use their creative resources to make inferences about the world and to construct linguistic forms that are quite similar to the figurative forms created by poets. This is true as well of immigrants coping with new cultural and social conditions. However, in the end, as Ludwig Wittgenstein so aptly put it (and whose ideas Casini examines in detail), it is true that "the limits of my language mean the limits of my world."

Acknowledgments

Language Creativity: A Semiotic Perspective is my first monograph as a single author. It is therefore the result of study and research that has seen me take my first steps in Italian and international academia. It is a work that ends in 2020, but was conceived a few years ago, and which took on from time to time different forms: initially it started as simple notes hastily written during trips between Rome and Siena, and then moved on to more thoughtful and reflective ideas, up to systematic and structured research in libraries and urban realities of different cities of the world spanning from Rome to Tokyo to Toronto.

Language Creativity: A Semiotic Perspective is published with a Canadian passport, but in its veins flows Italian blood: the book was borne in Siena and followed me throughout the years in Viterbo, sometimes with interruptions, other times with accelerations, but always on the front line as something that needed to be concluded. And that conclusion came in Toronto.

A monograph is certainly something personal; creative, I would say considering the object of research, but nevertheless it is also the result of sharing. Reports, relationships, advice, exchanges of thought, models, and views that I shared with some of the people I met in my academic (and personal) journey have all contributed to the final project.

For this, a few thankful considerations are in order. A first thank you to Professor Massimo Vedovelli, for his ability to guide me on the path of method and scientific research which I used to discuss linguistic creativity from the first months of my PhD at the University for Foreigners of Siena and with whom I spent important years of my postdoctoral training.

I owe to Professor Silvana Ferreri the attention with which today I consider the facts of theory as an integral part of a more general, practical, and expendable action, especially in a field such as education. On the human level, the constant encouragement for the book to be concluded was certainly an important sting that started in the years in Viterbo, continued to New York and Toronto, and has been one more source of encouragement to conclude this journey.

At the University of Toronto, I had the opportunity to meet Professors Salvatore Bancheri and Michael Lettieri, whom I thank for welcoming me to a new country and into the new reality, in a way far better than anyone could have expected. From both of my mentors, I have learned styles, models, and behaviors that are certainly life lessons far beyond academic fact. To Professor Bancheri then goes a thank you for the continuous reflections on Italian abroad, on Italiese, on teachings in Canada, and for opening the doors of the Italian community, the Sicilian community, and the Delian community (and in particular, to one of its parts) in Toronto, which represented (and continues to represent) an important reference point in North America.

A particular mention goes to the late Professor Tullio De Mauro, to whom I had the honor of having read some excerpts and rough notes of the volume (and of which I still keep the comments, the precious suggestions, and the forward-looking points).

Alongside my professors there are other people whom I want to thank: Michelle Galati and Jennifer Tatiana Fimognari, both undergraduate students who have taken all my courses held at the University of Toronto Mississauga and who over the years have acquired with dedication, attention, and rigor, a sensitivity to Italian linguistics that I hope can become in them a beacon for the years to come. To them my thanks, extended also to John Lewis, for important work done in the English revision of the text.

Last, *sed non ultimum,* I thank my family, who supported me in the professional choices made in Italy and Canada in order to achieve the goals that I set for myself, supporting me without hesitation and representing a port to be able to dock on days of stormy waters. And in these years, of course, there have been days like this. And then there is Sveva, to whom this book is dedicated.

Introduction

Cogere item pluris unus victosque domare / non poterat, rerum ut perdiscere nomina vellent. / Nec ratione docere ulla suadereque surdis, / quid sit opus facto, facilest; neque enim paterentur / nec ratione ulla sibi ferrent amplius auris / vocis inauditos sonitus obtundere frustra. / Postremo quid in hac mirabile tantoperest re, / si genus humanum, cui vox et lingua vigeret, / pro vario sensu varia res voce notaret?[1]

Titus Lucretius Carus, *De rerum natura*

A reflection on *creativity* could begin by focusing on a distant past, on the beginnings of Western thought. Specifically, it could attempt to reconstruct *ab initio* the philosophical, semiotic, and linguistic foundations for one of the essential questions of human speculation. What does creativity mean? What are its areas of relevance? And what are the developments that this *forma mentis* represents in being the first condition for human understanding and then a linguistic and semiotic property of man used for man?

From the aesthetic point of view, the term creativity is used in many different contexts, becoming today a cause for debate and sometimes misunderstanding. However, one fact is true: only since Romanticism has art benefited from the qualities of creativity. Prior to Romanticism, art had a predominantly negative connotation. The creative artist (or the craftsman, a term that adequately encompasses the functions of a pre-Romantic artist) was an idolater, a magician, a liar, and a creator of false hopes and promises (Givone 2010). Only in the post-Romantic period does art emancipate itself and the artist assume the role of aesthetic creator capable of extending his skills within a framework that defines artistic creativity as something extravagant and inventive. Nevertheless, creativity and creation seem to be intimately intertwined.

There is no sense of creativity that does not start from the concept of creation and, since the concept of creation has Christian origins, it is with Christianity that creativity becomes a thing of man and for man (as well as God).

If we want to define creativity within the global epistemological landscape, we must, therefore, start *ab initio*. This method allows us to examine creativity while analyzing areas and dealing with themes that have accompanied the intellectual (and physical) development of man. For this reason, creativity also has to do with the ethological scope and the phylogenetical development of the human species from the time of *Homo sapiens* and perhaps even *Homo neanderthalensis* (Leroi-Gourhan [1964] 1993).

This book aims to address the specific issue of semiological codes and proposes a theoretical systemization of creativity. To do this, we must circumstantiate the principles and assumptions of creativity within reference models, leaving out everything that is not directly relevant to these, but which inevitably affects them.

Questions regarding creativity underlie the general processes of symbolic management and the adaptation to the different forms of construction of meaning, particularly of the genus *homo*. So much so, indeed, that questions of creativity have represented for much of the twentieth century a peculiar characteristic of linguistic activity *sensu stricto*. The issues of creativity, without a doubt, have to do with language especially when language is conceived beyond its pragmatic function as a communicative tool. In the perspective of analysis and study that we want to undertake, the concept of creativity falls within a framework of reference that goes beyond applicational scopes and comes to a plan that could be defined as cognitive: creativity in this (Kantian and Aristotelian) sense means knowing, or rather, it is a prerequisite for knowledge. "Knowing" means classifying real entities into abstract schemes, which, given the unlimited nature of real things, must necessarily extend beyond the physical similarity to things of the world. Abstract schemes must be constructed through an abstract process, which is necessarily creative (Garroni 1976).

This classification within creatively defined schemes assumes a level of creativity that is at least twofold: first, creativity varies from species to species and what appears to be semi-relevant to one species may not be so for another. In addition, within the same living species, the classification of a class of physically different entities is not affected by the intrinsic characteristics of the entity itself, but is abstractly managed by the subject who classifies, identifies, and then initiates a semiotic process of creation and construction of sense.

Every form of semiosis, including language, therefore presupposes a spark of creativity and of freedom that characterizes the way of life of human beings since the emergence of the concept of language in Aristotle's *Politics*.

Within this vision, we find the social foundations of verbal language conceived not as an instrument of man for the use of man, but as a vital activity necessary to make man part of society. As a foundation of creativity, one can recognize the traces of the subject that processes the outside world by attributing meaning (Garroni [1978] 2010): in this sense, the elaboration of meaning is a cultural operation of pertinence (Prieto 1976) and is a creative and spontaneous operation carried out by the human and nonhuman subjects. The theoretically significant element of this concept is the mental (cultural and identifying) operation which consists of the identification of a semiotic situation (among the infinite available) and arbitrarily attributes meaning to this situation.

If we want to establish a point of conjunction between creativity and the subject, then creativity relates to a science called semantics, and it relates to the relationships between the sets of signs and the fields of content on which the signs are focused. We must inevitably relate to this; that is, to the science that considers the facts of meaning in order to be able to talk about creativity. The question is to define the scope of semantics and its convergence with creativity, where creativity, in some of its manifestations, seems not only to refer to the meaning but also to have profound evidence with the formal construction of each sign. In this case, can we discuss semantics? What are the relationships between semantics and creativity?

The answer to the two questions stems from a quite recent historical reference. We must first remember that toward the end of the experience of logical empiricism and coinciding with the disclosure of Peirce's semiotic theories (1960), semiotics (*semiotics* as a logical-philosophical basis and not *sémiologie*, Saussure's linguistic-communicative basis) as a science that studies the relationships between signs provided a reference framework of research on the language of pre-Saussurian mold. This semiotic conception of language considered semantics interested in the relationship of signs with things; it was a syntactic dedicated to the study of the relationships between signs to which was flanked (albeit marginally) the pragmatic that should investigate the relationship of signs with users. In fact, a reference view of the meaning was reiterated, and the meaning was conceptually separate from the historical socio-identity of the users. A separation was therefore consolidated between the moment of meaning and the moment of use to which the processes of interpretation of the semiotic act persist, but which has marginal and peripheral effects on the meaning. The meaning was given by the thing; the thing was the meaning.

On the other hand, from the linguistic and artificial intelligence sphere came, from the end of the 1950s, a massive attack on semantics (or rather its being part of language as a semiotic perspective) moved by Noam Chomsky, according to which the heart of the functioning of language was found in a syntactic-based generative device and the meanings (semantics) were pushed toward the field of linguistic behavior and were mainly related to the interpretation of grammatical models already realized, repeated, and repeatable.

Faced with the approach of a universal and innate foundation of linguistic behavior and its meaning, the Humboldian conception of creativity, for which the language we speak affects the world we perceive and in which we give meaning to experience, seemed to crumble. In short, in the logical and Chomskian vision, one would have lost the idea of creativity as the structuring of experience and, therefore, of the creativity of meaning.

In this context, the synthesis of the theory and method of Tullio De Mauro—one of the most important linguists and philosophers of language of the twentieth century in Italy and in the world—manages to hold together the instances of semantics (and creativity) without creating a fatal opposition: it denies neither the legitimacy of a formal semantics, nor a formal approach to semantics intended to define the logical components of meaning. The case of languages in which the meanings of the signs are predetermined (as is the case with calculations and signs) and that of verbal language is very distinct. And the creativity that operates in both, in verbal language it does not presuppose an opposition between the two ways in which it is realized, on the one hand in the creative construction (type of union of elements) of the linguistic signs, on the other in the creative construction of meanings from experiences. Creativity is therefore not realized in verbal codes as an opposition between different forms, but is determined in a parallelism devoid of convergences, overlaps, and obstacles that enhance its semiotic function.

To the contrary, in verbal language the idea of an engine carried out by meaning and with it by the historical and social dimension of communication is strengthened. In supporting this distinction, there are reasons we say *de iure*, that is, related to general theoretical issues. Natural historical languages do not seem to be any kind of code. They have a peculiarity that is precisely of a semantic order. It is a variously named feature, the importance of which is characterizing languages compared to other languages and has been defined with the idea of translatability (De Mauro 2019). In practice, a language is a semiotic in which every other semiotics—that is, every other language and any other conceivable semiotic structure—can be translated. This translatability is based on the fact that languages (and languages only) are able to shape any material; in language, and only in language, it is possible to fight against the inexpressible in order to express it (Hjelmslev [1961] 1963).

Since the idea of a *uniquely human* language (Lieberman 1991) has given way to different conceptions in which language is a characteristic of even nonhuman living species (Chomsky *et al.* 2002; Cimatti 2002), with good reason the issues of creativity (and of semantics) could be addressed from different perspectives, considering different languages and different codes. In mathematics, in music, in the figurative arts, in dance, in play: it might make sense to define the contours of creativity in each of these codes, establishing a ranking of greater or less creativity. Or simply establish, for each of these codes, when creative begins and when it becomes habit, practice, and is no longer creative.

To give meaning and order to this writing that looks at creativity from a scientific perspective, with results not only speculative, but empirical, we essentially examine verbal codes and consider issues of creativity related to the processes of communication, understanding, and creation of meaning in languages. We acknowledge that our reflections lack an important aspect of creativity (everything related to the creativity of the nonhuman and nonverbal world) that will be integrated as part of the epistemology of creativity. We continue our inquiry of language according to the lines of semiotic and linguistic analysis introduced in twentieth-century Europe and North America, starting with Saussure's *Course in General Linguistics* before moving to its subsequent exegesis and its previous theoretical references.

LANGUAGE CREATIVITY: A CONFUSED MASS OF HETEROGENEOUS AND UNRELATED THINGS

When Ferdinand de Saussure started working on symbolic codes and inaugurated a new model for modern linguistics, he faced a problem: no single perspective of analysis could characterize the integral object of linguistics against a set of different things. According to this perspective, we do not find the integral object of linguistics anywhere. The object of linguistics is presented as a confused mass of heterogeneous and unrelated things. Either procedure opens to several sciences such as psychology, anthropology, normative grammar, or philology which are distinct from linguistics, but, in view of the faculty methods of linguistics, may claim speech as one of their objects (CGL, 91[2]). Following the Saussurian effort to provide a unified framework to the problem of semiotic creativity, even "simply" in reference to verbal codes, a scholar wanting to limit the semantic field of creativity would find himself in a similar situation. Creativity is "a confused mass of heterogeneous and unrelated things." A 2019 Google web search highlighted over 15 million different results, and is a sign of the growing relevance and human interest regarding everything that is considered to be like *imagination, inventiveness, genius, ingenuity,* or *originality.*

If we consider the lexicography of both Italian and English, we obtain an interesting perspective that certainly limits the number of results, but not the areas of the relevance of creativity. The *English Language Dictionary* (Collins—COBUILD, 2019) describes *creativity* as "the ability to invent and develop new and original ideas," specifying that the area of relevance is predominantly regarding art ("especially in an artistic way"). Nevertheless, if we consider the adjective *creative,* other than its artistic dimension, the second acceptation recalls "the creative use of the language" within a context such as "the use of something in a new and imaginative way to produce interesting and unusual results."

In the Italian context, which represents the semiotic and linguistic fields from which our reflections began, the dictionary *Zingarelli* (2019) defines *creativity* as a "capacity" or an "inventive faculty" of production of "new ideas, inventions, works of art." This first meaning is accompanied by a second, restricted to the linguistic field, for which creativity is "the ability of the speaker to understand and to issue statements that have never been heard before." The noun *creatività* is derived from the adjective that recalls the act of creation. The second sense considers personal qualities: a *creative* individual is someone "who has or reveals the ability to create, who is rich in inventiveness." For example, a *creative child* is one whose personality is shaped by their "creative intelligence" or ingenuity. In Italian there is also a *finanza creativa* (embezzlement), seen as management of resources and goods, that is, "the result of imaginative choices, at the limits of regularity." And a *creative* (noun) in advertising is the one who "proposes the ideas that will lead to the realization of an advertising campaign" and therefore, the *creative* becomes the one who "shows gifts of inventiveness and originality."

The *GRADIT* (Dictionary of the Use of the Italian Language) indicates that the word *creatività* was first reported in 1920 and refers to the "ability to create, to invent" something (e.g., "stimulate creativity in children"). The synonyms of creativity are *inspiration*, *imagination*, and *inventiveness*. The adjective *creativo* has been used since 1406, while *creativo* (as a noun) has been present since 1970 with specialized use in the world of advertising. *Creativo* (and *creative* as well) traces its etymology back to *create*, the first appearance of which dates to 1276. The first accepted addition to the lemma has a generally ontological value: "creating" takes forms including "to give origin, to give rise from nothing: *God created the world.*" *To create*, in this case, is placed in relation to the synonyms *build*, *found*, *devise*, and *invent*.

In the economic sphere, new industries or new jobs are being *created*, including new laws in the legislative area. Similarly, a work of art, scientific discipline, or a figure of speech is also *created*. *Creating* as "origin" means "creating a new family, a new political party." In the economic sphere, you *create* a debt, or you *create* an account; that is, you open it. *To create* is also used figuratively: a behavior can "create embarrassment" or you can create problems or an atmosphere of intimacy. *To create* also means procreating, putting into the world. You can *create* a "knight" or a "prince" in the sense of electing him.

Creativity, therefore, truly is "a confused mass of heterogeneous and unrelated things," especially when we consider comparative lexicography. And if we then consider the verb *create*, our references return to creation from nothing, that is, in an ontological and universalist perspective at the beginning of the deepest forms of life: *In the beginning, God created the heaven and the earth. And the earth was without form and void, and darkness was upon the face of the deep. And the spirit of God moved upon the face of the waters* (Gen 1, 1–2).

This book is part of an attempt, incomplete but functional, to frame creativity with a common thread. We propose a linguistic and semiotic reading that defines the theoretical scope within which creativity may be used as a model to interpret linguistic facts and languages in contact. We aim to investigate the theoretical assumptions of semiotic creativity and the consequences, in terms of linguistic repercussions and the negotiation of sense, determined by contact in the social space. We reference contexts characterized by constant and continuous interaction between speech, language, forms of life, and identity.

Within the linguistic code, creativity is then the theoretical prerequisite for the opening and changing of meaning of derived words and phrases of shared linguistic use. Creativity results in the innovation, manipulation, and change of coded and historically fixed forms, through a process of *rule-changing* and *rule-governed* transformation.

Saussure defined a method of linguistic research that represents a paradigm for semiotic creativity. However, the concept of language on which creativity is based is not Saussurian (Garroni 1977): its theoretical basis recalls Humboldt ([1836] 1988) and the language as ἐνέργεια (*enérgeia*), as an activity that does not use signs already created but is a sign-creating activity in and of itself (Coseriu 1958). Language is an activity, therefore, that manifests itself in the multilingualism of yesterday and today, within the processes of interaction, understanding, and communication between users. Such users move linguistically within a language space, alternating formal and informal styles that potentially do not conform to the linguistic norm. This, for example, happens regularly in language learning and teaching processes.

What is important here is that creativity has a profound philosophical foundation in the concept of ἐνέργεια. This Aristotelian notion, linked to λόγος (*logos*), is attributed to social, political, and generally cognitive values (Coseriu 1958; Di Cesare 1987). According to this principle, creativity is Aristotelian.

Within the framework presented, we study the theoretical assumptions of creativity, its results, having as a theoretical and conceptual reference point the reflections advanced in the Italian field by Tullio De Mauro. Among the works mentioned in this study we consider in particular, but not only,

Minisemantica (1982) *Introduzione alla semantica* (1965), *Senso e significato* (1971), *Scuola e linguaggio* (1981), *Prima lezione sul linguaggio* (2002), and *Educazione linguistica democratica* (posthumous 2018), which study the characteristics—both in a strictly theoretical and semiotic analysis of language use, communication, and mutual understanding processes. According to De Mauro—it is our duty to introduce a fruitful dialogue on the subject of creativity between the two sides of the Atlantic and to the international semiotic landscape.[3]

However, in order to find a starting point, we find that the fundamental meanings of the linguistics and semiotics of creativity must be sought, on the one hand, within the notion of formativity with which Saussure and Hjelmslev eliminate the "superficial notion of the general public" that "people see nothing more than a name-giving system in a language" (CGL, 16). On the other hand, creativity is manifest in the way in which the human species adapts to various social and communicative environments, and therefore, creativity contributes to supporting the operational or cognitive tasks of the human species (Garroni [1978] 2010).

So, creativity is the basis of civil and political life; and if language is the prerequisite for civil and political life, then creativity is the foundation of language.

CREATIVITY: A UNIQUE TYPE OF INTELLECTUAL ORGANIZATION

We read in the *Politics* of Aristotle:

> Every state is as we see a sort of partnership, and every partnership is formed with a view to some good (since all the actions of all mankind are done with a view to what they think to be good). It is therefore evident that, while all partnerships aim at some good the partnership that is the most supreme of all and includes all the others does so most of all and aims at the most supreme of all goods; and this is the partnership entitled the state, the political association. . . .
>
> Again, the object for which a thing exists, its end, is its chief good; and self-sufficiency is an end and a chief good. From these things, therefore, it is clear that the city-state is a natural growth, and that man is by nature a political animal, and a man that is by nature and not merely by fortune citiless is either low in the scale of humanity or above it (like the "clanless, lawless, heartless" man reviled by Homer, for one by nature unsocial is also "a lover of war") in as much as he is solitary, like an isolated piece at draughts. And why man is a political animal in a greater measure than any bee or any gregarious animal is clear. For nature, as we declare, does nothing without purpose; and man, alone

of the animals possesses speech. The mere voice, it is true, can indicate pain and pleasure, and therefore is possessed by the other animals as well (for their nature has been developed so far as to have sensations of what is painful and pleasant and to indicate those sensations to one another), but speech is designed to indicate the advantageous and the harmful, and therefore also the right and the wrong; for it is the special property of man in distinction from the other animals that he alone has perception of good and bad and right and wrong and the other moral qualities, and it is partnership in these things that makes a household and a city-state. (1252a–1253a)

This Aristotelian passage is well known and echoes the fundamentals of the *Ethica Nichomachea* and *De Anima* (*Ethics* and *On the Soul*) in which the linguistic man is considered from a cognitive and behavioral point of view. Man is the most political animal ("in a greater measure than any bee or any gregarious animal") because only man, through the use of words, can choose what is useful or useless, just or unjust, good or bad, true or false. Through the λόγος, the word can move within those categories of values belonging only to linguistic animals, on which the ideas of social institution (from the Greek word πόλις, *polis*) and civil coexistence are founded.

The Aristotelian conception of language is profoundly ontological: it is necessary to bear in mind the decisive importance that this concept has in the construction not only of a political science but of a civic and state order that represents an alternative to Skepticism and is able to condition every principle of science and civil coexistence (De Mauro 1965). Language does not become an instrument of man, for the use of man, for communication with man. Language becomes a vital activity species-specific to man. Distancing yourself from language (putting it back in the toolbox and moving on to other occupations) is as impossible as moving away from the brain, heart, and lungs, and continuing to live (Lo Piparo 2003).

Aristotelian linguistic philosophy assigns to the language made of words a unique cognitive value compared to other activities that man shares or can share with other living beings. In the living human, every act is directly or indirectly dense with linguistic aspects. This Aristotelian lesson has many illustrious followers within modern and contemporary philosophical thought. We consider some that we believe to be functional to the principles of creativity.

Descartes proposed in *L'Homme* (1630–1633) and *Discourse on Method* (1637) a rigid distinction between man—characterized by the presence of a thinking mind (*res cogitans*) with the linguistic ability to express content—and animal (*res extensa*)—absolutely devoid of thought and able to define itself only in the sense of being able to live like a machine (Gensini 2010). Descartes therefore assigns to linguistic ability (together with intellectual and thinking abilities) the power to discriminate man from animal, linguistic being from that which is merely vocal or phonic, but non-linguistic and unthinking:

> Again, by means of these two tests, we may likewise know the difference between men and brutes. For it is highly deserving of remark, that there are no men so dull and stupid, not even idiots, as to be incapable of joining together different words, and thereby constructing a declaration by which to make their thoughts understood; and that on the other hand, there is no other animal, however perfect or happily circumstanced, which can do the like. (*Discourse on Method*, part V, 45)

The Cartesian influence has fed the idea that verbal language is an impassable boundary between humanity and animality, despite it being observed that Descartes did not use language to specifically characterize the human being, but the "reason" for which language was a simple tool. In the contemporary era, as we have briefly mentioned, the myth of the human uniqueness of language has collapsed (Cimatti 2002; Chomsky *et al.* 2002[4]). But we would like to point out that this myth was the basis of Chomskyan linguistics, which examined language and made arguments relevant to our consideration of creativity: Noam Chomsky, whose fundamental contribution to creativity in linguistics will be examined further in chapter 3, declared creativity within a dichotomy between "rule governed" and "rule changing," and in *Cartesian Linguistics* recalled precisely the ethological scope of creativity.

In *Cartesian Linguistics*, creativity becomes the specific capacity of the human species, "a unique type of intellectual organization which cannot be attributed to peripheral organs or related to general intelligence and which manifests itself in what we may refer to as the 'creative aspect' of ordinary language use—its property being both unbounded in scope and stimulus-free" (Chomsky 1966, 60). "Unbounded in scope" and "stimulus-free" represent the two cornerstones of Chomskyan creativity, linked from the beginning to the ability to make infinite use of finite means. This is the basis for the elaboration of a generative and recursive linguistic theory. It is a vision that Chomsky himself refers to Humboldt (*On Language*), Descartes (*Discourse on Method*), and consequently Aristotle (*Politics*), and which takes up an interest in creativity as a property *prima inter pares* (Danesi 2000; De Mauro 1974, 2008; Petrilli and Ponzio 2007).

If it is true that the greater power[5] of languages, when compared to other codes of communication, is a semiotic factor of interaction of the different properties that characterize the languages (De Mauro 1974; Hjelmslev [1961] 1963), then creativity appears to be its true essence. Creativity determines the diversity of codes (and therefore multilingualism) and allows us to address with a new scientific approach the principles of the development of *Homo sapiens*. Creativity is therefore rightly conceived no longer as the single property of codes, but, in fieri, as the possibility of humans changing habits and adapting to the cultural context in which they extend their relationships. It is, therefore, the ability to establish ever new forms of civil coexistence through the possibility of choice and which guarantees (within rules) forms of behavior that are not fixed and determined, but indeterminate and heterogeneous (Garroni [1978] 2010). In this sense, creativity abandons the condition of being "simply" a linguistic property of *inter pares* and becomes a theoretical approach, a model by which to manage and understand the dynamics of meaningful creation in relation to linguistic uses in social contexts.

We therefore place creativity in a particular reference framework, one in which semantic references can be outlined and in which the confusing cluster of heteroclite things mentioned at the beginning of this introduction can be solved through a semiotic approach to the problem of creativity. In this sense, expressions such as *work of art*, *invention*, or *new ideas* do not represent effective synonyms for creativity, unless they too are synonyms for a way of acting and organizing behavior and relationships of individuals within the frameworks of social, civil, and political reality. A creative way is such not because it is new or innovative (never done before). Creativity is the ability to innovate and to find new solutions—an example being the creative intelligence that Clumsy Hans (Klods-Hans) puts in place to win the heart of the daughter of the King of Denmark in Hans Christian Andersen's fable. It is an innate biological endowment, it is an integral part of the overall behavioral endowment of man as an innate capacity[6] in that it allows man to change the established rules and habits by crossing the "limbo" circumscribed between a rule (linguistic, semiotic, or behavior) and its multiple interpretations.

However, creative behavior, a creative act, is not anarchic, but must be included within a context made up of consolidated habits which are nothing else other than linguistic, civil, and social rules. In this sense, creativity is fully enclosed in the way we apply a rule in a particular case. In other words, creativity not only demands the existence of norms but also manifests itself exclusively in their presence, in the semiotic possibility of variation and new interpretation. The result is a significant consonance of thought, precisely in the field of creativity with the Wittgenstein of *Philosophical Investigations* (*Philosophische Untersuchungen, PU*), in which through the analogy between linguistic uses and linguistic games the recourse of rules as elements of subsistence of verbal activity is clarified. But what are the rules of verbal activity? What are the spaces of freedom (of creativity) in which the *animal loquens* follows or does not follow rules of linguistic use, or even modify them, without limiting the very possibility of one's own speech?

These questions are answered through reference to the forms of semiotic creativity that, on the one hand, seem to guarantee the possibilities of communication and understanding because they grant the individual the possibility to choose and the expressive potential capable of creating communication. On the other hand, by virtue of an ever-present possibility of change and disavowal of established uses (of social and semiotic rules), creativity requires the need to always confirm *upon the field* (De Mauro 1982) an understanding between the speakers in order to direct the intercourse of languages. We then follow Wittgenstein, who has made rules of language, and their ability to be edited *as we go along*, the basis of interpretation on which language games rest as the "whole process of using words" (PU §7). In what direction should we proceed between the (linguistic and non-linguistic) paths that open to human choice? Do we follow or ignore the rules or find different interpretations? Wittgenstein seems to anticipate the answers to these questions when he states that "speaking of language is part of an activity, or of a form of life":

> A rule stands there like a signpost.—Does the signpost leave no doubt open about the way I have to go? Does it shew which direction I am to take when I have passed it; whether along the road or the footpath or cross-country? But where is it said which way, I am to follow it; whether in the direction of its finger or (e.g.) in the opposite one?—And if there were, not a single signpost, but a chain of adjacent ones or chalk marks on the ground—is there only one way of interpreting them?—So, I can say, the signpost does, after all, leave no room for doubt. Or rather: it sometimes leaves room for doubt and sometimes not. And now no longer a philosophical proposition, but an empirical one. (PU §85)

This book consists of two sections. We are convinced that issues of language contact in the global world, of using words in communication, language learning, and the daily contexts of interaction, can be explained only if inserted within a theoretical model that can justify concrete facts. In this sense, the volume consists of a first section, essentially theoretical, in which the linguistic and semiotic references of the twentieth century about language, system, sign, linguistic play, arbitrariness, and creativity are reported.

We have made a field choice in the theoretical reconstruction of the semiotic process which, as already highlighted, does not have the ambition to be sympathetic to all the formal semiotic, philosophical, or linguistic theories on creativity, nor of all possible North American and European sources. We privileged a chronological anchor in the twentieth century and an approach in Saussurian linguistics and its critical analysis following the approach provided by Tullio De Mauro in defining the semiotic perimeters of creativity as part of semantic science. The scope of theoretical considerations and their value in the sciences of language make the Italian linguist's reflections an essential reference point for a universal, *ubicumque* scientific approach to the problem of linguistic and semiotic creativity.

The second part proposes an exemplification of the results of creativity, considering some dimensions of linguistic contact but also the general use of words for the creation of meaning in which creativity can represent a theoretical framework of reference to the concrete act.

In the exhibition, the use of technical terms was reduced to the essentials so that the volume could be adapted for different research and educational profiles. The conception of creativity straddling different fields of human knowledge allows an articulated analysis that does not limit its depth and theoretical accuracy, but is an added value.

English translations are used whenever possible. When no published English translation is available, quotations appear in their original language. Such quotations are always followed by a critical reflection in English.

NOTES

1. Likewise, one man could not force, overpower, and triumph over many men, so to make them consent to learn the names of things. And it is not simple to convince the deaf by any device and teach them what they must do; for in no way would they endure or allow strange vocal sounds to thunder meaninglessly upon their ears for a prolonged period of time. Finally, what seems so beautiful in this, if humanity with well-developed voice and tongue should express things by sounds that vary in accordance with the various feelings stimulated by each? (Our translation).

2. From now on, we will use CGL to indicate De Saussure ([1922] 1959) from which we have taken all the citations of the *Course on General Linguistics*. The English translation is of the original French text *Course de linguistique générale*. The English version consulted does not indicate the original pages of the *Course* and therefore we have used the English translation pages by Wade Baskin. For the critical and philological apparatus, we refer to the edition of the *Course* translated into Italian with comments by Tullio De Mauro ([1922] 1967).

3. We consider the texts of Umberto Eco: *A Theory of Semiotics* ([1975] 1976), *The Role of the Reader: Explorations in the Semiotics of Texts* (1979), *Semiotics and the Philosophy of Language* (1984), *The Limits of Interpretation* (1990), *La combinatoria della creatività* (2004).

4. It is important to remember the work by Hauser, Chomsky, and Fitch (2002) as it marks the conclusion of the research inaugurated by *Cartesian Linguistics* in which animal communication is given space within the framework of the FLB (broad language faculty) that represents a cognitive link between animal and man. Man remains the prerogative of the FNL (narrow language faculty), a faculty of language in the strict

sense, consisting of the innate mental device capable of allowing a syntactic and recursive management of verbal activity, an activity (in the strict sense) uniquely human.

5. It is important to consider the power that languages have to give shape to all human knowledge (Hjelmslev [1961] 1963).

6. We read in Garroni ([1978] 2010, 148) "essa è parte integrante della complessiva dotazione comportamentale dell'uomo come una capacità innata."

Chapter 1

A Creative *System*? Of Signs Named Language

Sed cum in eo magnus error esset, quale esset id dicendi genus, putavi mihi suscipiendum laborem utilem studiosis, mihi quidem ipsi non necessarium. Converti enim ex Atticis duorum eloquentissimorum nobilissimas orationes inter seque contrarias, Aeschinis et Demosthenis; nec converti ut interpres, sed ut orator, sententiis isdem et earum formis tamquam figuris, verbis ad nostram consuetudinem aptis. In quibus non verbum pro verbo necesse habui reddere, sed genus omne verborum vimque servavi. Non enim ea me adnumerare lectori putavi oportere, sed tamquam appendere. Hic labor meus hoc assequetur, ut nostri homines quid ab illis exigant, qui se Atticos volunt, et ad quam eos quasi formulam dicendi revocent intellegant.[1]

Marcus Tullius Cicero,
De optimo genere oratorum

THE FIRST FORM OF CREATIVITY

The notion of creativity plays a fundamental role in the conception of historical-natural languages. One of its main contributions to language sciences is the construction of semiotic codes based on four criteria: i) ability to articulate/not articulate; ii) finite/potentially infinite signs; iii) synonymy/non-synonymy; and iv) calculability/non-calculability of signs and synonyms. According to this principle[2] creativity is, in a general sense, the possibility of codes to vary and change. In the context of semiotic codes, creativity manifests itself in the construction of open codes. These are codes with a potentially infinite number of signs, starting with a limited number of basic units and rules of their operation: like natural languages, infinite codes are characterized by the opening and oscillation of the number of basic elements and rules of which they are composed and oppose non-creative codes (such as logic and arithmetic) for which no (even unexpected) variation of the elements is allowed. However, even before the action of creativity on codes can determine the outcomes and, with them, the nature of the codes themselves (whether creative or non-creative), the theoretically most relevant meaning of semiotic and linguistic creativity must be sought in the notion of Saussurian formativity.

In *Course*, languages are based on the notion of arbitrariness which refers not only to the relationship between the signifier and the meaning of the sign, but to the same structuring of the meaning and the signifier from a set of elements. Saussure's attempt to dismantle the idea of a language as a nomenclature defines the real functioning of language and inaugurates, perhaps unknowingly, a new scientific approach to the problem of creativity which, therefore, is no longer just about the symbolic code, but determines the existence of the code itself (or the codes themselves). In terms of languages, for example, without creativity, we would not be able to explain the existence of so many languages in the world, nor the correlation between the languages (Avalle 1973).[3]

Garroni ([1978] 2010) points out that the first form of creativity is linked to the arbitrary conception of language; that is, the principle for which the classification of concrete elements (signals: senses, expressions) within abstract classes (signs: meanings, signifiers) and the same constitution of the abstract classes takes place through a creative process and, hence, are not dictated by preestablished rules (Prieto 1976, 1995; De Mauro 2008). The need to establish the social and historical dimension of language is essential to highlight the role that the speaking mass has in structuring the classification of signifiers and meanings. For the assumptions of radical arbitrariness highlighted, the articulation of these classifications creatively differ from language to language, and this diversity pertains only to each language: if, however, the speakers are entities within the language, inevitably these formal relationships of articulation of abstract classes become essentially social. The structuring of meanings and signifiers is not defined based on the physical similarity of concrete expressions and senses, but always and only based on the judgment of commutability.[4] This social judgment, operated by the talking mass that determines variation, change, and linguistic configuration, varies from one linguistic community to another, changing through time and eras and assuming variations historically radical (De Mauro 1967). The commutation judgment is therefore contingent and has its foundation only in the collective behavior of a group of speakers at a given point in time (De Mauro 1971b). However, we ask ourselves some questions: To what extent can judgment be creative?

How creative can the code-building process be? What are the limits (if any) of this first creativity?[5]

In reference to natural historical languages, the answer lies in the traditional philosophical dichotomy by which languages are considered ένέργεια (*enérgeia*), a creative activity, or έργον (*ergon*), a product of this activity (Humboldt [1836] 1988). In his work dedicated to the division of mankind into peoples and ethnic groups and the consequent diversity of languages, Humboldt refers to a creative process, that is, "a living sprout of infinite variability" strictly intertwined with the activity of the spirit of men. In this sense, a single language should be depicted as a system aimed at creating a generative system (but not Chomsky's generativism) and not as a product already made. For example, German should be regarded as the sum of the possibility that the language offers, which are partly made historically and partly still to be realized in a process that is constantly changing (and thus creative) (Coseriu 1962). By interpreting these reflections through the categories closest to semiotic analysis, creativity can be the action that peoples and nations (i.e., the social partners linked to history) operate on a language inherited from past generations. In this sense, Humboldt's theoretical system recalls that concept of linguistic creation that is not the creation of the first words by men but which represents the (creative) bond that exists for every language with the nation and a historical era (Di Cesare 2005). As a result, from Humboldt to Saussure, arbitrariness as creativity has endless applications—some unpredictable and some unrealized—but limited only by the social, historical, and cultural dimensions within which it applies.

To this creative activity in a historical and social sense, De Mauro (1982) gives the name *creatività humboltiana* (Humboldtian creativity) or *creatività di langage* (creativity of language), understood as a human faculty to create, transform, and manage different symbolic codes.

IS LANGUAGE A CREATIVE *SYSTEM*?

The Humboldt concept of language as ένέργεια is the direct antecedent of Hjelmslev's language-scheme concept. It reads in the *Prolegomena* of Hjelmslev ([1961] 1963, 52–60):

> Each language lays down its own boundaries within the amorphous "thought-mass" and stresses different facts in its different arrangements, puts the centers of gravity in different places and gives them different emphases. It is like one and the same handful of sand that is formed in quite different patterns, or like the cloud in the heavens that changes shape in Hamlet's view from minute to minute. Just as the same sand can be put into different moulds, and the same

cloud take on ever new shapes, so also the same purport is formed or structured differently in different languages. What determines its form is solely the functions of the language, the sign function and the functions deductible therefrom. Purport remains, each time, substance for a new form, and has no possible existence except through being substance for one form or another. . . . We may conclude from this fact that in one of the two entities that are functions of the sign function, namely the content, the sign function institutes a form, the content form, which from the point of view of the purport is arbitrary and which can be explained only by the sign function and is obviously solitary with it. In this sense, Saussure is clearly correct in distinguishing between form and substance.

From Hjelmslev's perspective, the concept of an abstract scheme has important correlations with Saussurian's concept of *language—speaking* and *form—substance*. Saussure's linguistic considers the *parole* (speaking) as an "execution always individual, and the individual is always its master" and even that "speaking . . . is an individual act. It is wilful and intellectual. Within the act, we should distinguish between: (1) the combinations by which the speaker uses the language code for expressing his own thought; and (2) the psychophysical mechanism that allows him to exteriorize those combinations" (CGL, 13–14). The *parole* is an individual physical reality that opposes the sound image of language that on the contrary has a social value: "speaking is thus not a collective instrument; its manifestations are individual and momentary" (CGL, 19).

In describing the concept of language (*langue*), Saussure's theory does not have a clear position. The lack of clarity, argues Coseriu (1958), is due to the fact that *Course in General Linguistics* is the founding document of modern linguistics, but it is also a test bed, a theoretical laboratory which Saussure constantly confronts and to which univocal references are not always found. However, this lack of clarity is useful for highlighting how the idea of creativity, even if not directly, may have conditioned the same concept of language. To recall the characters of the Saussurian language, we follow the proposal of Coseriu (1958) that recalls three lines of thought: i) *Language* is "the sum of word-images stored in the minds of all individuals" and "it is a storehouse filled by the members of a given community through their active use of speaking, a grammatical system that has a potential existence in each brain, or, more specifically, in the brains of a group of individuals. For language is not complete in any speakers; it exists perfectly only within a collectivity" (CGL, 13–14); ii) *Language* is the "whole set of linguistic habits which allow an individual to understand and to be understood. . . . It is a social institution." Because the social part of a language cannot be completed by any one individual; "for the realization of language, a community of speakers is necessary. Contrary to all appearances, language never exists from the social fact, for it is a semiological phenomenon" (CGL, 77); and iii) *Language* is therefore "a system of arbitrary signs": a language "constitutes a system. In this one respect (as we shall see later) language is not completely arbitrary but it is ruled to some extent by logic; it is here also, however, that the inability of the masses to transform it becomes apparent. The system is a complex mechanism that can be grasped only through reflection; the very ones who use it daily are ignorant about it. We can conceive of a change only though the intervention of specialists, grammarians, logicians, and so on; but experience shows us that all such meddling has failed" (CGL, 73). Language, as well as being a social institution, is a system of relationships and functions. Within a language a term acquires its meaning only because it opposes one that precedes it or the one that follows it, that is, because it is opposite to both. Language signs "are above all else opposing, relative and negative entities" (CGL, 119). On the one hand, therefore, the language is a network of relationships and relationships between signs, that is, a reference system that welcomes all possible concrete ways of speaking and allows their categorization. But at the same time, language is a historical and social system linked to people's lives because it cannot exist outside of society. Abstract scheme and society are two concepts that characterize the language of Saussure and, even in their conception of opposite elements, we want to keep them together. Their union creates the space for semiotic creativity.

The Language: *A System of Pure Values*

Saussure uses the notion of a system, and with it the concept of a language as a system of united signs, to escape the theoretical difficulties of developing a linguistic and semiotic theory that is based on the notion of sign and its own nature.[6] The signs are united only because in the Saussurian model, all the elements (i.e., all the signs in it) support and condition each other, and so the change of one depends on the change of the other (and the internal system). We cannot describe a sign only in its relation to a meaning and a signifier—Saussure uses the word *sign* to designate the whole and to replace *concept* and *sound-image*, respectively, by *meaning* [*signifié*] and *signifier* [*signifiant*]. The signifier and meaning are intimately united, and each recall the other. To understand a semiotic relationship, it is necessary to add a new element (which still involves both levels): this new element is the *value*. Therefore, to define the sign, Saussure needs to introduce the notion of system, and with it the notion of value.

Saussure states:[7]

> Thus, it is only this community system which merits the name of signs, and which is such a system. . . . "The social nature" is one of its internal, not one of

its external, elements. We "therefore" recognize as semiological only that part of the phenomena which characteristically appears as a social product, "and we refuse to consider as semiological what is properly individual." . . . Any given semiological system is comprised of a quantity of units (more or less complex units, "suffixes, etc.," of different orders) and the true nature of these units "what will prevent them from being confused with something else" is that they are values. This system of units which is a system of signs is a system of values. (*Second Course of Lectures on General Linguistics*, 1908–1909, 14a)

Still in the *Second Course*, the system is the necessary condition for a sign to exist:

[In the language] all quantities [all signs] are mutually interdependent: thus if we want to determine what judgement ["judgement"] is in French, we can only define it "by" what it is so or rounds it, either to say what it is in itself, or to say what it is not. Similarly, if we wish to translate it into another language. Here appears the necessity to consider the sign, the word, in the whole of the system. Similarly, the synonyms *craindre*, *redouter* ["fear"] only exist side by side: *craindre* will acquire all the content of *redouter* as long as *redouter* doesn't exist. The case would be the same with *chien* ["dog"], *loup* ["wolf"], even though we think of them as isolated signs. (*Second Course of Lectures on General Linguistics*, 1908–1909, 11a)

For the purposes of this work, it is important to consider that Saussure resorts to a comparison between language and play that has remained present in Saussurian and post-Saussurian linguistic theory: in the game, and especially in the game of chess, every pawn assumes a value assigned to it not by the materiality of the pawn itself, but by the relationship it has with the other pawns necessary for the game to exist. We'll come back to this analogy between language and play in the next chapter.

What is proposed in the *Second Course* is still central to CGL and is the basis of the ability of a sign to create meaning and therefore of the existence of languages as systems of pure values in which nothing is material, but everything (both signifier and meaning) is made from abstract and radically arbitrary elements. In CGL (111–113) it reads that a language can be nothing different from a system of pure values composed of ideas and sounds. Thought is an amorphous, indistinct mass and without the use of signs man would be unable to distinguish two ideas clearly and accurately. In his analysis, Saussure highlights that, in the facts of the world, there are no predetermined ideas and nothing—although existing as a reality and element of matter—is knowable and analyzed without the support of languages. Thought is like a nebula in which nothing is bounded. In the face of this moving sea devoid of certainties, Saussure wonders: Do sounds offer greater stability than concepts? The answer is clear. Absolutely not. The sounds themselves are neither more fixed, nor more rigid, nor more stable than thought, and these too are configured as a material apparatus perpetually in need of semiotic instruments of analysis and determination. As a result, language can be represented as a series of adjacent subdivisions, marked off on both the indefinite plane of mixed ideas (A) and the equally vague plane of sounds (B). The thought, in fact, chaotic by nature, must be organized in the process of its decomposition. It's not about materializing thoughts or making sounds intangible. It is an aspect, somewhat mysterious, for which the thought-sound implies divisions, and, in this, language processes its units (of signs with signifier and meaning) constituting itself as a bridge between two amorphous masses. This bridge, that is, the link between the signifier and the meaning is, as we have already considered, arbitrary. If this were not the case, and therefore, something intervened in determining the length and characteristics of the bridge, then there would be something material and external to the sign capable of imposing a certain form. But values remain entirely relative, and that is why the bond between sound and idea is radically arbitrary.

The Saussurian passage emphasizes the arbitrary nature of language and for this reason it's being a social element, the fruit of collectivity and not individuality. Moreover, conceiving language as a system of values opens up a paradox: the paradox is that on the one hand, the meaning of a sign is the counterpart of its acoustic image (i.e., the meaning of a sign is the counterpart of the signifier); but on the other hand, the sign is also the counterpart of the other signs in the language system.

The arbitrary nature of the sign explains in turn why only the social fact is able to create a linguistic system. A community of language users is necessary if the values that owe their existence to the usage and general acceptance are to be defined; by himself, an individual is unable to define a single value.

In addition, the idea of value, as defined, shows that to consider a term as the combination of a certain sound with a certain concept is very misleading. To define it in this way would distance the term from its system; it would mean assuming that one can start from the terms and build the system by joining them together. On the contrary, it is from the interdependent whole that one must start and through analysis obtain its elements.

But here there is a second paradox: on the one hand, the concept seems to be the counterpart of the sound-image; on the other hand, the sign itself—that is, the relationship that links its elements—is also the counterpart of the other signs of language. Language is a system in which all signs are supportive and in which the value of one (which is not simply the meaning) results only from the simultaneous presence of the other. Therefore, the value of a sign is not fixed if one simply states that it can be "exchanged" for a given concept, that is, that it can mean this or that: one must also draw comparisons with other words of similar value that stand in opposition. Its content is really fixed only by the concurrence of everything that exists outside it. The content is not really determined without the intervention of what is outside the sign (i.e., the other signs) which determines the value of that sign. As part of a system, a word is coated not only by a meaning, but even more by a value that is much more important. Aware of the difficulty of accessing these issues, Saussure produces examples which, despite their theoretical difficulty, justify and give sense, for example, to the difficulties of translations, or the theoretical difficulties that occur in wanting to make the same content in different languages. This means making the same content in languages that, despite having words with similar meaning, these same words may not have a same value, and therefore severely limit (prevent) a *verbum de verbo* translation. The word French *mouton* may have the same meaning as the English *sheep*, but not the same value, because speaking of a piece of meat, cooked and served on the table, in English is *mutton* and not *sheep*. The difference in value between *sheep* and *mouton* depends on the fact that the first term is within a system (the one of English) that provides a second term (*sheep* and *mutton*), whereas in French this does not happen. From the words of the *Course*, it is clear that the value of any linguistic sign is therefore unfixed until the sign is put in comparison with the other opposed signs within a system of formal and only functional relations (which therefore consider the sign as a function and not contained). If signs of different languages with similar meaning may have different values, this is justifiable only within a plan of radical arbitrariness: an arbitrariness within the same language between the signifier and the meaning of a sign; arbitrariness between different languages; and an arbitrariness between language and the amorphous mass of thoughts and sounds.

These reflections were already present in the *Second Course* in which the concept of value so conceived—with this decisive role for the conception of language—exists only thanks to the collectivity.[8] The steps we have proposed make it clear that in order to define the identity of the sign, and to escape the paradox that we mentioned earlier, it is not possible to solve everything within the relationship between the signifier and the meaning, but it is necessary to change the elements of the combination by adding an additional element. For this reason Saussure introduces the concept of value, and of value of solidarity and therefore of a system, despite not being completely satisfied with the sign-system-value relationship (De Palo 2016). Saussure elaborates the theory of the system only to study this fact and not to compare language to a logical code[9] (De Mauro 1965). Having knowledge of this is important to better understand a fundamental aspect for linguistic theory.

The theory of the system, if considered without the doubts with which Saussure himself creates it (De Mauro 1965, 1971b, 1984, 2008), has a rigid, closed conformation: it is a *serré* system in which everything seems to hold up and in which the change or addition of a single element is the precondition of total change of the system itself. Saussure senses the problem and tries to find a balance to the *serré* system in the principle of immutability of the language for which the individual cannot act alone, but because a system changes; it is necessary to have a talking mass, and therefore a collective dimension. The CGL (72) states that a certain language-state is always the result of historical and social forces, and these forces clarify why the sign—or the system—is fixed, that is, why it resists any arbitrary substitution.

The social dimension supports and balances a *serré* system. From this perspective, Saussure has felt the inadequacy of a system as a communication tool: Can all people have the same *serré* language system? Even within the same community of native speakers, can you find people who have exactly the same language? And again: How is it possible to communicate between L1 speakers and L2 learners where the disparity and diversity of the s*erré* language system is evident? De Mauro (1965) considers how the rigid architrave that Saussure has placed as an attempt to guarantee communication and understand one another between individuals is perhaps one of those insights that led Saussure himself to state that not everything remained obscure, but not everything has been entirely elucidated. The dynamism of the system (the creativity of the system) is necessary as a guarantee of stability. It is a prerequisite of communicating and understanding between individuals because a minimal individual linguistic variation—which is the norm in daily communication—can jeopardize the structuring itself and the linguistic identity of the system, resulting in the impossibility of communication and interaction.

A *JEU DE SIGNES APPELÉ LANGUE*

The *Course in General Linguistics* concludes with these words: "*the true and unique object of linguistics is language studied in and for itself*" (CGL 232). Let us refer to De Mauro (1965, 1967) who highlights that the famous phrase with which the *Course* ends was written by the publishers of the *Course* and cannot be traced back to the notes made directly by Saussure (La Fauci 2011). In support of the theoretical and philological reconstruction of De Mauro (2005a), we consider the *Writings in General Linguistics*[10] (2006) which are a collection of texts useful to reconstruct an authentic intellectual and scientific image of Saussure and of his linguistic ideas. *Writings in General Linguistics* introduce new developments, some of which are terminologically compared to the other texts of the Saussurian tradition. First is the new concept of *quaternion*. The novelties are not only lexical, but above all theoretical:

The first formulation of the real situation would be to state that language (or rather the speaking subject) perceives neither idea a, nor form A, but only the relationship a/A; this formulation would still be entirely rough and ready. What he perceives is the relationship between the two relationships a/AHZ and abc/A or b/ARS and blr/B, etc.

This is what we term the LAST QUATERNION and, as far as the four terms in their relationships are concerned: the irreducible triple relationship. (6e)

As De Mauro (2005a) points out, the term *quaternion* is not widespread in Saussurian work, nor in his philology. This term, known in mathematics for defining hypercomplex numbers,[11] is used by Saussure to confirm that a word is not understood, not by speakers nor by scholars, if one does not correlate the signifier to its meaning. However, this is not enough: the form must also be linked with the other signifiers with which it coexists, which it recalls and from which it is invoked. The same process applies to the meaning to invoke and be invoked by the meanings of other words that are semantically close to them. Paraphrasing Saussure again, every form,[12] every sign should be an element of a quadruple relationship like that which mathematicians already call *quaternion*.

Up to this point, *Writings in General Linguistics* do not seem to add anything different from what has already been claimed in the CGL, even though Saussure may already appear aware of the charm, but at the same time of the limit of the *serré* system for the creation of a communication theory. The issue becomes more complex and delicate when Saussure must define the same form,[13] and that definition leads him to write all the limits of a systemic vision of a language, going so far as to hypothesize the replacement of the system with something more dynamic, less rigid, more open to change and a creativity not mathematical, but dynamic. When Saussure in *Writings in General Linguistics* defines the form as "element which alternates" incardinated inside a quaternion (i.e., a *serré* system), it proposes a question:

Form implies: DIFFERENCE: PLURALITY. (SYSTEM?). SIMULTANEITY. SIGNIFYING VALUE.

To sum up:

FORM = Not a *positive* entity in a given order, and a simple order; but an entity both *negative* and *complex* (lacking any material basis), born of *difference* from other forms COMBINED with the difference of meaning of other forms.

A question that is neither trivial nor random. Asking oneself a question about the symbol element of one's theory in which the signs (the forms) should coexist is a revolution of great novelty and interest. In this regard, De Mauro (2005a) notes that if the speaker (and even the linguist) were to consider all the forms of which the language system is composed every time he uses the language, a mechanism would be produced so complex that communication would be impossible.

These difficulties which Saussure confronts recall the linguistic perspective of the Aristotelian world (and Wittgenstein in *Tractatus*) in which words denoting equal things for all make communication impossible.[14] In the Aristotelian model, only an empirically and rationally indemonstrable coincidence, a mystical communion of souls, ensures that the meaning is understood by the other person; that is, it guarantees that the two (or more) linguistic systems are completely identical.

If, however, we believe that mysticism and non-rationality are not parameters on which to base a linguistic theory, we must admit that *sic stantibus rebus* communication is impossible.

For this reason, there are at least two different meanings of a system, albeit interrelated: a real meaning and a theoretical meaning.

Saussure had a clear and strong notion of a system, a concept that certainly fascinated him, because he was able to make communication between people logical and safe. In practice, this model would have led to the paradoxical consequences of non-communicability and the Aristotelian world. The summary of the nature of FORM in *Writings in General Linguistics*, and the question of the word *system*, gives a weak view of the systematicity of the form: a version that recalls "other forms," but certainly not the entire language system.[15] Saussure wonders whether the identity of a form really should go through the identification of all language units of the same system. In the very act in which the word system is put on the field, Saussure immediately distances himself from applications that are too literal: if a language was a system as is the game of chess and *the analogy with the game was radical*, then, exactly as in the game the addition or loss of a single piece should radically alter the mechanism of the game. If a language were exactly a system, the presence of different elements (or the absence of an element in a person's language) would correspond to system diversity and therefore the impossibility of playing the same game with the same rules, that is, the impossibility of understanding (De Mauro 1971a, b, 1984).

The "solution" identified by Saussure is, at this point, less radical than the *serré* system. The speaker cannot dominate the entire system of signifiers and meanings: the solution that Saussure then uses is that of a reference not total, but "regional" or "local" to the coexisting forms closest to the form in question. Saussure refers to those forms that are closer to the one considered in language's *jeu de(s) signes*: "A vocal figure becomes a form from the crucial moment at which it is introduced into the interplay of signs called *langue*" (*Writings in General Linguistics*, 6e).

Within Saussurian linguistics, there is an awareness that the language game is no longer a cage that is imposed on the speakers and is not described as a calculation. But it is the combination of forms built and rebuilt *upon the field*, on the road, to meet the needs of meaning and understanding of the speakers (De Mauro 1982, 1994; De Mauro and Fortuna 1995). It is not something closed and delimited, but something open and in the making on which semiotic creativity intervenes, or, perhaps, is thus in the making by virtue of the action of semiotic creativity. The game of signs does not escape the cultural, social, strongly anthropological dimension that is the result of the community which, using a language and playing with its forms and signs, creates meaning and communication between users. Talking among people, that is, language games on which Wittgenstein bases his *Philosophical Investigations* (*PU*), is the essence of a language (of all languages).

NOTES

1. Since it is possible to make serious errors in regard to this kind of saying (of making orations), I believed that I was suffering from an effort that might not be indispensable, but it is useful to lovers of matter. In fact, I translated two very well-known and authentic speeches made by two of Attica's most eloquent speakers, Eschine and Demosthenes: I translated as a speaker, not as an interpreter. I translated with the very expressions of thought, with the same ways of making thought with words, with a lexicon appropriate to the nature of our language. In these texts, I did not believe to give word for word, but I kept every character and every expressive effectiveness of the words themselves. Because I didn't think it was more convenient for the reader to give him one word after another. Rather I believed better give it a complete meaning, that it was as adequate as possible for the whole expression (Our translation).

2. We will further the reflection on these issues in chapter 4 when considering the work of Tullio De Mauro (1982).

3. In Garroni ([1978] 2010, 102–3): "la formatività saussuriana, (ciò che Saussure chiama arbitrarietà, ma in senso nuovo rispetto all'arbitrarietà del rapporto significante-significato . . . riguarda infatti non più soltanto quel rapporto, ma la stessa strutturazione del piano del significato (o del «contenuto», nella terminologia hjelmsleviana), oltre che ovviamente quello del significante, cioè l'analisi e la discretizzazione arbitraria dell'esperienza nonché del *continuum* fonico. La vigorosa polemica di Saussure contro l'idea di lingua come una nomenclatura si iscrive appunto in quest'ordine di considerazioni rivoluzionarie, le uniche che comincino a dar conto del reale funzionamento del linguaggio instaurando nello stesso tempo un nuovo approccio scientifico al problema della creatività. . . . Poiché—si badi—non si tratta semplicemente del nascere di una nuova «sensibilità» all'idea di formatività o creatività, ma di una prospettiva scientifica che è esplicativamente più adeguata

nei riguardi dei reali fenomeni linguistici. Basti dire che non riusciremmo altrimenti a spiegare neppure il fatto semplicissimo della molteplicità delle cosiddette lingue naturali, né quello correlativo della possibilità di traduzione da una lingua ad un'altra."

4. "Due fonie collegabili, in una data comunità di parlanti, ad uno stesso senso si dicono commutabili. . . . Due sensi collegabili, in una data comunità di parlanti, ad una stessa fonia si dicono commutabili" (De Mauro 1971b, 89). The judgment of commutability is the focus of Hjelmslev's philosophy:

> non si ripeterà mai abbastanza quanto importante sia, nella prospettiva hjelmsleviana, il procedimento della *commutazione*: il quale non è solo uno strumento di analisi linguistica, ma anche lo strumento di formazione, di apprendimento, di raggiustamento e comprensione continua (nell'uso e nella pratica) delle unità linguistiche. Ai fini del nostro discorso, è rilevante che le classi di identità, le invarianti, costruite attraverso la commutazione governano già, al loro interno, varianti, *applicazioni* nel senso impiegato da Hempel . . . che sono in relazione di reciproca vaghezza, e di non identità. (Prampolini 1997, 104)

5. In De Mauro (2008) the arbitrariness has a limit in the biological characteristics of living beings that use codes. We do not consider this form of arbitration called material arbitrariness. We consider formal arbitrariness as a property of historically natural languages.

6. In the lesson of Saussure, the definition of sign implies the definition of meaning; the latter in turn defined only by the sign. In De Mauro (1965, 19): "Così, se la definizione di significato implica quella di segno, la definizione di segno implica, a sua volta, quella di significato. Non sappiamo che cos'è il significato se non sappiamo cos'è il segno; ma non possiamo stabilire che cos'è il segno se non sappiamo già che cos'è il significato. È questo il primo e più grave circolo vizioso nel quale si aggira il tradizionale pensiero linguistico."

7. It is known that CGL is the editorial result of three general linguistics courses taught by Saussure at the University of Geneva between 1906 and 1911 (1906–1907, *First Course*; 1908–1909, *Second Course*; 1910–1911, *Third Course*). We refer to the critical apparatus, introduction, and commentary of the Italian edition of the *Course* curated by Tullio De Mauro (1967) for the philological reconstruction of the Saussurian text from the three linguistics courses held in Geneva and from the notes of students Bally and Sechehaye.

8. We make reference to Simone (1970, 45) and his philological reconstruction of the *Second Course*. However, the manuscripts R (by A. Riedlinger) and G (by L. Gautier) present even more radical lessons on the social conception of value: "appena si parla di valori è in gioco il loro rapporto (nessun valore esiste da solo), il che fa sì che il segno avrà valore in sé solo in forza della consacrazione della collettività. Pare che nel segno ci siano due valori: valore in sé e quello che gli viene dalla collettività—ma in fondo si tratta dello stesso." (R) "Le diverse unità hanno necessariamente dei valori che sono reciproci. Ma il valore è stabilito solo dalla forza sociale che lo sanziona. Se andiamo al fondo delle cose, questi due aspetti sono identici" (G).

9. In (De Mauro 1965, 128): "è solo per spiegare questo fatto e non per un astratto bisogno di concepire le cose in maniera logicizzante, che Saussure elabora la più celebre delle sue teorie: la teoria del sistema. A tale conformazione pur non restando

soddisfatto della soluzione che il riferimento al sistema sembra offrire al problema del valore il linguista ginevrino assegna una determinazione essenziale nella gestione segnica. Non si tratta di un affare di poco conto, né di un aspetto marginale per la teoria linguistica."

10. In addition to the English translation of the original text, *Écrits de linguistique générale* (En. Ed. *Writing in General Linguistics* 2002), we consider the Italian version with commentary and analysis by Tullio De Mauro (2005a).

11. In mathematics, the quaternions is a number system that extends the complex numbers. It was first described by Irish mathematician William Rowan Hamilton in 1843 and applied to mechanics in three-dimensional space. A feature of quaternions is that multiplication of two quaternions is noncommutative. Hamilton defined a quaternion as the quotient of two directed lines in a three-dimensional space or equivalently as the quotient of two vectors.

Quaternions are generally represented in the form:

$$a + bi + cj + dk$$

where a, b, c, and d are real numbers, and i, j, and k are the fundamental quaternion units (Conway and Smith 2003).

12. We consider the term *form* as it is considered by the Saussurian tradition (CGL) and in the *Prolegomena* of Hjelmslev. Sometimes form is considered as a signifier, other times as a sign as a whole. We do not consider the ways in which it is used in *Writings in General Linguistics* for which we refer to the critical apparatus of De Mauro (2005a).

13. "Crucially all *four things* implied by FORM are overlooked: 1. *Form*, first and foremost, means *diversity of form*; otherwise there would be no basis whatsoever, true or false, adequate or inadequate, for the slightest theorization about *form*. 2. Hence *Form* implies *plurality of form*; without this, the *difference* which is the basis for a form's existence ceases to be possible. 3. *Form*, or difference within a plurality." (6c)

14. In the concept of "solipsismo aristotelico" we see the *Tractatus* of Ludwig Wittgenstein expressed in the *Preface*: "This book will be perhaps only be understood by those who have themselves already thought the thoughts which are expressed in it—or similar thoughts."

15. In De Mauro (2005a, 32, n. 38):

davvero l'identificazione di una forma passa (per il linguista? Per il parlante?) attraverso l'identificazione di *tutte* le diverse forme coesistenti (dove? Nella coscienza o uso di chi?) *nell'intero* sistema? Se è così, come può il parlante come può il linguista capire e usare o, rispettivamente identificare una forma nella totalità delle sue relazioni? Della nozione di sistema esistono almeno due accezioni dominanti, distinguibili pur se interrelate nella storia del pensiero e delle scienza: un'accezione che può dirsi reale o realistica e un'accezione più accentuatamente epistemica . . . . Saussure disponeva di una nozione netta e forte di sistema, che lo affascinava, certamente, di cui avvertiva capacità esplicative, ma insieme conseguenze paradossali per la comprensione del parlare effettivo a entrambi i livelli, della comprensione tra locutori e della comprensione scientifica. Il riassunto FORMA ecc. dà una visione debole della sistematicità della forma: una versione per così dire 'locale' che evoca 'altre forme,' non la totalità sistemica delle altre forme.

Chapter 2

Language and Game Are Typical Creative Activities

Multa renascentur, quae iam cecidere, cadentque quae nunc sunt in honore vocabula, si volet usus, quem penes arbitrium est et ius et norma loquendi.[1]

Quintus Horatius Flaccus, *Ars poetica*

LANGUAGE AND GAME: SEMIOTIC ANALOGIES

Amongst the many meanings currently applied to the term creativity, it seems as though linguistics and semiotics are able to offer the most appropriate theoretical and methodological framework to the notion of creativity *in the full sense of this term* (Garroni [1978] 2010) by adopting the concepts of *value*, *system*, and *game* upon which the Saussurean lessons of the CGL and the *Writings in General Linguistics* are based (De Palo and Gensini 2018).

In fact, language activity and its operating conditions were often compared to the conditions of existence of a game: both the language and the game are manifested in principle as typical creative activities and, at the same time, they must obey certain conditions without which there would be neither language nor play.

Saussurean linguistics frequently resorts to the comparison of language and game, in particular the analogies between the *jeu de signes appelé langue* and a chess game (despite the specifications already mentioned about the game as a formal system). These similarities have been widespread since the *Second Course* and the following excerpt from the CGL (22–110), briefly illustrates this concept:

Among the different comparisons proposed by the *Course* between language and other semiotic systems, a comparison with the game of chess may help one understand what is meant by internal and external elements to the system, and again by system rule and ancillary rule. It is external and uninfluential that the game of chess was born in Iran and has arrived in Europe. On the contrary, everything that has to do with the game system and the rules of operation are internal. If, by playing, one replaces the pieces of wood with pieces of gold or silver, the change of material is indifferent to the system. But if the number of pieces decreases, the system changes radically. And with it, it radically changes the grammar of the game.

The change affecting the grammar of the game does not refer to the identity of the sign in relation to the material with which it is made (sound or symbol in language, wood or ivory in chess), but refers only to the relationship between signs. But of all comparisons that might be envisioned, the most effective is the one that might be drawn between the functioning of language and the game of chess. In both cases, one encounters a system of values and their observable modifications. Chess is like an artificial realization of what language offers in a natural form. First, the position of the chessmen corresponds closely to a state of language. The value of the respective pieces depends on their position on the chessboard, just as each linguistic term obtains its value from its opposition to all other terms. Also, the system is always momentary; it changes from one position to the next. It is also true that values depend on unchangeable convention: the set of rules that exist before a game begins and that persist after each move. Despite this, the moves influence the whole system; it is impossible for the player to predict exactly the extent of the effect. Resulting changes of value will be, according to the circumstances, either nothing, very serious, or of average importance. A certain move can transform the whole game and even influence pieces that are not immediately involved. We have just seen that the same holds for language. A new comparison with the set of chess pieces will clarify this point: *the meaning of value* [emphasis added]. Take a knight, for instance. By itself, is it an element in the game? Certainly not, for by its material make-up—outside its square and the other conditions of the game—it means nothing to the player; it becomes a real concrete element only when provided with value and wedded to it. Suppose that the piece happens to be ruined or lost during a game. Can it be replaced by another piece? Certainly. Not only another knight but even a figure that resembles a knight can be pronounced identical and provided the same value. We see then that in semiological systems, like in language, where elements maintain the others' equilibrium in accordance with fixed rules, the idea of identity mixes with that of value and vice versa.

The abovementioned passages have several points in common: the concepts of *rule*, *grammar*, and *unchangeable convention* are formal elements that characterise the *jeu de signes appelé langue* and are comparable to the conditions necessary for a game (like, chess, for example) to exist. These seem to be the elements capable of justifying the theoretical insistence on the semiotic relationship between language and game (Karlin and Peres 2016).

If we were to examine *Theory of Games and Economic Behavior* (Neumann and Morgenstern 1944), which is traditionally considered as the text that inaugurates the attempt to describe some types of games (such as board games) using a mathematical theory, we would come to similar conclusions. *Theory of Games* forms such strong analogies between games and the formal constructive conditions of language that it justifies the hypothesis that both game and language are activities that underline the same basic theoretical structure.

We will briefly recall some of these theories and will refer to Karlin and Peres (2016), Prampolini (1997), and Rasmussen (2001) for further details and a more thorough examination. First, we refer to an aspect of method that does not seem random: the authors of *Theory of Games* had the objective of extending their research on the theoretical and mathematical foundations of the game to different games in which the principle of competition was also present. This theory also intended to develop a mathematical procedure to ensure that one of the players wins. In this sense, the proposed theory also considers (as evident through its title) the economic dimension in which "winning" leads to a successful economic transaction with economic gain. Both the conduct of a game and the exchange of goods are considered a co-operation governed by a code or, in other words, by a system of rules: a negotiation from which one party will come out with losses, and another with gains.

In our opinion, identifying a perfect triptych between language (or game) economics is neither random nor dangerous considering that in order to develop the theory of value at the basis of the conception system of language and the identity of signs, Saussure provides an example of economic exchange and of the value of currency. The importance of the concept of value on the semiotic level of meaning creation has already been defined. Now the concept of value intervenes in reference to the game and the economic plan that is precisely linked to the game itself. To determine how much a coin is worth you need to know that you can exchange it with a certain amount of a different thing (e.g., with an object, with a material asset that through the coin you can buy). But likewise, the value of a coin is given by the fact that it can be exchanged for a currency of a different system such as the Euro to US dollars, US dollars to Canadian dollars. The Euro, US dollars, and Canadian dollars are all currencies, but they belong to different economic and monetary systems. And therefore, the value of each coin is given by the possibility (and quantity) of exchange with the other coins.

From a linguistic perspective, the value of a currency recalls the value of a sign: namely, it refers to the principle that an entity within a semiological framework does not validate itself but is validated in relation to what it stands for, that is, its value. The value is therefore determined in relation to dissimilar elements with which it can be exchanged or to similar elements with which it can be replaced. This "game" which regulates economic relations in trade simultaneously regulates the process of creating linguistic signs and, therefore, creates languages themselves. What could have appeared as an analogy of form between language (or game) economy proves to be a strong structural identity.

Let us examine this in detail: the first analogy considers the concepts illustrated in the paragraph *Explanation of the Termini Technici* of *Theory of Games* (48–49) and the concepts with which Saussure defines the particular object of linguistics in the *Course*:

> Before an exact definition of the combinatorial concept of a game can be given, we must first clarify the use of some termini. There are some notions which are quite fundamental for the discussion of games, but the use of which in everyday language is highly ambiguous. . . . First, one must distinguish between the abstract concept of a *game* and the individual *plays* of that game. The *game* is simply the totality of the rules which describe it. Every particular instance at which the game is played—in a particular way—from beginning to end, is a *play*.
>
> Second, the corresponding distinction should be made for the moves, which are the opponent elements of the game. A move is the occasion of a choice between various alternatives, to be made either by one of the players, or by some device subject to chance, under conditions precisely prescribed by the rules of the game. The *move* is nothing but this abstract "occasion," with the attendant details of description,—i.e. an opponent of the *game*. The specific alternative chosen in a concrete instance—i.e. in a concrete *play*—is the *choice*. Thus, the moves are related to the choices in the same way as the game is to the play. The game consists of a sequence of moves, and the play of a sequence of choices.
>
> Finally, the *rules* of the game should not be confused with the *strategies* of the players. Exact definitions will be given subsequently, but the distinction which we stress must be clear from the start. Each player selects his strategy—i.e. the general principles governing his choices—freely. While any particular strategy may be good or bad—provided that these concepts can be interpreted in an exact sense—it is within the player's discretion to use or to reject it.

It is obvious that the oppositions between *game* and *play*, *move* and *choice*, and *rules* and *strategies* are parallel to the oppositions between *langue* and *parole*, *signe* and *acte*, and grammar (made of rules) and linguistic use present in the CGL. Such oppositions are overlapping not only from a quantitative point of view, but mainly for the functions that they serve in the game and in the language.

The opposition system referred to recalls the Saussurean dichotomy between *form* and *substance* for which abstraction is the paradigm on which the functioning of each semiotic code is based. The relationship between signs is biplanar: There exist both the reality made of concrete realizations of *delie* (individual material expressions and individual meaning), phonetic, graphic, and gestural elements, and the abstract reference schemes (signifiers and meanings) that serve to recognize the totality of the *delie*.

Language, like a game, consists of a number of communicative possibilities. Some are accepted by the language system, whereas others are rejected due to historical-linguistic and cultural habits consolidated over time. Some communicative possibilities are not currently accepted, but maybe they were accepted in the past or will be in the future, whereas other possibilities will never be accepted because their realization is not permitted by the code which does not allow for communication.

The same analogy can be applied to a game in which the player creates his own game within all the games that the player could possibly create: Games that are allowed in the game or games that reinvent the game. There are also games that cannot be carried out because, by doing so, that game (or any other game) would not exist. Finally, in a game (and in language) there are rules (communicative rules); however, such rules are not strategies. Each speaker elaborates their own communication strategies in order to be understood by others, just as a player elaborates their own strategies to win the game they are playing.

However, there still seems to be more. Some games allow for the possibility to signal (*signaling*); that is, the possibility with which a player—only if abiding by the rules of the game—can update his teammate on his own conditions and on the possibility to make moves in the game. Alternatively, one can try to deceive the opponent. Informing, warning, deceiving, and making unexpected moves are all aspects integral to the modalities of the conduct of a game; in other words, they are some of the elements that characterize and distinguish a game strategy. Nevertheless informing, warning, deceiving, and making unexpected moves are also main aspects of linguistic use: the meaning of the word "strategy" acquires its full value when it refers to a new conduct each time (a creative conduct) which is unpredictable and able to evade not only the expectations of the speaker, but also the syntactic, morphological and semantic relationships between signs (defined by rules) in the language game.

We will now touch upon the last of the characters (possibly the main one for our prerogatives) that combines game and language. It is about defining the relationships between regularity (the rules of a game and of a language, its grammar, and the syntactic, morphological, and semantical rules) and creativity as a formal moment of variation and deviation (where possible) from regularity. This can be done in some (or all) games and it can also be done in language use (Ladusaw 1983; Lamb 1966).

In accordance with this last idea, it is necessary to read Antonio Pagliaro (1952, 1973), who argues that any game (including the *jeu de signes appelé langue*) exists in virtue of the existence of rules. Pagliaro's reflection proposes an important hypothesis on the nature of a rule: Pagliaro distinguishes the rules of a game, which attribute a value to signs and determine the functionality of the game, and the rules regarding the conduct of a game, rules which the player must keep in mind to avoid defeat. Such references are useful when considering the nature and identity of a rule: with the introduction of the idea of a normal rule and a constitutive rule, the concept of a rule loses some of its rigor if one considers that in a game a normal rule does not modify a constituent rule. A consistent rule remains unchanged until a legislator of the game, not a player, feels the need to modify it.

In languages (in a context without a legislator other than the speaking mass), the balance between rules is such that a clear distinction between them may not be fully functional. It is evident that one can speak of games, one can speak of languages and games, and one can speak of linguistic games only if rules are present. Essentially, the rules of a language are creative rules.

THE *JEU DE SIGNES APPELÉ LANGUE* AS A *LANGUAGE-GAME*

The comparison of a chess game to a language game is also related to Hjelmslev's linguistics ([1961] 1968), but it is with Wittgenstein's Philosophical Investigations (*PU*) that the comparison takes on systematic importance as the game becomes "the whole, consisting of language and the actions into which it is woven, the 'language-game'" (§ 7). The Wittgenstein of the *PU* systematically speaks of linguistic games as models of the linguistic behavior necessary to describe linguistic peculiarity and to frame the propositions within a plan of meaning. If the linguistic game is the entire process of the use of words, the meaning of sentences is only created within a linguistic game (Badiou 2011).

Although the game is a central concept of Wittgenstein's philosophy, it represents a classical open concept which is difficult to define in a unique and conclusive way. In other words, there is no *in nuce* identity of the linguistic game; instead, there exists a plurality of elements—known as linguistic games—which are interrelated in various ways. It is the *PU* itself that provides a non-exhaustive framework of the multiplicity of linguistic games (§

23) and recalls the impossibility of defining beforehand what is or is not a linguistic game (Gilmore 1999). Language games are terms of comparison used to shed light on the similarities or differences regarding the state of our language. The *PU* states:

> Here the term "language-*game*" is meant to bring into prominence the fact that the *speaking* of language is part of an activity, or of a form of life.

Review the multiplicity of language-games in the following examples, and in others:

> Giving orders, and obeying them—
> Describing the appearance of an object, or giving its measurements—
> Constructing an object from a description (a drawing)—
> Reporting an event—
> Speculating about an event—
> Forming and testing a hypothesis—
> Presenting the results of an experiment in tables and diagrams—
> Making up a story, and reading it—
> Play-acting—
> Singing catches—
> Guessing riddles—
> Making a joke; telling it—
> Solving a problem in practical arithmetic—
> Translating from one language into another—
> Asking, thanking, cursing, greeting, praying.

(§ 23)

For how is the concept of a game bounded? What still counts as a game and what no longer does? Can you give the boundary? No. You can *draw* one; for none has so far been drawn. . . .

"But then the use of the word is unregulated, the 'game' we play with it is unregulated"—it is not everywhere circumscribed by rules; but no more are there any rules for how high one throws the ball in tennis, or how hard; yet tennis is a fame for all that and has rules too. (§ 68)

One might say that the concept "game" is a concept with blurred edges. (§ 71)

Wittgenstein is aware that he is not able to provide a definition of a linguistic game because, if he had tried, he would have reconstructed the logical system of *Tractatus* that regulates the world and is an image of the world. Whatever solution Wittenstein would have found to define the game, he would have researched a primitive idea of the way language functions, which was at the basis of the logistical conception of language and of its inability to create meaning if not for the same person that uses the language. The linguistic game used by Wittgenstein allows him to bypass Saussure's logical and fixed *serré* system. The latter describes the capacity for language as if it were a mirror of the world, i.e., it sees in the subject the limit of the world, and, thus, the limit of communication outside the subject itself. We will not recall Wittgenstein's philosophy in *Tractatus*, for which we refer to Hacker (2001, 2019); Marconi (1997, 1999), Stenius (1960); Sullivan (2013) and Voltolini (1998). Instead, we refer to how the concept of a linguistic game has been developed by Wittgenstein as a solution to the semantic and communication paradox with which *Tractatus* considered the functioning of language and communication.

The linguistic game contrasts this method. By means of the linguistic game, *Tractatus* could have even been understood by those who would have never thought the thoughts expressed in the book. Unlike what is written in *Tractatus*:

> This book will perhaps only be understood by those who have themselves already thought the thoughts which are expressed on it—or have thought similar thoughts. (*Tractatus*, *Preface*)
>
> A picture is a fact. (§ 2.141)
>
> A sign through which we express a thought I call a propositional sign. And the preposition is the prepositional sign in its projective relation to the world. (§ 3.12)
>
> A prepositional sign consists in the fact that its elements, the words, are combined in it in a definite way. A propositional sign is a fact. (§ 3.14)
>
> A proposition is a picture of reality.
>
> A proposition is a model of reality and we think it is. (§ 4.01)
>
> *The boundaries of my language* mean the boundaries of my world. (§ 5.6)

Logic fills the world: the boundaries of the world are also its boundaries.

We cannot therefore say in logic: This and this there is in the world, that there is not.

> For that would appear to presuppose that we have excluded certain possibilities, and this cannot be the case since then logic must go beyond the boundaries of the world, as if it could also look upon these boundaries from the other side.

What we cannot think, that we cannot think; we cannot therefore *say* what we cannot think. (§ 5.61)

This remark provides a key to deciding the question, to what extent solipsism is a truth.

Namely, what solipsism *means* is quite correct, only it cannot be *said*, but it shows itself.

That the world is *my* world shows itself in that the boundaries of language (the only language which I understand) mean the boundaries of *my* world. (§ 5.62)

I am my world. (The microcosm.) (§ 5.63)

The subject does not belong to the world, but is a boundary of the world. (§ 5.632)

The extreme truth in *Tractatus* is precisely expressed through these fundamental concepts. Only a coincidence that is empirically and rationally unprovable, only a mystical communion of souls, guarantees that a sentence is understood by someone other than the person that originally enunciated it. Otherwise, if mysticism and irrationality are not scientific parameters for analyzing communication, we are forced to admit that in the world of logic—in the *serré* system—communication is impossible. The linguistic game changes the language model. The linguistic game interrupts the "crystalline purity of logic" and brings us "to the rough ground" where we are able to walk, because "we need friction" and mostly because "we want to walk."

THE LINGUISTIC RULE IN THE *PU*

The crisis of the concept of language as a calculation and logical system is realized through the discovery that language is not governed by rigid and rigorous rules that would guide communication on infinite tracks. Previously in the *Blue Book*, in the *Brown Book* and later in the *PU*, Wittgenstein rejects the notion of language as a calculation because that notion would lead to the risk that any form of language is governed by grammar rules that would act independently of its use. Each rule alone cannot determine linguistic use, since any use could be considered compliant to that rule or to a particular interpretation of that same rule (Stern 2004).

Wittgenstein realizes that no rule has only one meaning and that the meaning of a rule depends on the way it is used. It follows that the meaning of an expression is no longer its role in the language designed as a calculation, but its role in the linguistic game (its use). At the heart of Wittgenstein's philosophical interest lies the notion of rule as an element capable of supporting the essence of a game and, in a creative and renewed sense, the essence of language (Garroni [1978] 2010). In *PU*, § 81, Wittgenstein motivates, justifies, and resolves the inaccuracy in believing that speech and understanding are comparable to a well-defined calculation through the analogy between language and game. Understanding the nature of language games becomes central in recognizing that being able to pronounce a sentence or understand its meaning does not mean performing a calculation according to well-executed rules.

Furthermore, the *PU* states:

> Doesn't the analogy between language and games throw light here? We can easily imagine people amusing themselves in a field by playing with a ball so as to start various existing games, but playing many without finishing them and in between throwing the ball aimlessly into the air, chasing one another with the ball and bombarding one another for a joke and so on. . . .
> And is there not also the case where we play and—make up the rules as we go along? And there is even one where we alter them—as we go along. (§ 83)

From the perspective of *PU*, a rule stands there like a road sign. But the question at this point becomes: Does the road sign leave any room for doubt regarding which way to go? Does the road sign say which way to go once you've crossed? Does the road sign tell whether to continue the paved road, or take a different path? The conclusions Wittgenstein reaches are not an answer to questions in terms of purpose or paths to be taken. The answer is negative, that is, it tells us what the road sign cannot do. But the meaning of the answer is still clear and it is not a philosophical conjecture, but it is a fact: sometimes a road marker leaves doubts, sometimes not. Bringing the reflection back to the linguistic level, this means that the rule sometimes serves and indicates the communicative way to go, sometimes not. And therefore, the rule itself is not a guarantee of the possibility of communication.

The rule in the linguistic game is not always a valid guide: sometimes it leaves room for doubt, sometimes it changes *as we go along*, sometimes it is superseded by other rules that still allow the linguistic game to move on. Or, they allow for the creation of another linguistic game, because it is not said (and it is indeed impossible) that the first linguistic game is the only one possible (Barry 1996).

Wittgenstein continues to state that this axiom is an empirical proposition; it is a fact, not a syllogism or philosophical proposition. In the *PU*, the concept of a rule overlaps with what we mean by rule of use of a term, referring to the numerous uses to which a rule is applicable and interpretable and therefore allowing a sentence to be uttered. Following this reasoning, the grammar of a language is a set of rules with which the language is realized in use: knowing the grammar of a linguistic expression means knowing the identity of the sentence with a direct reference to the semantic aspect of the sign and to its meaning within the linguistic game.

Wittgenstein affirms, "*Essence* is expressed by grammar" (*PU* § 371) and "Grammar tells what kind of object anything is" (Theology as grammar) (*PU* § 373). The grammar of an expression therefore has both an ontological and a semantic value (Hacker 2019): not only are there morphological and syntactic rules, but according to Wittgenstein, there are also pragmatic and semantic rules. Simply stated, these rules are applicable to all dimensions of language. Wittgenstein highlights that in the field of grammar, and hence in the field of all the rules of language use, these rules do not work conclusively but only when they resolve comprehension issues; comprehension issues can only be tackled as they arise and not once and for all in their entirety (Messeri 1997). For a *considerable* class of instances—though not for all—in which we use the word "meaning" it can be defined according to the *PU* as: the meaning of the term is its use in the language. And the *meaning* of a name is something described by indicating to its *bearer* (PU § 43). For this reason, in language, one cannot speak of a single order that supervises its functioning. It is not only more correct, but dutiful, to speak about one of the many possible orders with which to operate and use the historical-natural languages (§ 132).

There is no complete grammar (a complete set of rules) that implies all the possible rules of use of a sign and that determines the meaning of the signs in the countless contexts of use (in the countless linguistic games). In light of the developed reconnaissance, the rule in the PU can be defined as conventional in an important sense and substantially unknown to the previous tradition of conventionalism (Messeri 1997): the rule is not constrictive; it is arbitrary. The rule is creative (Baker and Hacker 2009). The already cited § 83 is not only important for the analogy between language and game which we previously mentioned, but because it implies (according to the principle of *making up the rules as we go along*) that a game can be played by progressively creating the rules to be applied without them having been predetermined at the start of the game and, especially, without them being able not to change from the start of the game as a result of the game progressing (the uses of the language). This means that any game can exist by virtue of the existence of a desirable regularity.

Yet the very invention of a rule—only if it is a rule and not a random act, without impacting the game—is not in turn free of any regularity. It implies that there is at least one previous rule with which it is compatible and with which it must, in some way, be integrated. Garroni ([1978] 2010) highlights the fact that if, in a game, a player could invent at will the rule that grants him victory regardless of any previous rules, the game could not even begin;

whoever is first to say "I won" would win the game. This would, in its own way, be a rule but from a different game: the game could be a race or a competition to overcome an opponent.[2] In Wittgenstein's teaching, the identity of a rule in a game can only be determined through the totality of its possible applications, a totality that—inextricably linked to use—is conclusively never given in its entirety but is always open to new and continuous determinations.

The regularity of grammar in (linguistic) games is arbitrary, without any parameters and is therefore creative because he who (in language) adheres to different grammatical rules than those defined at the beginning does not speak falsely (or does not speak at all), but speaks about something else. In other terms, he plays a different game but plays nonetheless (Baker and Hacker 2009):

> The rules of grammar are arbitrary and not arbitrary, in the same sense as is the choice of a unit of measurement. This is also expressed by saying that these rules are "practical" or "impractical," "useful," or "useless," but not "true" or "false." . . .
>
> "The unit of measurement is arbitrary" (if this is not to mean "Choose the unit any way you want in this case") means nothing other than that the specification of the unit of measurement is not a specification of length (even though it sounds like one). And to say that the rules of grammar are arbitrary just means: Don't confuse a rule for the use of the word A with a sentence in which the word A is used. Don't think that a rule is answerable to a reality, is comparable to a reality, in more or less the way an empirical proposition about A is. . . .
>
> The importance of a game lies in the fact that we play this game. That we carry out *these* actions. It doesn't lose its importance by not being an action in another (superior) game.
>
> Why don't I call the rules of cooking arbitrary; and why am I tempted to call the rules of grammar arbitrary? Because "cooking" is defined by its end, whereas speaking a language isn't. Therefore the use of language is autonomous in a certain sense in which cooking and washing aren't. For anyone guided by other than the correct rules when he cooks, cooks badly; but anyone guided by rules other than those for chess plays a *different game*, and anyone guided by grammatical rules other than such and such doesn't as a different result say anything that is false, but is talking about something else. (*The Big Typescript TS 213*, VII, 235–238)

Creativity is represented by the rule itself which is determined in an open way only in use and in the course of work: a use that is in the creative, liberal, and autonomous (linguistic) hands of humans. It is therefore a use that cannot be reduced to the logical forms of a system: "no course of action could be determined by a rule, because every course of action can be made out to accord with the rule. The answer was: if everything can be made out to accord with the rule, then it can also be made out to conflict with it. And so there would be neither accord nor conflict here" (§ *PU* 201). "Accord" or "conflict" are thus not useful parameters to evaluate linguistic games because one cannot summarize what the possible applications for each rule will be, much less which applications will be correct and which will not. Only future use can demonstrate the content of the rule presented: the consequences of grasping the creativity thus understood in the functioning of the linguistic game puts us like savage and primitive people who hear the expressions of civilized men, a false interpretation on them, and then draws the queerest conclusions from it (*PU* § 194).

Creative Rules and *Masse Parlante*

The creative nature of the rule alone, however, does not justify a fact: How can a creative rule be able to guide a game, eluding the idea that there is a sort of anarchy being determined in the (linguistic) game? It remains to be emphasized how creative and individual freedom with regard to the rule (and the nature of the rule itself) can coexist with the necessity that this same rule functions as a framework of reference of use, and therefore does not determine behavioral (and linguistical) anarchy, but is at the same time a point of reference that can be innovated. The *PU* Wittegenstein asks whether a rule can demonstrate what one person must do at *this* point. What a person does can always be made compatible with the rule through some sort of interpretation. A rule, if it imposes something, does not do so because that thing could not be done otherwise or could not be interpreted in any other way. The imposition that the rule produces is such because there is a stable use, a socially shared habit of using that rule, and in interpreting that rule in that way (§ 198). Moreover, what we call "following a rule" could not be done by a single man, once in a lifetime. Following a rule, communicating, giving an order, playing a game of chess, are habits; that is, uses (shared) in a language that represent real institutions (§ 199).

The creative freedom to violate or modify a rule in order to make a new rule and a new game does not push the game toward forms of communicative chaos: if any course of action can become a rule and, *sic stantibus rebus*, every rule can lose its power of being a rule and ruling, the only element capable of addressing some form of regularity is the (shared) practice, the (shared) use, the (shared) habits and thus, the behavior of the *masse parlante*. And therefore, "obeying a rule" is a practice, and to *believe* one is obeying a rule is not to obey a rule. Hence, it is not possible to obey a rule "privately": otherwise believing one was obeying a rule would be the same thing as obeying it (*PU* § 202).

Even though it is a linguistic choice of individuals—just as the moves in a game are a result of individual choices—in order for a linguistic (or non-linguistic) game to exist, it must be substantiated by rules (susceptible to change and redefinition) which exist only by virtue of social sharing: it is the uses of the *masse parlante* which determine what is regular and what is not, what allows the communication game to proceed and what hinders it and therefore, not permitting the game to exist. Obeying a rule is the same as obeying an order. We are trained to do so; we react to an order in a certain way. But what if one person reacts one way and another person reacts in a different way? Who is right? Suppose you arrive in an unknown country with a language quite strange to you; under what circumstances would you say that the speakers there gave orders, understood them, obeyed them, rebelled against them, and so on? The standard behaviour of mankind is the system of reference by means of which we interpret an unknown language (*PU* § 206).

This element becomes more evident if we consider the semantic dimension of the language.

Looking for the meaning of a sign within a game of uses is not a strategy that can be applied "privatim," but requires a community dimension. This means placing oneself in a perspective of sharing, that is, giving the concrete uses of the language and the modes of linguistic behaviour the ability to be a frame of reference, the ability to make itself a rule and not only a simple interpretation of the rule (*PU* § 201).

Individual interpretations of the rule do not offer a solid basis upon which to build the constitution of the concepts of correct application of a rule in particular singular cases. In contrast, it is through the attribution of a pragmatic (collective) role to a single interpretation of the rule that one can define what a rule is. For example, if the community believes that the result of 1.002 is achieved through the correct application of rule 1.000 plus 2, then, only thanks to this, would a different result, as of not having applied the rule (or applying the rule incorrectly), be called an incorrect result. It must be said that it is either an incorrect application of that rule or it is not at all an application of that rule[3] (Frascolla 2000).

The volume *Wittgenstein on Rule and Private Language* (Kripke 1982) highlights the profound changes that the Austrian philosopher has made in the conception of language, starting from the truth-conditions of the proposition—that is, from its meaning—the aspect that most interests Wittgenstein. The philosophical analysis of language moves from conditions of truth to conditions of justification: a proposition therefore goes from being true (meaning it does not have to be demonstrated) since a meaning exists as an axiom, to conditions of validity of a sentence (or non-validity) in a linguistic game following a judgment of use by speakers. Kripke (1982, 72–92) claims:

The simplest, most basic idea of the *Tractatus* can hardly be dismissed: a declarative sentence gets its meaning by virtue of its *true conditions*, by virtue of its correspondence to facts that must obtain if it is true. For example, "the cat is on the mat" is understood by those speakers who realize that it is true if and only if a certain cat is on a certain mat; it is false otherwise. The presence of the cat on the mat is a fact or condition-in-the-world that would make the sentence true (express a truth) if it obtained. So stated, the *Tractatus* picture of the meaning of declarative sentences may seem not only natural but even tautological. . . . In the place of this view, Wittgenstein offers an alternative rough general picture. . . . Wittgenstein replaces the question, "What must be the case for this sentence to be true?" By two others: first, "Under what conditions may this form of words be appropriately asserted (or denied)?"; second, given an answer to the first question, "What is the role, and the utility, in our lives of our practice of asserting (or denying) the form of words under these conditions?"

. . . We can say that Wittgenstein proposes a picture of a language based, not on *truth conditions*, but on *assertability conditions* or *justification conditions*: under what circumstances are we allowed to make a given assertion?

. . . An individual who claims to have mastered the concept of addition will be judged by the community to have done so if his particular responses agree with those of the community in enough cases, especially the simple ones (and if his "wrong" answers are not often *bizarrely* wrong, as in "5" for "68+57," but seem to agree with ours in *procedure*, even when he makes a "computational mistake"). An individual who passes such tests is admitted into the community as an adder; an individual who passes such tests in enough other cases is admitted as a normal speaker of the language and member of the community.

According to Wittgenstein's philosophical thought, following a rule is a communal act in the same way that such a rule could be fragmented or modified. The static nature of Saussure's *serré* verbal system is supplanted by the dynamism of the linguistic game that is reflected in the community and from which derive the judgments of argumentation and justification. The individual dimension of the linguistic rule (or rule of the game) has no specific weight on its own; weight which, on the contrary, is attributed only to a community dimension. There exists a consideration of language that is founded on the judgment of communicative acceptability on behalf of the community as the only indication of communicative possibility; that is, as the only beacon toward which the communication can and must trend.

The proposed philosophical and semiotic references have highlighted how the analogy between language and game represents the best contribution to address the theme of linguistic and semiotic creativity. The reference to Wittgenstein has broadened the perspective of the study not so much by looking directly at the concept of creativity, whose term does not explicitly appear either in *Tractatus* or in *PU*, but by theoretically grounding the idea of language as a game in which violations and changes to the rules are possible without them preventing the game from continuing and thus allowing the communication to proceed.

Wittgenstein did not dive directly into the nature of the rule; however, each language consists of a "part" deeply characterized by rules: this is the grammar of a language, for which current linguistic sciences are unable to provide a clear definition (Bruni 1984; Serianni 2006; 2012; Serianni and Antonelli 2017), but which, on the basis of Wittgenstein's philosophy, is characterized by the forms that a language takes on a phonetic, morphological, syntactic, lexical, and pragmatic level (De Mauro 1965). This is a non-restrictive concept of grammar, a concept linked to the use of a language and therefore to the creativity of a language. It is a grammar that changes and that is able to change and be violated without the communication being affected (or affected so much so that it creates misunderstanding and therefore no communication at all).

Although indirectly, Prampolini (2001, 132–144) creates a profile on creativity that can be found in Wittgenstein's philosophy and seems to identify a formulation of deep interest for our purposes. We could say it is an ontological interest, in that creativity is nothing extraordinary, but is an intrinsic part of language (and of life):

> creativa è l'azione per cui un fatto (linguistico e non) entra in un gioco, in una regola; creativa è l'azione per cui lo stesso fatto può entrare in giochi e regole diverse; la creatività sta sia nella creazione sia nell'applicazione delle regole. E come accade in ogni partita, una mossa è allo stesso tempo ripetizione e novità, atto prefigurato (regolare) e nuova figurazione.
> ... Ma in questo modo la creatività non ha più nulla di straordinario; essa è parte intrinseca della vita.
> Le regole, poi, non sono scritte una volta per tutte: esse vivono fin quando sono applicate. Nel linguaggio come in ogni altro comportamento, ad ogni applicazione una regola si rinnova, si ricrea. E ugualmente ogni accadimento è pronto ad entrare in una regola e in un gioco diverso. La forza di una regola, la sua iussività (non poter agire diversamente), come pure la sua produttività (la quantità di atti che governa) non sono dati da qualche potere intrinseco al suo dettato: essa vive nell'estensione delle sue applicazioni.
> In altre parole, si deve seguire la regola perché altri la hanno adottata e la stanno applicando.
> ... Il soggetto *(singolo)* resta figura non sufficiente per l'attuazione dei giochi.
> ... Anche le regole non sono il prodotto di un agente o di una causa efficiente, tanto meno di un atto individuale, ma di un concerto complessivo di

azioni e di reciprocità. E tuttavia, ci sarebbero ancora giochi ove non ci fossero giocatori? Chiameremmo ancora giochi le attività in cui non c'è chi fa le mosse?
 . . . La creatività è un *conatus*, affermazione di qualcosa che fa segno di sé.[4]

Wittgenstein's acquisitions, albeit from a philosophical and theoretical perspective, have implications in the formal consideration of a language, in its creative use within the linguistic space, and also in the teaching and learning process. These are the theoretical elements that, in our opinion, can be functional in considering linguistic creativity not as a "simple" semiotic property, but as a theoretical approach to the creation of meaning and theoretical assumption for communication and understanding.

NOTES

1. Many terms that have fallen out of use shall be reborn, and those now in repute shall fall, if usage so will it, in whose hands lies the decision, the right, and the rule of speech (our translation).

2. As written in Garroni ([1978] 2010, 105): "se un giocatore—quando tocca a lui la mossa o l'azione—potesse decidere d'inventare indipendentemente da ogni regola precedente proprio la regola che gli attribuisce la vittoria, il gioco non potrebbe neppure cominciare e vincerebbe—prima di ogni gioco—colui che semplicemente avesse inventato la regola a lui favorevole: o meglio vincerebbe chi per primo dicesse «ho vinto». Che sarebbe a suo modo una regola, ma di un gioco diverso: il gioco della rapidità e della sopraffazione—come accade nel gioco o quasi-gioco infantile del 'Pizzico a te, fortuna a me.'"

3. As written in Frascolla (2000, 231–232): "qualunque tentativo di estrarre da una formulazione generale di una regola, o da una serie di esempi di applicazioni, il concetto di ciò che costituisce la sua corretta applicazione in un nuovo caso poggerebbe su qualche interpretazione della formulazione della regola o di espressioni del tipo "essere identico a," "essere in accordo con," "essere conseguenza di," ecc. Le interpretazioni, però, non offrono una solida base su cui poter fondare la costituzione dei concetti di corretta applicazione di una regola nei singoli casi particolari. Al contrario, è attraverso l'attribuzione di un ruolo paradigmatico ad una data applicazione che si costituiscono tanto quei concetti quanto, pezzo per pezzo, l'identità stessa della regola: ad esempio, se all'applicazione con cui si ottiene per risultato 1.002 è affidato l'ufficio di paradigma della corretta applicazione al numero 1.000 della regola di addizionare 2, allora, in forza di quest'attribuzione, *e solo in virtù di essa*, di un processo segnico che porti ad un risultato diverso, dovrà dirsi o che costituisce un'applicazione scorretta di quella regola, oppure che non è affatto un'applicazione di quella regola."

4. This is an excerpt from Prampolini (2001) inserted directly in italian, its original language. Referring to Wittgenstein, Prampolini emphasizes how creativity in the

linguistic game model is nothing extraordinary but is part of the life of a language. Therefore, the grammar rules of a language are not written conclusively but live only as long as they are applied. In addition, each rule is renewed and recreated though its use. Prampolini highlights that creativity is the action for which a fact (whether it be linguistic or not) enters a game, a rule. The action for which the same fact can enter into different games and rules is creative and creativity lies both in the formation and in the application of rules. As in every game, a move/an action represents both repetition and novelty; a prefigured (regular) act and a new figuration. Nevertheless, in this way creativity is not extraordinary, it is an intrinsic part of life. The rules, therefore, are not written once and for all; they live so long as they are applied. In language, as in any other behaviour, a rule is renewed and recreated each time it is applied. Likewise, every event/fact is ready to enter into a different rule and game. The strength of a rule, its force (not being able to act otherwise), as well as its productivity (the number of acts it governs) are not given by some power intrinsic to its dictation; the rule lives in the extension of its application. In other words, one must follow the rule because others have adopted it and are applying it. The subject (single) remains an insufficient figure for the implementation of the games. The rules are neither the product of an agent nor of an efficient cause (let alone an individual act) but of an overall collective agreement of actions and reciprocity. However, could games exist without players? Would activities in which there is no one to make the moves still be called games? Ultimately, creativity is a *conatus*, an affirmation of something that makes a sign of itself.

Chapter 3

The Language between *Rule-Governed* and *Rule-Changing Creativity*

> La facoltà imitativa è una delle principali parti dell'ingegno umano. L'imparare in gran parte non è che imitare. Ora la facoltà d'imitare non è che una facoltà di attenzione esatta e minuta all'oggetto e sue parti, e una facilità di assuefarsi.[1]
>
> Giacomo Leopardi, *Zibaldone di pensieri*

> Ora l'Uso è l'arbitrio, il signore delle lingue, come tutti affermano; anzi, si può dire, è le lingue stesse. Quest'arbitrio però è mutabile: qualità la quale è un vantaggio e un inconveniente insieme; ma ad ogni modo è ingenita, e pur da nessuno posta in dubbio. Vantaggio, perché può recare e reca nelle lingue aumento e miglioramento; inconveniente, perché dove cade toglie loro quella certezza, quelle unità di che hanno tanto bisogno, di che vivono.[2]
>
> Alessandro Manzoni, *Sentir messa*

The concept of creativity proposed by Wittgenstein in the *Philosophical Investigations* (*PU*) is centered around the concept of rule which shifts from a dimension of application of the rule itself to a dimension in which the rule is undetermined and continuously open to change as a result of the user's application of the language.

In line with Prampolini's (2001) argument, we believe that Wittgenstein's creativity opposes precision in logical space (this is *Tractatus*'s plan, without the possibility of creative acts) to the imprecision in the grammatical space of propositions which are life forms that are achieved within linguistic games (this is the *PU's* plan, with continuous creativity).

This principle brings out at least one fundamental consideration whereby Wittgenstein's linguistic game combines two complementary concepts: that of the game as a birthplace or change of rules and as a space of creation and freedom (similar to Noam Chomsky's *rule-changing creativity*); and that of the game as a place of adhesion of linguistic facts to the obligations and constraints established by the rules, that is, of the game as a space of adaption to given elements (similar to Chomsky's *rule-governed creativity*).

If these two complementary dimensions are not considered, the notion of game is not fully capable of examining the theme of creativity.[3]

THE *RULE-GOVERNED CREATIVITY*

In the field of linguistics, the American linguist Noam Chomsky insisted more than anyone else on the idea of language creativity, thereby distinguishing *rule-governed creativity* from *rule-changing creativity*. Referring to Descartes in *Cartesian Linguistics*[4] (1966, 59), Chomsky observes that language is the mechanism of analysis and the determination of thought whose possibilities of expression are such because the creative aspect of language use exists: "The fundamental property of a language must be its capacity to use its finitely specifiable mechanisms for an unbounded and unpredictable set of contingencies." *The Creative Aspect of Language Use* ensures infinite expressive potential starting from finite base units through the use of recursive training rules that are the foundations of generative grammar: this creativity model is defined by the *rule-governed creativity* formula (Horrocks 2016).

Following Garroni ([1978] 2010), we highlight how the reflections that Chomsky calls *Cartesian Linguistics* only generally pertain to Descartes and the Cartesians' school. However, it is true that "cartesian linguistics" is a label indicating how in Descartes (particularly in the *Discourse on Method* and *L'Homme*), we find the first clear references to a conception of creativity as *rule-governed creativity*, although technically, this idea had not yet been considered (Den Ouden 1975).

Chomsky addresses the phenomenon of linguistic creativity by indicating the unprecedented character that linguistic signs may have, derived from combinations of basic elements (the morphemes of the language) with a limited number of morphological and syntactic rules. The *rule-governed creativity* is used to produce and recognize a potentially infinite number of sentences, many of which have never been formulated before but are still usable and understandable by those who are familiar with the vocabulary and syntax of the language (Chomsky 1980[5]).

In *Aspects of the Theory of Syntax* (1965, v-6) Chomsky considers the creative aspect of languages to be a common property of all verbal systems and provides the means to express thought by reacting appropriately to infinite new situations:

The Language between Rule-Governed *and* Rule-Changing Creativity

The idea that a language is based on a system of rules determining the interpretation of its infinitely many sentences is by no means novel. Well over a century ago, it was expressed with reasonable clarity by Wilhelm von Humboldt in his famous but rarely studied introduction to general linguistics. His view that a language "makes infinitive use of finitive means" and that its grammar must describe the processes that make this possible is, furthermore, an outgrowth of a persistent concern, within rationalistic philosophy of language and mind, with this "creative" aspect of language use. . . .

Within traditional linguistic theory, furthermore, it was clearly understood that one of the qualities that all languages have in common is their "creative" aspect. Thus, an essential property of language is that it provides a means for expressing indefinitely many thoughts and for reacting appropriately in an indefinite range of new situations.

The grammar of a particular language, then, is to be supplemented by a universal grammar that accommodates the creative aspect of language use and expresses the deep-seated regularities which, being universal, are omitted from the grammar itself.

The proposed model gives a philosophical significance to Chomsky's creativity (as if the Cartesian reference were not sufficient), so as to build a grammatical theory of languages with a philosophical foundation in language theories (Di Cesare 2005).

The Philosophical Foundation of Linguistic Creativity: Language As *Enérgeia*

Following Di Cesare (2005), we consider how the philosophical reference to Humboldt in the theme of language creativity—presented in the passage of *Aspects of the Theory of Syntax*—is an attempt to offer further philosophical reference to Chomsky's thought, since the link between Chomsky and Humboldt is not a real theoretical sharing point between the two perspectives.

Chomsky was strongly criticized for this interpretation because he considered Humboldt to be the precursor of generative grammar. Generative grammar is not what Humboldt refers to as *form of language*, namely the generative principle of each language. As written in *Cartesian Linguistics* (19–22):

> The Cartesian emphasis on the creative aspect of language use, as the essential and defining characteristic of human language, finds its most forceful expression in Humboldt's attempt to develop a comprehensive theory of general linguistics. Humboldt's characterization of language as *enérgeia* rather than *ergon*, extends and elaborates—often, in almost the same words—the formulations typical of Cartesian Linguistics and romantic philosophy of language and aesthetic theory.

> For Humboldt, the only true definition of language is "eine genetische." ... There is a constant and uniform factor underlying this "Arbeit des Geistes"; it is this which Humboldt calls the "Form" of language. ...
>
> In developing the notion of "form of language" as a generative principle, fixed and unchanging, determining the scope and providing the means for the unbounded set of individual "creative" acts that constitute the normal language use, Humboldt makes an original and significant contribution to linguistic theory—a contribution that unfortunately remained unrecognized and unexploited until fairly recently.

Chomsky attempts to draw a parallel between the fixed and the unchallengeable generative principle of generative grammar with what Humboldt calls the *form of language*. In Chomsky's model, linguistic use is unlimited and indefinite, but the form that is found below and acts as its base—the underlying generative principle—is closed and definite because it is made up of fixed mechanisms: "The fixed mechanisms that, in their systematic and unified representation, constitute the form of the language must enable it to produce an indefinite range of speech events corresponding to the conditions imposed by thought processes" (20). In line with this idea, Chomsky (1965, 9) proposes a terminological parallelism between Descartes and Humboldt when he argues that

> confusion over this matter has sufficiently persisted to suggest that a terminological change might be in order. Nevertheless, I think that the term "generative grammar" is completely appropriate and have therefore continued to use it. The term "generate" is familiar to the sense intended here in logic, particularly in Post's theory of combinatorial systems. Furthermore, "generate" seems to be the most appropriate translation for Humboldt's term *erzeugen*, which he frequently uses, it seems, in essentially the sense here intended. Since this use of the term "generate" is well established both in logic and the tradition of linguistic theory, I can see no reason for a revision of terminology.

We refer to *Coseiru* ([1952] 1971), Di Cesare (2005), and Aarsleff (1988) to further explore the relationship between Chomsky's *generate* and Humboldt's *erzeugen*. However, we highlight how the form of language cannot be considered as a limited set of fixed mechanisms because, if that were the case, it would prove to be something static, at least in its founding principles (Di Cesare 2005).

The following is an excerpt which illustrates what Humboldt calls *Form of language*[6] ([1836] 1988, 48–50):

> We must look upon *language*, not as a dead *product*, but far more as a *producing*, must abstract more from what it does as a designator of objects and

instrument of understanding, and revert more carefully, on the other hand, to its origin, closely entwined as it is with inner mental activity, and to its reciprocal influence on the latter.

From the words of Humboldt, *language*, considered in its real nature, is a long-lasting thing, and at every moment a *transitory* one. Even its preserved written form is always just an incomplete and mummy-like maintenance, only required again in attempting to picture the living speech. It is no product (*ergon*), but an activity (*enérgeia*). The true description can therefore only be a genetic one. For it is the continual *mental labor* of making the *articulated* sound capable of expressing *thought*.

The continuous and consistent element in this mental labor of promoting articulated sound to an expression of thought, when viewed in its complete possible comprehension and systematically presented, constitutes the *form of language*.

The characteristic forms of languages rests on every *single* one of their smallest *elements*; however mysterious it may be in detail, each is in some way determined by that form. It is barely possible, however, to find points of which it can be maintained that this form has attached to them, taken individually.

The fixed mechanisms of Chomsky's generative principle are not comparable to Humboldt's *enérgeia* because, if they were, there would be something static in the creation of languages (something that is not considered by the *form of language*). According to Humboldt, the mechanisms would be *forma formata* instead of *forma formans*; they would be a product as opposed to an activity (Formigari 1977a,b). Moreover, Humboldt ([1836] 1988, 61) clearly states that the grammar of languages cannot appear to be stable even if apparently made up of previously formed elements:

> A language in its whole compass, contains everything that it has transformed into sounds. But just as the matter of thinking, and the infinity of its combinations, can never been exhausted, so it is equally impossible to do this with the mass of what calls for designation and connection in language. In addition to its already formed elements, language also consists, before all else, of methods for carrying forward the work of the mind to which it prescribes the path and the former. The elements, once firmly fashioned, constitute, indeed, a relatively dead mass, but one which bears within itself the living seed of a never-ending determinability. At every single point and period, therefore, language, like nature itself, appears to man—in contrast to all else that he has already known and thought of—as an inexhaustible storehouse, in which the mind can always discover something new to it, and feeling perceive what it has not yet felt in this way.

As previously mentioned in the introduction, Coseriu (1962) maintains that studying the semiotic and theoretical functioning of a language through the dichotomy between *ergon* and *enérgeia* is linked (on a conceptual and purely lexical level) to Aristotle's interpretation of *enérgeia*; this is a creative and free activity in all its forms, without purpose if not for the creation itself, with fine value to production and a strong teleological implication (Di Cesare 1987; Di Cesare 2005).

In relation to the emphasis placed by the German philosopher on the creative aspect of languages, Coseriu (1962, 1958) proposes some clarifications that are appropriate to resume in order to appropriately consider *enérgeia* and to treat a language as if it were *érgon* (Coseriu 1958, 25[7]):

> Ahora, la lengua funciona y se da concretamente en el *hablar*. Tomar como base de toda la teoría de la lengua este hecho significa partir de la conocida afirmación de Humboldt de que el lenguaje no es *érgon* sino *enérgeia*. Esta afirmación se cita a menudo, pero, en la mayoría de los casos, para olvidarla rápidamente y refugiarse en la lengua como *érgon*. En cambio, es necesario, en primer lugar, tomar en serio la frase de Humboldt, es decir, tomarla como fundamento, pues no se trata de una paradoja o de una metáfora, sino de la desnuda aserción de una verdad. Realmente, y no en algún sentido metafórico, el lenguaje es *actividad*, y no *producto*.

Moreover:

> Casi siempre se dice que Humboldt quería poner de relieve lo "vivo" en el lenguaje, que consideró el lenguaje ante todo como "habla," como actividad de hablar, y hasta se hace coincidir la distinción humboldtiana entre *ergon* y *enérgeia* con la distinción de Saussure entre *langue* y *parole*, que en realidad tiene un sentido totalmente distinto. Y casi siempre se olvida lo más importante, o sea que Humboldt era un pensador aristotélico y que en esta frase aludía, precisamente, a sus fundamentos aristotélicos. En efecto, Humboldt no escribe simplemente *Werk*, "producto," y *Tätigkeit*, "actividad," sino que añade las expresiones técnicas de Aristóteles *ergon* y *enérgeia*, con lo cual muestra claramente que por *Tätigkeit* no entiende una actividad cualquiera, sino un tipo especial y determinado de actividad, precisamente, la ενέργεια aristotélica: la actividad anterior a la potencia, es decir, la actividad creadora o "libre" en el sentido filosófico de la palabra libre. . . .
>
> Entender el lenguaje como *enérgeia* significa, en consecuencia, considerarlo como actividad creadora en *todas* sus formas. *Enérgeia* es tanto el lenguaje en general como el lenguaje en cuanto habla. Todo acto de hablar es, en alguna medida, un acto creador. . . .
>
> Pero *enérgeia* son también las lenguas, que no son sino modalidades particulares del lenguaje en cuanto determinado históricamente. Por ello también las

lenguas hay que interpretarlas en sentido dinámico. Una escuela norteamericana de lingüística que, en parte, acepta formalmente principios humboldtianos ha llegado en los últimos tiempos a interpretar las lenguas como sistemas de producción lingüística. Pero los representantes de esta escuela no han entendido correctamente a Humboldt, se quedan en la separación entre sincronía y diacronía y hasta le reprochan a Humboldt el no haber distinguido entre la actividad creadora que aplica reglas y actividad creadora que modifica reglas (de las lenguas). En contra de tal reproche hay que advenir que, si el lenguaje se entiende como *enérgeia*, esa distinción está fuera de lugar y, más aún, carece simplemente de sentido, puesto que, en realidad, el funcionamiento de las reglas y el "cambió lingüístico" no son, en la lengua misma, dos momentos, sino uno solo. (Coseriu 1977, 20–22)

The above excerpts highlight both the need to interpret Humboldt's categories under Aristotle's philosophical sphere and the theoretical impossibility of studying Chomsky's generative principle though Humboldt's theory. From Humboldt's perspective, the creativity of language is indeed a founding principle of language as a faculty of idioms: however, creativity as *enérgeia* is not the same as Chomsky's creativity. Therefore, creativity governed by fixed and limited mechanisms is not adjoined to Humboldt's creativity which modifies the grammar of the language: what Chomsky considers *rule-governed creativity* is not considered as creativity at all by Humboldt. According to Humboldt, linguistic creativity can change and, while in use, it can modify the rules of a language: having established a certain number of linguistic rules, this will always be modifiable by violating those rules and establishing different ones. This cannot occur at the discretion of the individual speaker but occurs on a social level.

In the most radical exegesis of Humboldt's thought, the rule itself has no real determination, thus it is impossible to contemplate the possibility (even if only theoretical) of altering something which itself is not determined (Di Cesare 2005). Humboldt's creativity that changes the rules manifests itself in every individual act, surpasses the linguistic system and creates its constituent characters[8] (of the system) (De Mauro 1982; Garroni [1978] 2010). Language changes, but in order for it to be a completely creative system it is nevertheless determined by the history and society in which it was founded. Every language is free from constrictive ties that are not determined by the historical character of the languages themselves.[9] Linguistic creativity is thus achieved between adherence to the history and the individual act:[10]

> I have already pointed out earlier on that in our study of language we find ourselves plunged throughout—if I may so put it—into a historical milieu, and that neither a nation nor a language, among those known to us, can be called *original*. Since each has already received from earlier generations material from a prehistory unknown to us. (Humboldt [1836] 1988, 49–50)

Humboldt's lesson[11] also includes references that could be political and current.

We consider how the theoretical and philosophical base of what Humboldt and Herder define as *triunity of Language-Prince-Nation* is to be found within the romantic lesson. In *Filosofia della Romantik* (Formigari 1977b), language is a circumstance that determines the nation, along with the climate, the geographical situation, the religion, the political constitution, and the customs and uses. Unlike the latter elements, which can be, to some extent, separated and distinguished, the language is the soul of the nation and it proceeds hand in hand with its development alongside that which it cannot be separated from.[12] The principles of linguistic contact from Weinreich's ([1963] 1967) lesson aim to limit this concept in which the principles of contact were exhausted between multilingualism and bilingualism. Broadening the perspective of analysis to multilingualism and super diversity (Vertovec 2007) demonstrates how the romantic system was more often linked to a social and political model as opposed to a linguistic, theoretical, and semiotic model.

THE *RULE-CHANGING CREATIVITY*

In *Aspects of the Theory of Syntax*, Chomsky highlights the objectives of modern linguistics by proposing a radically different version from the semiotic concept proposed by Saussure. According to Saussure, linguistics was part of a general science to which he applied the name semiotics. Chomsky (1965, 3–6) argues that the "linguistic theory is concerned primarily with an ideal speaker-listener, in a completely homogeneous speech-community, who knows its language perfectly and is unaffected by such grammatically irrelevant conditions as memory limitations, distractions, shifts of attention and interest, and errors (random or characteristic) in applying his knowledge of the language in actual performance."

The attention toward an ideal speaker-listener leads Chomsky to make "a fundamental distinction between *competence* (the speaker-hearer's knowledge of his language) and *performance* (the actual use of language in concrete situations)." In this framework of reference "the problem for the linguist, as well as for the child learning the language, is to determine from the data of performance the underlying system of rules that has been mastered by the speaker-hearer and that he puts to use in actual performance. Hence, in the technical sense, linguistic theory is mentalistic, since it is concerned with discovering a mental reality underlying actual behaviour."

The focus of the linguist that intends on scientifically studying a language is to look at a system, a grammatical apparatus, "to be a description of the ideal speaker-hearer's intrinsic competence." This type of grammar is called generative grammar. The grammars of individual languages have limitations which the linguist, the modern theoretician of the language, must realize: "The peculiarities of individual tongues are explained in their respective grammars and dictionaries. Those things, that all languages have in common, or that are necessary to every language, are treated of in a science, which some have called *Universal* or *Philosophical* grammar."

Chomsky admits that taking the fundamental property of languages as a reference, namely their creative aspect (of creativity as recursion and therefore generative), "the grammar of a particular language is to be supplemented by a universal grammar that accommodates the creative aspect of language use and expresses the deep-seated regularities which, being universal, are omitted from the grammar itself." Considering the regularity of linguistic forms with the aim of constructing a grammatical theory is a much more important question for the linguist than the study of performance: determining whether an utterance is grammatical (if it respects the condition of regularity according to a logical-mathematical model) is more important than the analysis of the acceptability of the utterance in a social context.

Despite the fact that the proposed theoretical model is founded on grammar and on its regularity, Chomsky's linguistics still believes that a form of creativity that betrays the universal logical recursion is possible: If language were only creative in a logical sense, it would be impossible to represent any innovation according to a pattern that fully respects those rules. However, not only are we far from having demonstrated the existence of universal rules in languages, any linguistic rule can be changed and replaced by other rules. If a rule cannot be altered or substituted, it is not a linguistic rule (Garroni [1978] 2010).

Albeit with milder justifications compared to Garroni, Chomsky admits the possibility of a form of creativity that modifies the rules. Just as the philosophical base for the *rule-governed creativity* was Humboldtian, it is Humboldt himself who does not recognize that alongside regular creativity there exists a creativity that changes the rules and escapes the recursive generative process:

> For all his concern with the creative aspect of language use and with form of generative process, Humboldt does not go on to face the substantive question: what is the precise character of "organic form" in language. He does not, so far as I can see, attempt to construct particular generative grammars or to determine the general character of any such system, the universal schema to which any particular grammar conforms. In this respect, his work in general linguistics does not reach the levels achieved by some of his predecessors, as we shall see directly. His work is also marred by unclarity regarding several fundamental questions, in particular regarding, the distinction between the rule-governed

creativity which constitutes the normal use of language and which does not modify the form of the language at all and the kind of innovation that leads to a modification in the grammatical structure of the language. These defects have been recognized and, to some extent, overcome in more recent work. Furthermore, in his discussion of generative processes in language is it often unclear whether what he has in mind in underlying competence or performance. (Chomsky 1966, 27–28)

According to Chomsky, the technical tools to deal with rule-governed creativity separately from *rule-changing creativity* have become accessible only in the last decades in the course of logical works and on the foundations of mathematics.

On the topic of linguistic and semiotic creativity, one cannot speak only of *rule-governed creativity*, which also represents an important aspect of linguistic creativity. After having established a certain set of linguistic rules, this will always be modifiable, violating those rules and establishing different ones. This process—especially in terms of deeper regularities—will not be naturally fulfilled at the discretion of the individual speaker but takes place on a social level and holds significant consequences with regard to a linguistic theory. One must come to terms with what Chomsky calls the *rule-changing creativity*, which he does not technically deal with[13] (Garroni [1978] 2010).

In *Current Issues of Linguistic Theory* (1964), Chomsky recalls the fundamental distinction between creativity that leaves the language completely unchanged and the creativity that changes the set of grammatical rules. This distinction will not be developed or resumed and will therefore disappear from Chomsky's theoretical interests. Instead, Chomsky will argue that the foundation of the faculty of language is a combinatorial faculty, but this faculty will not be recognized as a form of creativity because in the very idea of creativity (starting from the philosophical references previously proposed) we still find an individual factor that could pertain to the idea of an *ex novo* creation—an idea that would obviously not be relevant to Chomsky's creative model.

In the book that contains the most refined version of Chomsky's theoretical project, *The Minimalist Program*, creativity is no longer mentioned but it has been replaced by a much more abstract and formal concept known as *merge* which is defined as "the simplest computational operation" (Chomsky 2015, IX). *Merge* no longer holds the idea that something can be created (but that it can only be transformed) and from this perspective, even a lexical change allows for a greater formulization of the theory (Cimatti 2018). In fact, Chomsky is interested in a scientific theory of language which is predominately mathematical: *merge* refers to an operation which "takes a pair of syntactic objects (SO_i, SO_j) and replaces them by a new combined syntactic object (SOij)" (Chomsky 2015, 208). Chomsky is interested in a completely abstract and calculable device that allows for the creation of new syntactic objects by combining preexisting syntactic objects.

In his theory, Chomsky argues that anything that is not syntactical (semantic and pragmatic) in language is not required to account for the logical and computational nucleus of language. According to Chomsky, *merge* is the syntactic engine that produces an infinite variety of potential linguistic expressions that guarantee the communication between people:

> The most elementary property of human language is that knowing some variety of, say, English, each speaker can produce and interpret an unbounded number of expressions, understandable to others sharing similar knowledge. Furthermore, although there can be four- and five-word long sentences, there can be no four and a half word sentences. In this sense, language is a system of discrete infinity. It follows that human language is grounded on a particular computational mechanism, realized neutrally, that yields an infinite array of structured expressions. (Berwick *et al.* 2013, 90)

That which for logical mechanisms is considered "discrete infinite," therefore calculable and logical, cannot be subjected to indeterminate and variable foundations through which the meaning is realized through its use (or in the linguistic games). Take for instance the vagueness of a sign: according to Chomsky it is a pathology of the language but according to other theories that refer to De Mauro's idea, vagueness is not a pathology of the language but one of the constitutive feature which allows for its anchorage to context and users. In languages, the response to the speakers' communicative needs and to the needs of the creation of meaning is given by the expandability, retractability, and transformability of the meaning of any morpheme. The indeterminacy of the meaning and of the signifier as potentiality of multiple determinations of a sign constitutes vagueness (De Mauro 2008). Indeterminacy is a semiotic characteristic that is always in power because the vagueness is continuously realized in use according to the attitude of reciprocity between the users defined upon the field.[14]

SISTEMA, NORMA, AND *HABLA*: THREE CONCEPTS BETWEEN *LANGUE* AND *PAROLE*

The CGL, which in this study has been invoked for the definition of language as a sign game to which the concept of value and sign determination is linked in relation to the other signs of the system, offers important perspectives, beginning with the dichotomy between *langue* and *parole*:

> Una segunda serie de sugerencias acerca de la posibilidad y necesidad de distinguir entre *norma* y *sistema*, así como acerca del lugar donde hay que establecer la distinción, nos ha llegado De la Fuente misma de la oposición fundamental entre *lengua* y *habla*, es decir, del *Curso* de Saussure. El extraordinario libro póstumo del maestro ginebrino contiene, también bajo este aspecto, precisas ideas e intuiciones susceptibles de desarrollo—en sentido positivo o negativo—así como contiene el embrión y semilla de tantas doctrinas y actitudes de lingüística actual. (Coseriu 1962, 43)

First, Coseriu highlights that it is not possible to oppose something (the *langue*) to the *parole* which is detached from it. In other words, *langue* and *parole* do not describe autonomous sections of the same object (nor do they describe two separate objects) but they represent different viewpoints of the same faculty of language. This entails that in the continuum between *langue* and *parole,* abstraction and concreteness, there may be room for a third element: norma. Linguistic acts can be unprecedented acts of creation, but also acts of recreation: speaking is not always an *ex novo* invention of the individual but often the speaker adapts to previous models which were created and shared by a community of speakers.

The individual creates the linguistic act on previously realized models: the individual is linked on the one hand to language as a functional system that represents the highest level of abstraction and on the other hand to the common and widespread uses that have been realized by a community throughout history. These "communal" uses constitute the norma; that is, they represent the linguistic customs to which a speaker must comply in order to be a part of the community. The norma is a secondary level of abstraction because, in practice, only the *speaking* exists. This premise is useful in developing the concept of creativity: we use Coseriu's tradition as a primary source, while not neglecting the results proposed by Hjelmslev ([1961] 1963, 1971) and Rasmussen (1993), which sees the moments articulated in the triptych *sistema, norma y habla*.

The third element *habla* is in line with Saussure's linguistics: *habla* is the act actually produced: however, the salient fact is not the analogy between Saussure's *habla* and *parole*, but the distinction between *sistema* and norma.[15] This distinction derives from the empirical analysis of language. The phonological, morphological, syntactic, and semantic innovations that an individual can produce in speech can be perceived as "strange" by the community, but may not be perceived as real system errors:

> Para aclarar mejor la naturaleza y la distinción entre *norma y sistema* . . . otra analogía es la que asemeja un sistema lingüístico a un tren. Es evidente que "el expreso de París de las 8 y 20," si mantiene ciertas características

funcionales (como la de salir a una hora determinada, de llegar a París a una hora determinada, de parar en determinadas estaciones), es siempre el mismo tren, aun cambiando el número, el orden, la forma y el color de los vagones, y los vagones mismo, el personal etc. Sin embargo, los que viajan en el expreso saben que los elementos no-funcionales no son todos indiferentes y ocasionales, por ejemplo, que el tren tiene siempre diez vagones, que los vagones D, E, A, B se encuentran siempre en ese orden, que el segundo y el quinto vagón, contando desde la locomotora, son siempre de primera; que todos los sábados cambia el turno del personal, etc. Es decir que conocen toda una serie de aspectos que caracterizan el expreso de París, aun no teniendo valor funcional, y encontrarían anormal un tren que no lo presentara: aquí también, entre el tren abstracto, como función, y el tren concreto que el señor X ha tomado ayer o tomará mañana, se interpone la realización *normal* y mas o menos constante del tren mismo. . . .

Ya hace algunos años, al estudiar la lengua de un poeta rumano, en una comunicación leída, en diciembre de 1948, ante el "Sodalizio glottologico milanese," observábamos que las innovaciones, sobre todo sintácticas y semánticas, comprobadas en la expresión de dicho poeta, aunque absolutamente inéditas, audaces y sorprendentes y, de alguna manera, anormales, no resultan aberrantes desde el punto de vista del sistema, no se perciben como errores, no chocan el sentido lingüístico de los lectores homoglotas. . . . Por otra parte, ¿no son de ese mismo tipo casi siempre violaciones o ampliaciones de la norma, permitidas por el *sistema*? (Coseriu 1962, 60–63)

The distinction between norma and *sistema* can be found in all fields of language and develops as a result of the use (not according to the rule) of ideal means that the system provides and that the community has fixed, codified, and classified in traditional models of actualization (models that follow the norma).

The distinction between norma and *sistema* is emphasized in the field of phonetics, morphology, syntax, and vocabulary: Spanish, for example, does not distinguish between long and short vowels (*sistema*). However, all final vowels of words are long vowels (norma).

On the morphology level, we will refer to an example from English in order to clarify the sociocultural character of the *norma*. If a child says *ox*, plural *oxes* (instead of *oxen*) it is because the system requires an *s* for the construction of some plural words. In the case of *ox*, however, the social norm has established that it be *oxen* instead of *oxes*: from a functional point of view, *oxen* and *oxes* are interchangeable (because they are both opposed to *ox*) but the norma admits only *oxen*. From a syntactic perspective, the distinction between norma and *sistema* is the difference between regular models of sentence construction: for example, in Spanish the sentence *se me ha dado* is norma but the sentence *me se ha dado* is not norma but nevertheless retains all the features of the system[16] (Coseriu 1962).

In conclusion, we can affirm that the system is a system of possibilities: of linguistic routes which when open are possible and when closed are impossible. It is a system of possibilities of expression of phobia and of possible senses that are offered to the speaker and within which one finds the prerequisites for creativity according to norma or against norma, of *rule-governed* creativity or of *rule-changing* creativity. The *norma* is the collective realization of the system: it contains the system itself and has a shared, social character. The *parole* is the individual-concrete realization of the norma: it contains the norma itself as well as the expressive originality of the individual speakers. An analogy exemplifies the model of Coseriu: a system does not impose itself on the speaker any more than the canvas and colors impose themselves on the painter. The painter cannot paint beyond the confines of the canvas and cannot use colors that he does not have. But when remaining within the limits of the canvas and using the colors that he possesses, he has absolute freedom of expression. We could therefore say that rather than imposing on the individual, the system is offered to him, providing him with the tools to comprehend the unprecedented expression which is understood by those who use the same system. In the linguistic activity, the individual could know or not know the norm and have a greater or lesser knowledge of the system. If one does not know the norm, the individual is guided by the system, whether he or she is able to stay in accordance with the norm. If one knows the standard, one can repeat it or reject it deliberately, and go beyond it, taking advantage of the possibilities made available to the system. In this sense Coseriu, taking on Humboldt and Croce, repeats that we do not actually learn a language, but we learn to create a language, that is, we learn the norms that guide the creation of a language. That is, we learn about the guidelines, the arrows that drive in the system, and the elements that the system provides us for our unpublished expressions.

In Coseriu's conception, the norma is in toto a social dimension of speaking: It is a norm, not formal correctness, but it is the norm that we follow in order to be part of a linguistic community, and not the norm according to which one judges whether we speak correctly or incorrectly within the community.

From this perspective, the naturally concrete, creative, and heteroclite linguistic act can go beyond the norm and modify it while remaining within the limits allowed by the system: the norm reflects the equilibrium of the system at a specific moment and by changing the norm, this equilibrium also changes. In this way, the speaker becomes the starting point for the creation of the system which derives from the violation and nonacceptance of the norma.

The Language between Rule-Governed and Rule-Changing Creativity 61

But the distinction between norm and system seems important above all to understand the process of linguistic change. For Coseriu (1962) what is imposed on the speaker is not the system (which is offered to him) but the norm. The speaker has a conscience of the system and uses it: on the other hand, he knows or does not know, obeys or does not obey the norm while remaining within the possibilities of the system. But the expressive originality of an individual who does not know or obeys the norm, can be taken as a model by another individual or can be imitated and consequently become the norm:

> El individuo, pues, cambia la norma, quedando dentro de los límites permitidos por el sistema en un determinado momento y, cambiando la norma, cambia ese equilibrio, hasta volcarse totalmente de un lado o de otro. De esta manera el individuo hablante aparece como punto de partida también del cambio en el sistema, que empieza por el desconocimiento o la no-aceptación de la norma. (Coseriu 1962, 107)

The distinction between norma and *sistema* appears particularly important when considering the mechanism of linguistic change in light of the creativity concept. We have examined that what is imposed on the speaker is not the system, but the norma. On the one hand, the speaker knows the system and uses it; on the other hand, the speaker can know or not know the norma, obey or not obey the norma, while still remaining within the possibilities of the system. But the expressive originality of the individual who does not know or does not obey the norm can be taken as an example by someone else; it can be imitated and could eventually become the norm. Thus, the individual changes the norma while remaining within limits allowed by the *sistema*. In this way, the individual is also the starting point for the change of the system, a transformation that begins with the nonacceptance of the norm and that is implemented through the model of semiotic creativity.

This chapter concludes the theoretical corollary to consider semiotic creativity in the science of languages. We believe that the proposed linguistic, semiotic, and philosophical references are functional in considering the complexity of creativity as a semiotic property *prima inter pares* of languages and languages in contact. However, creativity has significant consequences on contemporary linguistics: not only on the semiotic level, but also on the educational level, of educational linguistics and of languages in contact. Therefore, it is not a menace for us to study the contribution of creativity in the different levels of the sciences of language, particularly considering the rule-changing outcomes of creativity. We have established that creativity is the primary foundation of languages and that the fundamental principles of language, such as the value of a sign, arbitrariness, and vagueness are linked to creativity. We have ascertained on a theoretical level that creativity is not only *rule governed* but in languages and in the creation of meaning it is *rule changing*. We therefore follow Tullio De Mauro's references to consider how this property is functional, not only in the theoretical description of a potentially infinite code, but in the principles of educational linguistics, which are the formal prerequisites for a language to be understood, used, and learned.

NOTES

1. The imitative faculty is one of the most important parts of human intelligence. In most cases, learning is nothing more than imitation. Now the ability to imitate is none other than the capacity for paying attention to the objects and its parts, and a capacity to become habituated (our translation).

2. Now the use is the decision, the use is the Lord of languages, as everyone says: indeed, one can concur that the use is the languages themselves. The decision, however, can change: the fact that the judgment can change is both a benefit and a difficulty: in any case, it is not questioned. This characteristic is beneficial because it improves languages and increases its words; it is difficult because it strips languages of their assurances (our translation).

3. Prampolini (2001, 136) argues that "l'idea di creatività, nella filosofia di Wittgenstein, sembra articolarsi, in sintesi su due piani: alla determinatezza nello spazio logico delle proposizioni contingenti (piano del *Tractatus*, senza possibilità di atti creativi), si oppone l'indeterminatezza nello spazio grammaticale delle proposizioni che ingranano con la forma di vita (piano delle *Ricerche filosofiche*, con una creatività continua e immanente). Nella indeterminatezza dello spazio grammaticale e nel passaggio alla determinatezza delle singole applicazioni possiamo ritrovare la creatività o, per usare la terminologia di Wittgenstein una "intuizione' o 'una nuova decisione." Alle conclusioni appena esposte . . . merita . . . mettere in evidenza *una prima considerazione*: la prima considerazione è quella per cui l'idea wittgenstiana di gioco riunisce due concezioni complementari: quella del gioco come luogo della nascita o del cambiamento delle regole, del gioco come spazio di creazione e di libertà (analogo alla *rule changing creativity* di Noam Chomsky); a questa si affianca la concezione del gioco come luogo di sussunzione dei fatti agli obblighi e ai vincoli che dalle regole sono già istituiti, del gioco come spazio di atti e fatti che si adempiono sotto necessità già configurate (analogo alla *rule-governed creativity* chomskiana). Se non si tengono presenti queste due dimensioni complementari, l'idea di gioco non è adeguata per prendere in considerazione un tema come quello della creatività."

4. In Garroni ([1978] 2010, 112): "ciò che Chomsky chiama Linguistica cartesiana è per la verità qualcosa che con Descartes ha che fare solo al livello generalissimo e che va ben al di là del pensiero di Descartes e dei cartesiani in senso stretto. . . . In prima istanza "linguistica cartesiana" è un'etichetta che sta ad indicare che in Descartes è dato ritrovare i primi e chiari sintomi di una concezione della creatività come *rule governed creativity*, anche se tecnicamente non ancora specificata."

5. Consider Chomsky (1981) as well.

6. Please read what twentieth-century glossematics proposes, in particular Hjelmslev ([1961] 1963). Consider Thrane (1980) as well.

7. Coseriu's quotes are taken from the original Spanish editions.

8. Refer to Saussure's concepts of *espirit de clocher* and *force d'intercourse* in the CGL.

9. "Pero el lenguaje tiene también otra dimensión, que está dada por la alteridad del sujeto, por el echo de que el sujeto creador de lenguaje presupone otros sujetos. . . . el lenguaje está siempre dirigido a otro, incluso como creación lingüística primaria. Los significados y los signos no se crean sólo para que sean (como el arte), sino que se crean para que sean también para otros . . . . A este respecto se ha dicho y se dice que el lenguaje es un hecho social y que la lengua simplemente se impone a los hablantes. En realidad, el lenguaje es más bien fundamento y, al mismo tiempo, manifestación primaria de lo social, del ser con otro" (Coseriu 1977, 31–32).

10. Coseriu (1958) maintains that Humboldt has never linked his own linguistic idea to absolute subjectivism. He has always maintained a dialectic between the individual and the historical dimension.

11. Humboldt ([1836] 1988, 42, 81) describes the romantic principle of the *cuius regio eius lingua* for which language-nation-people-identity represent the unity of living in a community*:* "In languages, therefore, since they always have a national form, nations, as such, are truly and immediately creative. . . . The intellectual merits of language therefore rest exclusively upon the well-ordered, firm and clear *mental organization* of peoples in the epoch of making and remaking language, and are the image, indeed the direct copy, of this. It may seem as if all languages would have to be *like* each other in their intellectual procedure. For the sound-form, an infinite, uncountable multiplicity is conceivable, since the sensuous and bodily individual arises from such differing causes that the possibility of its gradations cannot be calculated. But that which rests solely on mental self-activity—as the intellectual part of languages does—seems to have to be alike in all men, given the similarity of purpose and means; and this part of language does, indeed, preserve a large degree of uniformity. But from various causes there also arises a significant diversity. . . . Imagination and feeling engender individual shapings, in which the individual character of the nation again emerges, and where, as in everything individual, the variety of ways in which the thing in question can be represented in ever-differing guises, extends towards infinity."

In fact, the triunity proposed by Humboldt and Hereder's romantic philosophy is surpassed by the principles of language contact. As an example, please refer to Giorgio Raimondo Cardona's work from 1974 in the *Introduzione* in the Italian translation of *Languages in Contact* by Uriel Weinreich ([1963] 2008, LXXV-I): "è una delle nostre più radicate abitudini quella che ci fa considerare la lingua come un qualcosa di unico: si ha una sola lingua come si ha una sola patria, una sola anima e così via. Tutta la letteratura romantica e no sul concetto di lingua e nazione non ha fatto che rafforzare questa concezione monolitica dei rapporti tra individuo e lingua. . . . Il risultato di questa tendenza costante è stato quello di dare della distribuzione delle lingue sulla terra una rappresentazione ben sistemata: *cuius regio eius lingua.*

Come poi si passi da una lingua all'altra, è compito lasciato semmai ai dialettologi. Tutto ciò potrebbe essere accettabile se la situazione normale fosse il monolinguismo, e il plurilinguismo fosse un caso particolare in fondo quasi patologico. Invece il plurilinguismo è diffuso in tutte le parti del mondo. Basta puntare il dito a caso su un planisfero, e subito si toccherà una zona in cui il plurilinguismo è la norma."

12. "Le diverse lingue sono in realtà organi del modo di pensare e sentire delle nazioni; molti oggetti vengono creati solo per mezzo delle parole che li designano; gli elementi fondamentali delle lingue . . . imprimono al pensiero una foggia suscitatrice di nuovi pensieri e connessioni di pensieri, secondo affinità elettive specificamente nazionali. La lingua guida il cammino della nazione" (Formigari 1977b, 86–7).

13. In (Garroni [1978] 2010, 123–24): "è insomma difficilmente contestabile che, a proposito di creatività linguistica, non si possa parlare soltanto di *rule-governed creativity*, che pure costituisce un aspetto rilevante della creatività linguistica, e inoltre che, stabilito un certo insieme di regole linguistiche, questo sarà sempre modificabile, violando quelle regole e instituendone di diverse. Il che non accadrà naturalmente— soprattutto nel caso delle regolarità più profonde—ad arbitrio del singolo parlante, e tuttavia accade ad un livello opportuno (sociale e non individuale), ha riflessi importanti nei riguardi di una teoria linguistica e va in qualche modo spiegato. Bisogna appunto fare i conti con ciò che Chomsky chiama *rule-changing creativity*, e di cui però non si occupa tecnicamente."

14. On the vagueness as semiotic property according to what became De Mauro's linguistic model, we refer to Burns (1991), De Mauro (1982; 2008), Di Cesare (1997), Machetti (2006), and Prampolini (1997).

15. For the definition of the concept of norm, we will mainly refer to Coseriu (1962) and to Hjelmslev's ([1959] 1981) lesson. We particularly recall the interpretation of the latter given by Siertesema and presented by Prampolini (1981) in the notes to the essay *Lingua e parole*.

16. In Hjelmslev ([1959] 1981, 94) it is written: "Cominciamo con la lingua. Può essere considerata a) come *forma pura*, definita indipendentemente dalla sua realizzazione sociale e dalla sua manifestazione materiale; b) come una *forma materiale*, definita da una certa realizzazione sociale, ma indipendentemente ancora dal dettaglio della manifestazione; c) come un semplice *complesso di abitudini*, adottate da una certa società e definite dalle manifestazioni osservate. Per prima cosa distinguiamo queste tre accezioni . . . . Chiameremo: a) *schema*, la lingua come forma pura; b) *norma*, la lingua come forma materiale; c) *uso*, l'insieme di abitudini."

In a passage from Hjelmslev's first work the *Principles*, (1928), it is argued that the norm is an ideal imposed on all subjects belonging to the same social group and the norm does not correspond to grammatical correctness. The norm contains nothing prescriptive but indicates what is part of the appraisal system of the subjects belonging to the same social group (Prampolini 1981, 109).

Chapter 4

Educational Linguistics
From Education to Language Creativity

Ex qua mea disputatione forsitan occurrat illud, si paene innumerabiles sint quasi formae figuraeque dicendi, specie dispares, genere laudabiles, non posse ea, quae inter se discrepant, eisdem praeceptis atque una institutione formari. Quod non est ita, diligentissimeque hoc est eis, qui instituunt aliquos atque erudiunt, videndum, quo sua quemque natura maxime ferre videatur. Etenim videmus ex eodem quasi ludo [summorum in suo cuiusque genere artificum et magistrorum] exisse discipulos dissimilis inter se ac tamen laudandos, cum ad cuiusque naturam institutio doctoris accommodaretur. Cuius est vel maxime insigne illud exemplum, ut ceteras artis omittamus, quod dicebat Isocrates doctor singularis se calcaribus in Ephoro, contra autem in Theopompo frenis uti solere: alterum enim exsultantem verborum audacia reprimebat alterum cunctantem et quasi verecundantem incitabat. Neque eos similis effecit inter se, sed tantum alteri adfinxit, de altero limavit, ut id conformaret in utroque, quod utriusque natura pateretur.[1]

Marcus Tullius Cicero, *De oratore*

INTRODUCTION

The scientific approach to creativity *in the full sense of this term* involves considering the forms with which linguistic creativity manifests itself in the dynamics of the creation of meaning and in the general dynamics of understanding. This assumes to consider the relationships and interconnections between the creativity governed by rules and the creativity that changes the rules: even *rule-governed creativity* seems to assume, as a condition of existence, a *rule-changing creativity* (Garroni [1978] 2010).

In Italy, and in the second half of the twentieth century, Tullio De Mauro was the intellectual who treated creativity as a conception of the first property of the semiotic universe and languages by proposing a reflection that goes far beyond the "practical" conception with which creativity can manifest itself through the creation of new words or new meanings in a language. De Mauro was a multifaceted intellectual who viewed linguistics as one with history and society (Berruto 2018). He was the one who most authentically followed the lessons of Saussure's *Course*, attributing value, and therefore identity, in the languages to the *speaking mass* which is the engine and at the same time subsistence of each language (and of each semiotic system).

For De Mauro, *Storia linguistica dell'Italia*[2] is not only the story of the Italian language in its creation from Latin through the centuries, but it is the story of Italians, of the social, economic, and cultural events of Italians that have, by their nature, linguistic consequences on the language that Italians have used and use. At the foundation of De Mauro's fundamental sociolinguistic conception (reflecting the same Saussurean vision) is the arbitrary basis of languages. De Mauro (1982) calls it formal semiotic arbitrariness and it represents the first form of creativity for which a semiotic relationship between individuals exists, only if the issuer and the receiver manage to classify concrete elements within abstract classes or schemes. In other words, they are able to identify the relevant traits of concrete entities (the things of the world), and on the basis of these traits build mental models within which to recognize and classify the infinite diversity of the world. The choice of relevant traits is only very generally related to the material nature of the actual entity.

The establishment of a sign is a creative operation because it does not depend on how the world is made (it is not a subordinate operation to the things that exist in the world), the semiotic subject chooses what to make relevant, and therefore chooses what to identify as a relevant trait and as a sign, that which is (or can be) a sign and that which is not (but can be). This is a conceptual, semiotic operation—a creative operation. It is a creativity that involves the entire universe of signs, the signifier, the meaning, the languages, and other symbolic systems. Without making something relevant, without arbitrariness, without creativity, we would not have semiosis. We would have no languages, codes, and communication; that is, we would have no identity. It is therefore understood why creativity is not a semiotic property, but a postulate: if there were no creativity, semiosis could not exist.

But why is it so important for De Mauro to reiterate that there can be no semiosis without creativity? Because if at the base of semiosis in general, and languages in particular, there is creativity, then semiosis is not a calculation, it is not mechanizable (Gargani 2018). The stakes in the concept of creativity are therefore not simply the property of *inter pares*, but is the first property that initiates semiosis and is therefore a source of subsistence. On the contrary, a calculation is characterized by two fundamental postulates: *non-creativity* and *syntax*. In order for a calculation to be such, its symbols (i.e., its vocabulary) and its rules of connection of symbols must have the requirement not to vary in the course of the operations for which the calculation takes place (De Mauro 2002). The rules must be closed sets, and symbols must have a unique and stable (*non-creative*) meaning. The rules must be applicable to symbols, and symbols must be able to connect to each other through rules (*syntax*). Taken together, these two postulates define a semiotic system that "works" without the subject of semiosis.

In fact, every move of a calculation depends only on the moves that precede it and is needed for the moves that follow it (De Mauro 2008). A calculation therefore does not depend on semantics or pragmatics; that is, it is not linked to what a calculation means or to what can be done with calculation, nor from the situation in which the calculation is carried out and is located. Calculation works on it's own. Calculation works as long as the formal (non-creative) conditions for its operation are met.[3] All that is necessary for a calculation to work and have meaning is within the calculation itself; therefore, a calculation does not have a historical, social, or cultural dimension. Calculation has no identity, if by identity we mean a form of life. The calculation is creative, but it is creative in the mathematical sense, which, therefore, ultimately is not creative. A language, on the other hand, is a not-not-creative semiotics (De Mauro 2002). That is, language is a creative semiotics because it combines the given and fixed units according to certain rules (Danesi 2008, 2016).

But it is also a non-non-creative semiotics because it admits the abandonment of old forms, the introduction of new forms, and foresees the convergence of different intellectual forms. It is a generally combinatorial ability, as in a calculation, that manifests itself in many communicative occasions and in the production of many signs, but also a creative intelligence in a general sense, capable of producing and managing new signs and senses to adapt to the communicative needs of users and the social circumstances in which the intervention of languages is requested (De Mauro 2002). But the one and the other form of intelligence could not be realized in semiotic facts without the intervention of the ability to imitate others: we imitate others around us and those who have used the language before us while being a source of imitation for others.

At this point it is clear what is at stake when it comes to creativity: Is a language a calculation? Is a language creative (not-not-creative)? That is, does the functioning of a language need a semiotic subject? For De Mauro, the answer is clear. Language needs a semiotic subject: the ability to identify the *dictum* does not exist without identifying the *dicens*. It is a mistake to believe that linguistic forms have an intrinsic semiotic capacity and meaning. If the linguistic forms are isolated from the subject that uses them, and that performs the semiotic act of creativity, they do not have the ability to create meaning. Linguistic forms acquire the ability to create meaning only in relation to those who use them[4] (De Mauro 1965). In this context and on the need to define creativity in relation to its ontological scope, it is evident why creativity is even assumed as a parameter of classification of the semiotic codes that De Mauro proposed starting from *Minisemantica*.

FOR A CLASSIFICATION OF SEMIOTIC CODES

Through a procedure that we could define "according to the Aristotelian method," De Mauro in *Minisemantica* proposes a classification of codes based on relevant parameters.[5] Therefore, as in Aristotelian doctrine, the categories are a doctrine of speakable things, that is, of the more general concepts under which identity is given to every reality. De Mauro proposes, with an Aristotelian rigour, a classification of semiotic codes that take into account the relationship between a sign (or a phrase) and other possible signs (or other possible phrases) of the code. Additionally, it considers the semantics of the sign (or phrase) in relation to the meanings of the other signs and other possible phrases. In contrast, a classification that targets the identity of a sign and a code cannot refer to the material nature of the sign or the code.

A classification that looks after the material of which the signs are made is not entirely satisfactory. Any sentence can be said out loud by means of acoustic signs. We can also write it with a pen on a sheet of paper, therefore by chemical preparations. We can translate it into a sign language; that is, we can transmit the message through gestures. We can engrave it using braille, according to the writing system invented by the French Louis Braille (1809–1852), with which the blind can read via touch. Yet, by whichever materials the signifier signs are made, the phrase remains the same (De Mauro 1980). Classification according to material types obliges us to consider the same sentence as belonging to different semiotic codes: to an acoustic code, such as whistling, in the first case; to a chemical-visual code, such as painting, in the second; to a gestural-visual code in the third case; and to a tactile code in the fourth. But we know that, in all cases, it is the same phrase belonging to the same semiotic code: the verbal language. Certainly, a classification of semiotic codes will also have to take into account the relationship of signs with material reality. You should also keep in mind the sign report with users who produce or receive the sign and the code. But the choice that De Mauro operates by and which he proposes to follow is to reorder the semiotic codes on the basis of the internal, syntactic aspects of the signs and the code and on the basis of the semantic relationships between senses and meanings in the codes. A semantic classification of semiotic codes that is unique and exhaustive can be built on the basis of no more than five semantic-formal criteria, of which creativity is the fifth and final criterion[6] (De Mauro 1982).

Through the identification of the semantic-syntactic criteria for the classification of semiotic codes, De Mauro creates a Porphyrian tree that, starting from the tradition of ancient Greece, represents a pattern or model that relates classes (i.e., open sets of elements) and in fact, is made for opposition. The universe of semiotic codes is therefore divided into open classes, each of which is characterized by the presence or absence of a semantic-syntactic classification parameter. One of the classes selected by the first parameter—the class in which the parameter is present—goes on to the second parameter which gives rise to two other classes (one in which the selected property is present and the other in which it is absent) and so proceeds with the third, fourth, and fifth until all the parameters are identified for the classification of semiotic codes. The first criterion of code classification identified by De Mauro in *Minisemantica* is the articulation (I) of the signs of the code and their senses.

Aristotle in *De Interpretatione* (*On Interpretation*) had highlighted how man was able to handle codes composed by *grámmata*, that is, smaller parts of the language, where other living species operated only codes whose signs were *agrámmatoi*, that is, not able to be decomposed into smaller parts. In the twentieth century and in Europe, André Martinet (*Éléments de linguistique générale* 1964) was the one who insisted most on the natural articulation and double articulation of language signs: in languages, most linguistic signs are formed by a combination according to rules of smaller parts (the morphemes, units of first articulation with meaning), which in turn consist of combining second and even smaller parts (phonemes, meaningless second-articulation units). And yet the phrases of our languages are made up of different signs; and oral or written texts consisting of combining different phrases and so on. The articulation of linguistic signs, and its combinatorial component, plays a fundamental role in the functioning of languages. Articulation affects the potential infinity of the sentences of a language and the fact that the different combinations of the same signs in a sentence give rise to totally different sentences (the sentence *Michelle loves Luis* is different from the sentence *Luis loves Michelle*[7]).

Articulation affects both the signifier and the meaning of the sign: the letters of the alphabet, used to construct words, represent perhaps the most intuitive element to understand the articulated character of signs. However, the semantic dimension is also articulated: the meaning of the phrase *Michelle loves Luis* is given by the "arithmetic" sum of the meaning of each sign according to the model *Michelle + loves + Luis*. In addition, if we take a sign of the English language, for example *cars*, this consists of the lexical morpheme *car-* with a plural grammatical morpheme *-s*: the *cars* sign is the "arithmetic" sum of the *car- + -s* morphemes.

Most linguistic signs work through this articulated and combinatorial process, although, in languages, articulated signs are joined by non-articulated signs that are not decomposable and for which the meaning is not given by the "arithmetic" sum of the meaning of the signs that make up this expression (i.e., polirematic expressions[8]). From the point of study of articulation and combinatoriality, languages are real mathematical operations and do not differ much from calculations and logics, which are also governed by principles of articulation and combinatoriality. (In mathematics, the sign *21* consists of the signs 2 + 1, and the sign *21* is different from the sign *12*. In addition, operation 4:2 is quite different from operation 2:4 etc.) We can therefore conclude that articulated codes have signs that are grouped into morphemes and the different arrangement of the morphemes gives rise to different signs: an articulated code can be defined as combinatorial.

On a pragmatic level, the advantage of an articulated code is obvious: with just nine numbers plus zero it is possible to make signs of infinite number, and with fewer than thirty letters of the alphabet, in most historical-natural languages, you can create signs of infinite number. You can create and manage infinite number signs, even with non-infinite memory capacity, through a combinatorial and recursive process. In reality, we do not need to remember all the possible signs: we can make infinite numbers of signs remembering, possibly, only ten basic elements and recursive rules. For the purposes of classification of signs and codes, an articulated sign code opens the door to the second classification criterion, the infinity of code signs (II). As we have seen with a limited number of basic units, a language gives rise to a potentially infinite number of sentences and meanings. This applies not only to languages, but also to codes that behave such as languages and arithmetics where the position and repetition of an element affects the number of signs and their meaning.[9]

The third criterion identified for code classification is the existence of synonyms (III). Finished number codes of signs are created to classify a narrow semantic field so that each sign cannot be replaced by another. Thus, for example, the signs of the traffic light work with the alternation of the three colors of red, yellow, and green each linked to a specific meaning. Another example are the codes with which the chemical elements present in nature are identified: these exclude synonyms, that is, the possibility of identifying two different signs with the same meaning. Languages and even arithmetic are instead equipped with synonyms: the sign 10 is synonymous with the signs 9 + 1, or 5 + 5 or 12 - 2. In English, for example, *home* and *house* are synonyms, while being used to construct different phrases. Even *apartment* and *unit* are synonyms, as are the adjectives *excellent, wonderful, terrific,* and *great*. In codes without synonyms, we are sure that the meanings of two different signs never overlap. If this were not the case, (i.e., a synonym occurs) the code would not work, as for example in traffic lights. If the red sign suddenly became synonymous with the green sign, it would create chaos on the streets and the code would not work. In contrast, in synonym codes, two signs can cover the same semantic field, through a process of calculability or non-calculability of the synonyms of a code; that is, through a logical operation that can determine in advance the number of synonyms or reduce synonyms to predefined formal patterns.

Synonym calculability is the fourth criterion for semiotic code classification (IV). Synonym calculability is the criterion for which you define the formal characters of a code, potentially defining the number of synonyms that can be calculated. Or, however, if these codes are infinite signs, the criteria of the calculability of synonyms detected (potentially infinite) are still attributable to basic units and recursive rules. This is the case if the parameters for which a code is reducible to a calculation are respected. In paragraph 1 of this chapter we semiotically defined what is meant by calculation: a calculation is a code that, in order to exist, must respect the criterion of syntax and not change its elements and its rules during communication. A calculation is such if the value of the sign *3* will always remain equal to *three units*, and the value of the *+* sign will always be the value of the *sum*. If this were not to happen, and therefore, we were faced with codes in which initially the sign *3* has a value of *three units* and then, in other contexts, it has a value of *five units*, it would be a non-calculation code. The same reflection applies to the *+* sign: in a calculation the plus sign cannot represent a *sum* in one context, in another context a *multiplication*, and in a third context a *division*. In these situations, that is, in front of codes that change their elements in the conduct of communication (in the conduct of the calculation) we would be faced with the last principle of semantic-syntactic classification of codes: creativity (V).

CREATIVITY

In *Minisemantica*, De Mauro defines creativity as the possibility to change elements of a system or a semiotic code that is present within the mechanisms of the system and is recognizable as the property of the system or code.[10] Based on this general conception of creativity as a theoretical paradigm for the variation and change of semiotic codes, the articulation of creativity is determined within four dimensions—each with its own name and function—that through interrelationships characterize the linguistic use:

 i) Creativity of Croce or creativity of *parole*
 ii) Chomskian creativity or creativity of *langue*
 iii) Creativity of *language*
 iv) Creativity of "psychologists"

The first form of creativity (i), supported philosophically by *L'Estetica* by Benedetto Croce (1945), and the CGL by Saussure, has to do with language as a set of unique and unrepeatable acts, as are the deeds of *parole* that define a necessarily different character from every sense and every emission of voice in *parole*.

Each of us, and not only the poet, in every linguistic act creates and recreates phonic elements (or graphics) and senses with nuances that can be unedited. It is not, however, a creation *ex nihilo*, but a creation on the basis of a social and historical tradition which falls within a norm (in the sense expressed by Coseriu, 1962) and a community: in *L'Estetica*, Croce thought of the concrete character of the individual linguistic act, never identical to a previous act and that will never be identical to a subsequent act.[11] In CGL, this form of ever-different individual creation is called *parole*. However, it is clear that this form of creativity does not characterize any language and is not a characteristic that determines how the signs work within a code.[12]

The Chomskian creativity or *creativity of langue* (ii) refers to the Chomskian language model that we discussed in chapter 3 and which results in a *rule-governed creativity* and a *rule-changing creativity*. This form of creativity, especially *rule-governed creativity*, is useful for producing and recognizing a potentially infinite number of different phrases from a vocabulary that can be limited and by rules that can also be limited.[13] The verbal language, however, is creative (or is non-non creative, for what we said in paragraph 1) also (and above all) in another sense.

The third form of creativity (iii), the creativity of *language*, recalls creativity that is based on the human ability to manage different symbolic codes, and therefore to manage plurilingualism. It is not about the creation of languages from nothing, but about the creative link that exists between a language and its community of users. Relying on the idea of language as *enérgeia*, this form of creativity associates the construction of a plurality of languages and semiotic codes through *rule-changing creativity*. The *creativity of lang*uage gives the speaker the possibility to pass from one code to another according to techniques and rules that, when necessary and according to use, can be changed to create new rules and new uses (Nuessel 2010, 2017).

And finally, we consider that form of creativity, defined by "psychologists" (iv), which recalls both the human capacity to manage different codes and a capacity for divergence. It is the ability to solve a problem by modifying the terms or modifying the usual rules used to resolve analogous problems. That is, an ability to stand out from the established rules, to innovate them, and to change the data of the problem to solve it, representing an extension (or a close relative) of rule-changing creativity. All this is done for the purposes of communicating, understanding, and creating shared meaning.[14]

In this sense, the different forms of creativity—starting from the creativity of *parole*, to the creativity of *langue*, to then pass to the *creativity of lang*uage at the base of plurilingualism, up to the rule-governed creativity and the mathematical creativity—are, in their entirety, the elements able to determine the functioning of language. These forms recall actions that are sometimes contrary, which in languages represent not an exception or malfunction, but are the norm and are specific to languages, in relation to other semiotic codes (De Mauro 2008). The set of these forms of creativity is what we call not-not-creativity (*non-non creatività*).[15]

Semantically, not-not creativity has the most immediate consequence of extending the human capacity of speaking and thinking through a language so that there are no limits to the semantic capacity of a language (Hjelmslev [1961] 1963). There is, however, another linguistic and semiotic dimension that is involved by creativity as a parameter of code classification: it is the pragmatic dimension that assumes a supporting function within the classification and identity processes of the semiotic universe (Danesi 2004).

In short, by taking creativity as the fifth and final parameter of classification and identity of semiotic codes, we draw connections to users, to history, and to society as a central element of that mechanism. The question of the pragmatic value of creativity seems even more interesting if we consider languages from a not only theoretical, semiotic, and formal perspective, but also from an educational perspective that therefore looks at the processes of use and learning of languages (of choosing a communicative possibility among the infinite possibilities made available by the code) under the lens of creativity.

ISSUES OF CREATIVE LANGUAGE EDUCATION

One of De Mauro's great formal and methodized merits has been to look at theoretical linguistics not as a separate element of reflection on language and languages, but only as a theoretical prerequisite so that linguistics could outline social outcomes that are also very concrete and particular (Vedovelli 2017). With the aim of outlining the identity of educational linguistics as an autonomous science in the language sciences landscape, De Mauro (2012) points out how inseparable the link between educational and theoretical linguistic issues is, an aspect that in the Italian context had already been highlighted by Berretta (1978) and Berruto (1988).

In the context of North America, a fundamental contribution to the foundation of *Educational Linguistics* was made by Spolsky (1978, 1) who, while continuing to study *Educational Linguistics* within the dimension of *Applied Linguistics* (Spolsky 2008), outlines the object of *Educational Linguistics* by highlighting:

> Many linguists believe that their field should not be corrupted by any suggestion of relevance to practical matters; for them, linguistics is a pure science and its study is motivated only by the desire to increase human knowledge. Others, however, claimed that linguistics offers a panacea for any educational problem that arises quickly and offer their services to handle any difficulties in language planning or teaching. Each of these extreme positions is, I believe, quite wrong, for while it is evident that linguistics is often relevant to education, the relationship is seldom direct.

Spolsky argues that today it is not possible to consider the educational issue disconnected from theoretical-linguistic issues. He maintains that this aspect is today an urgency of the contemporary social context, particularly considering the area of language policies that has essentially made clear how important the theoretical foundation within the educational dimension is (Grin 2015). In this sense, the *language policy* consists of three distinct but interrelated components: the regular language practices of the community (such as choice of varieties); the language beliefs or ideology of the community (such as the values assigned to each variety by various members of the community); and any language management activities, namely, attempts by any individual or institution toward claiming authority to modify the language practices and language beliefs of other members of the community (Spolsky 2008). It is interesting to note that the recourse to users is central to the definition of a linguistic policy, and that this dimension that we define semiotic is also a fundamental element of the definition by which De Mauro and Ferreri (2005) have given a theoretical and Italian status to *Educational Linguistics* as a particular science in the framework of language sciences[16] (Danesi 2000, 2002).

The object of *Educational Linguistics* is therefore the language to be learned, and the learner-user is considered a semiotic subject or a human being engaged in a process of processing meaning to be expressed through language and languages: a process that has roots in the general symbolic faculty and that in the history of Western civilization has been placed within the specific and institutionalized context of education and school.[17]

The semiotic and formative question on which we have dwelled is not a random element inconsequential to the issues of creativity: De Mauro (1971b) defines the sign creativity (what will then be the creativity of *langue*) in reference to the process of using a language that can make a user anticipate from a formal premise, a strictly educational question. According to De Mauro (1971b, 153[18]):

> Anche in questo caso si osserva che nell'aria rarefatta delle astrazioni teoriche si può reperire qualche cosa di molto concreto: per molti secoli si è preteso di insegnare una lingua insegnando "i bei parlari," le frasi e i segni già usati da Tizio e da Caio, da questo o da quello scrittore. Questo era (ed è in molti luoghi ancor oggi) il metodo più stimato per insegnare una lingua. Ma se la conclusione di 4.2.3 è esatta [con una lingua è possibile generare un numero infinito di segni] (e si attende dai puristi di ogni razza e colore una smentita) insegnare una lingua significa, bene al contrario, insegnare a produrre il maggior numero di segni possibile che *non* siano mai stati usati prima da nessuno. Soltanto una accorta educazione alla più sfrenata licenza fraseologica ed espressiva può dare il reale, profondo possesso di una lingua.

Although from an essentially theoretical and formal perspective, De Mauro highlights in a very clear way how to teach languages; today, we say "do language education," meaning educate people to use and respect all sorts of linguistic varieties and the use of all sorts of linguistic creativity (De Mauro 2018) where creativity therefore assumes a semiotic and social value.

Educational Linguistics is therefore an education of creativity and the variety of languages and different symbolic forms—from numbers to historical-natural languages, through graphic, chromatic, artistic forms in general—are all conceived as possible forms of semiosis and are useful to regulate the production and reception of signs with which users classify and communicate the experience (and their identity). In the Italian context, we refer to Ferreri (2002, 2005a, b, 2013) to clarify the theoretical relationship between *Educational Linguistics* and *Linguistic Education*;[19] but to consider linguistic education as an education of creativity means elevating all languages and their varieties to the dignity of "able to be taught" and thus making education to creativity a plurilingual education.

If creativity is more than the regular production of sentences, but creativity invests "without pre-determined rules" the whole process of communication and understanding, then educating creativity means on the one hand, opening up the expressive possibilities of users, but on the other, providing all the semiotic tools so that communication can achieve its goal of understanding. In the language space, which is a multilingual space, the compass that governs the communicative movement does not refer to the canons of adherence to a language model *prima inter pares*. On the other, it is *inter linguas pares* that the communicative function guides users in choosing between the creative possibilities of the language of what is the idiomatic variety, dialectal, slang, etc., socially and at the same time more functional (no longer correct but more functional) to the creation of meaning and to the achievement of the communicative end.

Educating to creativity as a variety therefore means educating to the variety of phrases, the variety of vocabulary that you can have in a language, and the variety of styles in which a language is realized: knowing a *lingua* and knowing how to handle it (in the sense of semiotic creativity) also means knowing how to juggle stylistic varieties, knowing and using appropriately what is needed in speech and what is needed in written text. What do we need to write a newspaper article, or a university essay? What do we need in order to communicate with friends in an informal context as opposed to a formal context? We do these with the rush of having to respect deadlines and we do these for our professors. In the Italian context, the perspective of education in creativity is found in the *Dieci Tesi* Giscel[20] (1975), the moment when the premise of language education exceeds the philosophical and pedagogical plan to embrace a more institutional dimension.

The text of the *Dieci Tesi* can be summarily divided into at least 4 parts: a) character thesis (Theses I–IV); *pars destruens*, analysis and criticism of traditional linguistic pedagogy (Theses V–VIII); *pars construens* principles of a democratic linguistic education (Theses VIII–IX); conclusions (Thesis X). The literature on the analysis of the *Dieci Tesi* and their scope in the international context is extensive; we therefore refer to the contributions of De Mauro (1998, 2006, 2018), Vedovelli and Casini (2016), and Casini (2019a) for international reach. However, here we want to mention the X principle of the *Dieci Tesi*, which is perhaps where semiotic creativity has the greatest implications:

> In ogni caso e modo occorre sviluppare il senso della funzionalità comunicativa di ogni possibile tipo di forme linguistiche note e ignote. La vecchia pedagogia linguistica era imitativa, prescrittiva ed esclusiva. Diceva: "Devi dire sempre e solo così. Il resto è errore." La nuova educazione linguistica (più ardua) dice: "Puoi dire così, e anche così; e anche questo che pare errore o stranezza può dirsi e si dice; e questo e quest'altro è il risultato che ottieni nel dire così o così." La vecchia didattica linguistica era dittatoriale. Ma la nuova non è affatto anarchica: ha una regola fondamentale e una bussola, che è la funzionalità comunicativa di un testo parlato o scritto e delle sue parti a seconda degli interlocutori reali cui effettivamente lo so vuole destinare.[21]

There will be more objective language solutions, solutions that are less adequate but always allowed, or solutions that do not allow a result of communication: the latter will not be inherently wrong (or may not be); they will only be non-functional in that context, for those particular users, at that precise moment. It follows that the process of renewed teaching according to semiotic creativity outlines a reinvigorated, more arduous language education, which supports multiple possibilities and that which seems to be error or strangeness can be said. This is the result that you get in saying one way as opposed to another. Within the concept of communicative functionality lies precisely the revolution in the field of language teaching. This revolution is not only instrumental to the objectives of the educational process, but responds primarily, and in a different way from tradition, to the following questions: What is a language? Is there a model of language, established and universal, to be referred to always and anyway?

Traditional language education has been a pedagogy of imitation of past linguistic models considered socially elevated. Such teaching models (and therefore this view of the language system) were linked to the "evaluative" concept as a criterion that discriminates against what is good and linguistically correct, separating it from what is not based on criteria outside the language. But by failing the concept of rule, and indeed considering the semiotic value of the concept of creativity as we outlined in this study, teaching also becomes variation of the system and violation of its grammatical rules (Berretta 1971). In traditional education we had a binary system of fairness versus incorrectness. There was no other option but the predetermined one: no creativity was allowed in forms and structures, even where a creative solution could be functional to the communicative intent.[22]

Now, the rule to be followed is first of all a social rule for which a speaker will be faced with a kind of continuum of possibilities within which to choose the linguistic solution that can guarantee, or at least direct the communicative end: it can be chosen on the basis of various parameters ranging from the language skills already possessed, to those being acquired, or according to the context in which it is found, but whatever behavior is chosen, there will never be a case in which one can say that one has evidently been wrong (Simone 1979). From this there was a fundamental consequence: since the grammar of a language not only has the function of embellishing the language, but on the contrary, it also contributes (as Aristotle had already guessed) to determine the concrete meaning of a statement (De Mauro 2009), grammar *in nuce*, and its teaching, must be based on the implications of variety, creativity, and social norm as we have mentioned them. This is a difficult task. The position and role of creative grammar are far more complex than the imitative intent of the past educational tradition. But this is the challenge between creativity and language education. An educational challenge that is not only of yesterday, but that can represent an important model of development for the current issues that see in Europe and North America a common desire to define objectives, strategies, and educational approaches in line with the needs of the new global citizen.

In Casini (2019a) we consider how the fundamental points of *linguistic education*, born in Italy in the 1970s and which gave rise to the *Dieci Tesi*, today represents the inspiring principles of the most important documents of linguistic policy both in Europe and North America. In a limited way to the European context, we pointed out that with the use of *linguistic education,* the *European Framework (Common European Framework of Reference for Languages—CEFRL)* develops on the one hand an action-oriented approach and, on the other, the profile of a user/learner seen as a social actor who is capable of performing tasks of a non-solely linguistic type, putting a range of skills in place both general and specifically linguistic-communicative. We also looked at the multilingual model proposed by *CEFRL* through the idea of semiotic multilingualism present in the *Dieci Tesi* and through which education must aim to integrate different semiotic codes, different languages, and different varieties of the same language. To these elements was added a third, which took into account the skills of the teacher, to be renewed and to be expanded to a multiplicity of skills not only linguistic, but linguistic theory, cognitive skills, evolutionary psychology, pragmatic, pragmalinguistics, sociology, and sociolinguistics.

Of course, we cannot and do not want to argue that there is an explicit direct link between Italian linguistic education and the European educational model. However, the convergences are so widespread and so important that they assume that the important theoretical elaboration to which language education had come, also thanks to the formalization of the concept of creativity, anticipated a linguistic policy that in Europe and North America took place at least thirty years later.

In the North American context, the issue is even more subtle and interesting: the ACTFL (*American Council on the Teaching of Foreign Languages*), which represents the most important association for the teaching of foreign languages in North America, since the mid-1980s has developed tools and guidelines that can support educational needs of teachers and students in line with current language and educational research. The way in which a language is learned can be different (e.g., a language can either be learned in a formal context such as school or not through an institutionalized process) and the language skills that develop in the learner may appear to be similar but, in reality, they are different; in the case of schooling, we must also consider the curriculum carried out in the classroom. This differs from non-institutional learning which does not follow a specific curriculum.

For this reason, the ACTFL has also developed alongside the *Proficiency Guidelines* (which we have analyzed in relation to linguistic education in Casini (2019a) as well as the *Performance Descriptors for Language Learners 2012* document that focuses on the level of skills to be acquired) distinguishing the concept of *performance* from that of *proficiency*. Proficiency "is the ability to use language in real-world situations in a spontaneous interaction and non-rehearsed context and in a manner acceptable and appropriate to native speakers of the language. Proficiency demonstrates what a language user is able to do regardless of where, when, or how the language was acquired. The demonstration is independent of how the language was learned; the context may or may not be familiar; the evaluation of proficiency is not limited to the content of a particular curriculum that has been taught and learned" (p. 4). *Proficiency* therefore represents the linguistic competence that can be obtained, even after a formal course, but is not linked to a specific curriculum, or to specific notions; what is linked instead is language use in real contexts—for example, *proficiency* is assessed not by a school exam but by a certification exam (Purpura 1999, 2004).

That is, *proficiency* represents the competence in the creative language space in which people are naturally inserted: a linguistic space of possibilities (a linguistic game, to recall the Wittgenstein model) that is creative, *in fieri*, and never regulated by fixed and immutable rules for the theoretical assumptions that we have invoked in this writing. For example, the *proficiency* of the skill level allows the learner to produce "highly sophisticated and tightly organized extended discourse. At the same time, they can speak succinctly, often using cultural and historical references to allow them to say less and mean more." That is, it allows the speaker to move between well-made phrases in the higher linguistic variety and then move on to sentences with a lower register, less formal, but which at the same time can be semiotically functional to the communicative action and the social context in which it takes place.

On the contrary, *performance* is:

> the ability to use language that has been learned and practiced in an instructional setting. Coached by an instructor, whether in a classroom or online, or guided by instructional materials performance refers to language ability that has been practiced and is within familiar contexts and content areas. The practice and assessment of performance should reflect authentic, real world use of language, even though the language is learned and practiced in some type of learning environment. Best practices for assessment of performance suggest that assessment be conducted in the same communicative manner in which the language was learned, practiced or rehearsed. To prepare for an assessment of performance, language learners need to practice the language functions, structures, and vocabulary they will apply on the assessment tasks, rather than practicing and memorizing exactly what will be on the assessment. Educators should provide language learners with practice of a variety of tasks related to the curriculum. In this way, learners will be ready to apply these elements in the context of the new tasks they will face on the performance assessment. To help language learners transfer their language skills, instruction needs to focus on real world-like tasks

with the anticipation that learners will be prepared to do the same outside the instructional setting (as in a demonstration of proficiency). In assessing performance, a language learner is evaluated against the description of the features of the domains of a given range within those contexts and content areas that have been learned and practiced. Demonstration of performance within a specific range may provide some indication of how the language user might perform on a proficiency assessment and indeed might point toward a proficiency level, but performance is not the same as proficiency. The language a learner produces on a collective set of performances generally correlates to a proficiency level, that is, the ratings that a language learner receives on a variety of performance assessments provides evidence of how the learner will be rated on an assessment of proficiency. (p. 4)

This distinction, which takes into account the skills that learners must develop, identifies the need for teachers to facilitate the development of performance by learners and to develop activities in the classroom that reflect multiple and different tasks and objectives: that is, the same tasks and objectives that characterize *proficiency*. In other words, teachers are asked to provide a creative teaching, educating students in a language creatively understood. That is creativity learned in the classroom, reflecting the creativity of the real language space as authentically as possible. Just as we have argued for *CEFRL*, we believe that the model of creativity represents, although it is not explicitly stated, the theoretical principle for teaching in North America and the inspiring model of educational linguistics and linguistic research (Casini and Bancheri (2019) point out to the creative educational processes in particular of Italian as L2 in North America).

As we begin to conclude this reflection on linguistic education and creativity, it is clear that reflection on language becomes a reflection on users, their linguistic and social role, and their ability to create meaning and language in the semiotic and social universe in which they live. At this point, however, we ask ourselves a question which is the basis of language use and language education: What is the purpose of communication? What is the purpose of language education? We respond using the words of Tullio De Mauro (2018, 84) and we see in these words the guiding principle of linguistic education as an education in creativity (in variety and diversity):

possiamo dire una cosa disegnando, cantando, mimandola, recitando, ammiccando, additando e con parole; possiamo dirla in inglese, in cinese, in turco, in francese in greco, in piemontese, in siciliano, in viterbese, romanesco, trasteverino, e in italiano; possiamo dirla con una sintassi semplice, per giustapposizione di proposizioni, o con una sintassi contorta e subordinante; con parole antiche o nuove, nobili o plebee, usate o specialistiche; possiamo dirla come uno scienziato o un poliziotto, un comiziante o un cronista, un gruppettaro o un curato di campagna; possiamo gridarla, scriverla a caratteri cubitali o in appunti frettolosi—possiamo dirla tacendo purché abbiamo veramente voglia di dirla e purché ce la lascino dire.[23]

NOTES

1. From my discussion, someone could draw this conclusion. Since the ways of the art of saying are almost infinite, different in their appearance but all worthy of praise, such manners of the art of saying so different cannot be valued with the same criteria and placed in the same schools. But this is not the case, and those who are tasked with educating and teaching young people must study each other's inclinations very carefully. We see that different disciples, all worthy of praise, have come out of the same school, for the teacher's teaching has adapted to the disposition of the student. Of this we find a truly illustrious example: Isocrat, a truly exceptional teacher, said that with Ephorus he used spurs, with Teopompo instead, he used brakes. This is to say that one who overshowed even too bold language had to be restrained, the other, who was instead hesitant, had to be spurred. The teacher did not teach them using the same technique; but to one he added and to the other he took something away, to enhance the qualities inherent in the disposition of each (our translation).

2. *Storia linguistica dell'Italia unita* (1963); *Storia linguistica dell'Italia repubblicana* (2014).

3. In De Mauro (1982, 83): "In conseguenza di quanto si è qui finora detto, dato un calcolo è possibile e necessario descriverne il suo funzionamento in termini di pura relazione tra segni, cioè in termini puramente sintattici, indipendentemente dalle possibili saturazioni semantiche ed espressive e dalle possibili destinazioni pragmatiche."

4. In De Mauro (1965, 151): "la possibilità di identificare il *dictum* non sussiste se questo è isolato dal *dicens*. . . . è un errore credere, come tutta la tradizione ha ritenuto, che le forme linguistiche hanno una intrinseca virtù semantica: isolate dal parlante che le adopera, esse non hanno capacità di garantire la trasmissione di un significato univoco: acquisiscono tale capacità soltanto in relazione a chi le usa." Further insights into this on the creativity of psychopedagogists are proposed in chapter 5 in relation to the analysis of Italiese.

5. In *Minisemantica,* De Mauro scientifically analyzes the language. "Scientific" means the study and the analysis of those semiotic properties that makes a language a semiotic first *inter pares*. Creativity, vagueness, ambiguity, possibility to widen the meanings thanks to the use of the masses: these are the properties that allow languages, all the languages, to create meaning and communication. Through a meticulous journey between points and counterpoints that allow for balance and substantiate the process of understanding, De Mauro examines the linguistic properties that on one side seem to impede the comprehension process and on the other side, through the mutual self-determination, enable the users to create an understanding that manages to direct the understanding between people. Each language is the kingdom of creativity and change.

Through the 187 pages, the text reconstructs the relationship between languages and verbal and nonverbal codes. The volume represents a great asset for the consideration of the languages, for the semiotics and on the philosophy of the language, besides a theoretical basis for anyone who is questioning on the principles of communication and comprehension. Lastly the title: *Minisemantica* is not a limited semantics but is called *mini* because it is the core, the key principle of the meaning and therefore of the communication.

6. In (De Mauro 1982, 32–33): "La scelta che facciamo e ci proponiamo di seguire è quella di riordinare quel che è possibile delle nostre conoscenze di codici semiologici in funzione di una classificazione, d'una tipologia che privilegi il riferimento agli aspetti interni, sintattici dei segni e codici e che, in subordine a ciò, badi in modo specifico al rapporto tra forme dei significati e sensi possibili per dati segni e dati codici. In altri termini intendiamo offrire un saggio di tipologia semantico-sintattica dei codici. . . . Un classificazione semantica dei codici semiologici che sia univoca e tenda ad essere esaustiva (allo stato attuale delle nostre conoscenze) può essere costruita sulla base di non più di quattro criteri semantico-formali."

7. The examples we propose have exemplary function and we do not consider the details of any exceptions, even of a semantic nature which often have to do with the sociolinguistic criterion of acceptability. The phrase *the cat is on the table* is sociolinguistically more accepted than the phrase *the table is on the cat*. The limits of this combinatorial and recursive process are linked to the morphologic-syntactic rules that are functional in the realization of communication and understanding between users.

8. The Italian polirematic expression *bestia nera* (difficulty to overcome) cannot be translated into English as a *black animal*. But the sense of *bestia nera* is expressed in English of the expression *pet hate* or *pet peeve*. However, if, in a specific context, *black beast* means *big black animal*, then the translation *verbum de verbo* is acceptable: *bestia nera = black animal*.

9. For example, the sign *1* is different from *11* and is different from *111* and so on. *The book of friends* is different from *the book of friends of friends* and is different from *the book of friends of friends of friends etc.*

10. In De Mauro (1982, 53): "Una nozione fondamentalmente unica di creatività intesa come disponibilità alla variazione delle forme di un sistema, o di un codice semiologico, insita negli utenti del sistema o codice, e riconoscibile come proprietà del sistema o codice stesso."

11. According to Coseriu (1962) Croce did not want to come up with a theory of the whole language. Although Croce still speaks of language, Croce refers to what is creative and poetic. In other words, Croce's linguistic interest is aesthetic in nature—toward art and poetry—and not towards the common (and daily) uses of the language.

12. This form of creativity, called expressive creativity, was already present in De Mauro's reflection (1971b, 126) when it reads: "In conseguenza del carattere continuo dei sensi e delle fonie ogni significante include un numero di fonie (o grafie ecc.) che, anche se finito di fatto, è potenzialmente infinito (nel senso in cui sono infinite le applicazioni di un qualsiasi numero intero a gruppi di oggetti); similmente è potenzialmente infinito il numero di sensi di un significato; infine ogni segno può includere un numero infinito di espressioni. Quante sono le espressioni (i diversi sensi e le diverse fonie o grafie ecc.) comprese in un qualsiasi banale segno, ad esempio # prendi questo! #? Esse sono potenzialmente infinite. La possibilità di realizzare un segno in un numero infinito di espressioni può essere detta creatività espressiva."

13. In De Mauro (1971b, 152–153) it reads: "Siamo dunque autorizzati a identificare un nuovo tipo di infinità connessa ai fenomeni linguistici: con una lingua è possibile generare un numero infinito di segni. Accanto alla creatività espressiva veniamo così a definire una creatività *segnica* inerente all'utilizzazione che di una lingua può fare un utente: essa consiste nella capacità dio produrre, data una lingua, un numero infinito di segni." We will come back to reflect on the role that users (as a social and historical dimension) play in linguistic creativity also in reference to the creativity of *Langue*.

14. Consider also Vygotsky (1966).

15. De Mauro (1982) considers another variation of creativity—the creativity of logicians—whereby a semiotic code is defined as a calculation. We will not add any more details because we have already given all the necessary references for creativity as a calculation.

16. In De Mauro and Ferreri (2005, 26–27): Educational Linguistics is a "settore delle scienze del linguaggio che ha per oggetto la lingua (una lingua, ogni lingua) considerata in funzione dell'apprendimento linguistico e del più generale sviluppo delle capacità semiotiche. Della lingua o delle lingue da apprendere (lingua madre, lingue seconde, lingue straniere, lingue letterarie, microlingue, lingue specialistiche ecc.) o di loro parti pertinentizza quegli elementi linguistici che potenziano lo sviluppo del linguaggio, a partire dall'incremento del patrimonio linguistico già in possesso di chi apprende. Le pertinenze si misurano in base al grado di funzionalità rispetto alle potenzialità di espansione dello spazio linguistico e culturale dei singoli parlanti e apprendenti. La linguistica educativa definisce ed elabora inoltre per il suo oggetto approcci, metodi, tecniche, risorse tecnologiche utili per facilitare lo sviluppo delle capacità semiotiche e l'apprendimento linguistico, ivi compreso l'insegnamento a scuola o in altri luoghi educativi."

17. Consider Vedovelli (2003) for a reflection in Italian educational context.

18. We include the quotation in the original language text. De Mauro argues that for many centuries, it has been commonplace that a language be taught through the "the beautiful speech," those phases and signs already used by Tizio and Caius, by this and that writer. This was (and in many places continues to be) the most prestigious language teaching method. If however, with language, it is possible to generate an infinite number of signs (and we are still waiting for a refutation), then teaching a language means teaching to produce as many signs as possible that have never been previously formulated by anyone. Only a careful education to the most unrestrained phraseological and expressive license can give the real, deep possession of a language (our translation).

19. Consider also De Mauro 2009 in reference to the birth and diffusion of *Educational Linguistics* in Italy.

20. The *Dieci Tesi per l'educazione linguistica democratica* (1975) is the most important document of the G.I.S.C.E.L. (Gruppo di Intervento e Studio nel Campo della Educazione Linguistica), founded by Tullio De Mauro in 1973 and represents a linguistic policy document that promoted a project developing the expressive abilities of the Italian population. The *Dieci Tesi*, therefore, do not only respond to educational purposes: they have behind them the theoretical depth of a semiotic and sociolinguistic approach to language facts and the knowledge of the importance that

the intertwining of language, school, cultural and social life are at the basis of the civil constitution of modern society. The document is not a teaching manual or a guide for teachers: it is a short document (containing "only" ten programmatic points), which collects the inspiring principles of creativity to then broaden the perspective to the new educational principles, when the pedagogical translation based on respect for grammatical, lexical, syntactic and morphological rule systems.

21. We include the quotation in the original language text. It is always necessary to develop the communicative functionality of every possible known or unknown linguistic form. An old model of language teaching was imitative and prescriptive: its principle was "to say always and only in a certain way." Everything else was error. The new language education (more to be implemented) has a different principle. The new language education teaches that things can be said in many different ways, and must also teach the linguistic and social effects that are achieved by saying one thing one way or another. The old linguistic teaching was dictatorial. But the new one is not anarchic: it has a fundamental rule. The only rule that must follow is the communicative functionality of a spoken or written text and its parts depending on the real interlocutors.

22. Consider the words from *Lettera a una professoressa*, an important Italian text written by the students of *Scuola di Barbiana* (Barbiana's school. Barbiana is a small village in the province of Florence, Italy) under the guidance of Don Lorenzo Milani: "Il compito di francese era un concentrato di eccezioni. Gli esami vanno aboliti. Ma se li fate, siate almeno leali. Le difficoltà vanno messe in percentuale di quelle della vita. Se le mettete più frequenti avete la mania del trabocchetto. Come se foste in guerra coi ragazzi. Chi ve lo fa fare? Il loro bene? Il loro bene no. Passò con nove un ragazzo che in Francia non saprebbe chiedere nemmeno il gabinetto. Sapeva solo chiedere gufi, ciottoli e ventagli sia al plurale che al singolare. Avrà saputo in tutto duecento vocaboli e scelti col metro di essere eccezioni, non d'esser frequenti. Il risultato è che odiava anche il francese come si potrebbe odiare la matematica.Io le lingue le ho imparate coi dichi. Senza neanche accorgermene ho imparato prima le cose più utili e frequenti. Esattamente come si impara l'italiano." The French assignment was a mass of exceptions. Exams must be abolished. But if you administer them, at least be honest. Difficulties must be put as a percentage of those in life. If you put them more frequently, you have a devious mania. As if you are at war with the kids. For what? Their good? Not for their good. A boy, who in France could not even ask for a bathroom, passed with a nine. He could only ask for owls, pebbles and fans, in both the plural and the singular. He knew in all two hundred words and chosen due to their nature of being exceptions, not of being frequent. The result is that he hated French just as one could hate math. I learned the languages by speaking. Without even realizing it, I learned the most useful and frequent things first. Exactly how you learn Italian (our translation).

23. We include the quotation in the original language text. We can say one thing by drawing, singing, mimicking, acting; we can say it in English, Chinese, Turkish, French, Greek, Piedmont, Sicilian, Vineyard, Romanesque and Italian; we can say it with a simple syntax or with a twisted syntax and many subordinates. We can say something with old or new words, noble or simple, with common or specialized words. We can tell you what a scientist or a policeman, or a journalist, or a priest would say. We can shout it, write it in capital letters or in hasty notes—we can say it by being silent as long as we really want to say it and as long as others, the social and political context allow us to (our translation).

Chapter 5

Open Questions for Semiotic Creativity

Gallia est ominis divisa in partes tres, quarum unam incolunt Belgae, aliam Aquitani, tertiam qui ipsorum lingua Celtae, nostra Galli appellantur. Hi omnes lingua, institutis, legibus inter se differunt. Gallos ab Aquitanis Garunna flumen, a Belgis Matrona et Sequana dividit.[1]

Julius Caesar, *De Bello Gallico*

E come, per fuggir questo male è necessario dar giusta e ragionata (non precipitata, e illegittima, e ingiudicata e anarchica) cittadinanza anche alle parole straniere, se sono necessarie, molto più bisogna e ricercare con ogni diligenza, e trovate accogliere con buon viso, e ricevere nel tesoro della buona e scrivibile e legittima favella, sì i derivati delle buone e già riconosciute radici, sì le radici che non essendo ancora riconosciute, vanno così vagando per l'uso della nazione, senza studio né osservazione, di chi le fermi, le cerchi, le chiami, le inviti, e le introduca a far parte delle voci o dei modi riconosciuti, e a partecipare degli onori dovuti ai cittadini della buona lingua.[2]

Giacomo Leopardi, *Zibaldone di pensieri*

INTRODUCTION

The theoretical reflection on semiotic and linguistic creativity represents the reference time within which to consider the phenomena of linguistic contact and multilingualism, being the dynamics of the contemporary global world, in which people, values, languages, and life forms meet at levels of quality and quantity much higher than in the recent past (Vertovec 2007). The objective of this volume is not to offer an answer to the issue of the early language, nor to consider, as Humboldt had done ([1836] 1988), that each language carries the speaker directly within the story. Therefore, it seems unreasonable to go so far back on the axis of time in search of the *first* language from which the others would then be born. If anything, a good starting point may be to look at the linguistic history of humanity with the advantage of being able to begin ab initio (Eco 1995) to see how ab initio human reality is characterized by the diversity that is the static result of semiotic creativity as a dynamic property. And so, with the advantage of considering things ab initio from a theoretical perspective we consider how, at the beginning of history, humanity was characterized by the seed of linguistic and semiotic diversity. And so, starting from ab initio, it reads in Genesis (11, 1–9):

> The whole world spoke the same language, using the same words. While men were migrating in the east, they came upon a valley in the land of Shinar and settled there. They said to one another, "Come, let us mold bricks and harden them with fire." They used bricks for stone, and bitumen for mortar. Then they said, "Come, let us build ourselves a city and a tower with its top in the sky, and so make a name for ourselves; otherwise we shall be scattered all over the earth." LORD came down to see the city and the tower that the men had built.
>   Then the LORD said: "If now, while they are one people, all speaking the same language, they have started to do this, nothing will later stop them from doing whatever they presume to do. Let us then go down and there confuses their language, so that one will not understand what another says." Thus, the LORD scattered them from there all over the earth, and they stopped building the city. That is why it was called Babel, because there the LORD confused the speech of all the world. It was from that place that he scattered them all over the earth.

We refer to Eco (1995) for the linguistic literature starting from the biblical tradition. However, this is an opportunity to highlight how since man loses the ability to live the life of the universe, the condition that emerges, with reference to both Babel and Pentecost, is the societal multilingualism: not only the states, but also the social environments themselves, the same *masses parlantes* have been characterized by the coexistence of different languages. It is not just a widespread case of bilingualism resulting from learning and studying in schools or universities, it is a kind of environmental, native multilingualism. The idea that the speaker should adhere to a language seen as unique, unified, massive, immovable, unwavering, and unemotional is replaced by the more realistic vision that speakers (all speakers) freely use of the means that the languages they know provide to express themselves

(De Mauro 2006a). In this sense, creativity is the theoretical prerequisite that determines linguistic variation, and with variation, a *societal multilingualism*.

Creativity is the engine that generates variation and variation is the *conditio diversitatis*. From this, it emerges that variation is not something that affects languages from the outside: it settles at every point of the language as a consequence of its semantics and pragmatics. Each speaker of each language has in itself, in the actual use that makes a language, the principle and variation and it is only the external social forces and factors that "oblige'" to establish and limit the unlimited potential of differentiation of languages. In languages themselves, and within languages, the uses are inevitably countless because the only universal *faculté du langage* must meet the semantic-pragmatic requirements of the communication needs of human beings; from them descends the continuous variability of the language repositories in which the language is realized[3] (De Mauro 1994). As if that were not enough, Martinet's words (VII–IX) in the Preface of *Languages in Contact* (1967) describe linguistic diversity as an intrinsic part of both society and the singular idiom:

> There was a time when the progress of research required that each community should be considered linguistically self-contained and homogeneous.... Linguists will always have to revert at times to this pragmatic assumption. But we shall now have to stress the fact that a linguistic community is never homogeneous and hardly ever self-contained.... But it remains to be emphasized that linguistic diversity begins next door, nay, at home and within one and the same man. It is not enough to point out that each individual is a battlefield for conflicting linguistic types and habits, and, at the same time, a permanent source of linguistic interference. What we heedlessly and somewhat rashly call "a language" is the aggregate of millions of such microcosms, many of which evince such aberrant linguistic comportment that the question arises whether they should not be grouped into other "languages." What further complicates the picture, and may, at the same time, contribute to clarify it, is the feeling of linguistic allegiance which will largely determine the responses of every individual. This, even more than sheer intercourse, is the cement that holds each one of our "languages" together.

In the previous chapter, we considered creativity from the particular perspective of the personal language space, considering how this property is the basis of the process of language learning and language management and use in relation to the communication, semiotic, and social goals that a user sets in his/her daily life. In this chapter, we compare the theoretical system of linguistic creativity with a possible practical and application dimension, in order to test the theoretical principles of creativity with its results in the contemporary world. We do not wish to state that this "concrete reflection" on semiotic creativity is exhaustive both for the areas of relevance and for the exemplifications it proposes; however, we support the theoretical assumption that creativity can represent the semiotic foundation to consider the linguistic phenomena arising from contact between people and life forms. And in this sense, a linguistic stud that wants to start from the speaker, and the speaker as a semiotic and social subject, would benefit from creativity as a theoretical and interpretive model of reference for both the birth and use of the language, both in terms of the interaction and contact between these languages (Blommaert 2010).

Among these particular areas within which to consider creativity, we take into account two phenomena of linguistic contact, partly different, but which have a common matrix. For the interests that this study has shown in wanting to keep together an international and American framework with a European and Italian dimension, we consider two areas in which the Italian language space comes into contact with other languages and whose results are interpretable according to the model of semiotic creativity. Consider the phenomenon of Italianisms (Italian words) and pseudo-Italianisms (words not Italian but linguistically constructed as if they were Italian) present in the urban landscapes of global cities whose semiotic uses outweigh the interaction between languages (in our case, predominantly Italian-English).[4]

The second area which we will refer to is the contact between the Italian language space (including the set of linguistic varieties, such as dialectal) and English that occurred as a result of the migratory phenomena of the Italian community that took place post–World War II in Ontario (Canada). This linguistic contact gave rise to Italiese, the koine spoken by Italian emigrants in Ontario and in other parts of English Canada which is, according to Clivio (1976), Danesi (1982), and Pietropaolo (1974), the result of contact among Italian, Italian dialects, and English. In this sense, Italiese is a unique Canadian member of the Italian linguistic community, and we will argue for its inclusion in the global Italian "language space," on par with Italian dialects and immigrant languages in Italy.[5] In both cases, creativity is a theoretical prerequisite and an interpretive model of linguistic contact and multilingualism, since the traditional categories of bilingualism and interference (Weinreich 1967) seem not to fully respond to the principles of linguistic contact in the global world. For multilingualism, we adopt the macro-definition proposed by De Mauro (1981), for which multilingualism is the coexistence within the same social and linguistic context of both different types of semiosis, different idioms, and different norms of realization of a single idiom.[6]

Starting with Weinreich (1967, 1–2), according to the tradition of studies on language contact, "two or more languages are said to be in contact if they are used alternately by the same persons. The language using individuals are thus the locus of the contact":

the practice of alternately using two languages will be called bilingualism and the persons involved, bilingual. Those instances of deviation from the norms of either language which occur in the speech of bilinguals as a result of their familiarity with more than one language, i.e., as a result of language contact, will be referred to as interference phenomena. It is these phenomena of speech, and their impact on the norms of either language exposed to contact, that invite the interest of the linguist. . . . Language contact and bilingualism will be considered here in the broadest sense, without qualifications as to the degree of difference between the two languages. For the purpose of the present study, it is immaterial whether the two systems are "languages," "dialects of the same language," or "varieties of the same dialect." . . . the mechanism of interference, abstracted from the amount of interference, would appear to be the same whether the contact is between Chinese and French or between two sub varieties of English used by neighboring families.

In addition, according to traditional contact categories, the mechanisms of interference lead to innovation (a standard and system innovation), but an innovation in which one of the two varieties is "supported" by the other (the language which has the freest grammatical categories). It reads in Weinreich (1967, 41–42):

Significantly, in the interference of two grammatical patterns it is ordinarily the one which uses relatively free and invariant morphemes in its paradigm—one might say, the more explicit pattern—which serve the model for imitation. This seems to be true not only in the creation of new categories . . . but also in those changes due to language contact where a new set of formants is developed to fulfill a pre-existing grammatical function. . . . Language contact can result in such far-reaching changes that the affected language assumes a different structural type.

In this sense, and considering the link between interference and contact (the second as the place of the first), Orioles (2008[7]) considers the hypothesis of Coseriu on the nature of exogenous interference on the assumption that it constitutes "eine Form der sprachlichen Kreativität" to be considered on the same level as creations that exploit the internal resources of the language. As for the outcome of the contact,[8] Weinreich notes that in power a prolonged phase of contact can have such significant repercussions that it can determine "a different structural type"; however, he is also aware that an even more advanced interpenetration can lead to the formation of a third language, structurally irreducible to the two originals[9] (Orioles 2008). The aim is therefore to consider how the results of linguistic contact and multilingualism are not only interpretable in terms of interference but can be studied and considered in their general semiotic complexity using the principles of linguistic creativity. In other words, we want to consider whether the processes of creation of meaning can be reduced to dynamics of interference between languages in which there are elements of deviation from the norm of one to the norm of the other, as is the case in the discourse of bilinguals as a result of their familiarity with more than one language (Weinreich 1967). Or rather to complement this, these same processes of negotiation of meaning can be interpreted through the category of semiotic creativity.

ITALIANISMS AND PSEUDO-ITALIANISMS IN THE GLOBAL CONTEXT

Sections 2 and 3 are a novelty in terms of linguistic and semiotic research. The innovation is not caused by the addition of new data, that is, new linguistic examples that have never been mentioned and commented on before. The novelty is the framework for analysis and interpretation of the data. If with regard to Italianisms and pseudo-Italianisms we had already introduced a reading of the linguistic phenomenon through the paradigm of creativity, albeit in a limited way (Vedovelli 2005; Casini 2012; Vedovelli and Casini 2013; Casini 2018), for Italiese the issue is of absolute novelty and originality. We therefore do not add new linguistic elements to what has already been proposed by Clivio, Danesi, and Pietropaolo. In this writing, Italiese is interpreted as a creative language not only because it is the result of linguistic contact, but it is eminently creative—that is creative to the highest degree—because it collects in itself all the meanings of creativity: from the formal and lexical ones of code mixing, to those of lexical enlargement through calques and loans, to semantic, cultural, and of thought. Italiese collects all forms of semiotic creativity.

Recently, there has been a growing focus on the uncultivated ways of spreading Italianism, within a general framework that has long been strongly oriented toward the only historical reconstruction of the spread of Italianism in the world by "other means." De Mauro et al. (2002) had already proposed a reconnaissance and interpretive framework of considerable scope; in other words, it is a matter of taking note of the systematic, dense, and widespread presence of new paths of mutual contact between the languages of the world, and therefore, also of those concerning Italian. The presence of Italianism and pseudo-Italianism in urban linguistic landscapes is non-marginal to consider the diffusion of a language in the world and such beyond their actual claim as exoticisms in the lexicon of the language of the country of reference, already marginal element to consider the linguistic scope of the processes of immigration and emigration (De Mauro 1963). The linguistic traces which we refer to are the written texts (plurilingual or monolingual) of public social communication—the signs of shops, street names, restaurant menus, and so on—that are all factors of linguistic visibility and at the same time, a powerful indicator of the social vitality of languages. The reflections that we advance start from theoretical assumptions and methods different from those that guided Franco Pierno (2017) in his work on Italianism in Canada starting from the lexicographic tradition, an element that is important to verify the degree of sedimentation of the lexicon of a language, but that we do not take into consideration.

The framework within which to inscribe the processes of contact moves to the level of the language market (Calvet 2002; De Mauro *et al.* 2002), that is, of the "competition" between different languages that is the demonstration of "strength" and "armor" (symbolic) that an idiom puts in place to be used and chosen, learned and spent in social contexts by users. The competitive plan concerns the general symbolic value the idiom possesses as a form of life and an identity factor, that is, it refers to the value it evokes in the processes of interaction and use: competition takes place, therefore, between linguistic systems that are the function of "language-culture-society-economy. These dimensions are identity plans ranging from the recognition of the symbolic values of a language to the semiotic ability that it has to direct (or support) the choice made by a user to use precisely that language, to learn it. In choosing a linguistic element, the semiotic implant goes beyond the pragmatic implications, but embraces semiotic phenomena and identity recognition; in particular if the choice is counted by a foreigner who sees in the linguistic use of an L2 the possibility of creating, evoking, and transmitting cultural values to which to refer. From this point of view, Italian has manifested in different phases that are related to its most recent history (De Mauro 2014; Vedovelli 2010, 2011, 2018): before being L1 in Italy for more than 95 percent of the population who today, if they want, can use Italian in the contexts of use, Italian was L2 for Italians and foreign learners, that is, a language to search for, research, and create as a shared communication module within and outside national borders.

The sociolinguistic framework within which we insert analyses on Italianisms in urban spaces considers those who, Italian or non-Italian speakers, perhaps without a kinship or Italian descent, embrace Italian values, lifestyles, and models and do so through the choice and use of the Italian language (Bassetti 2015). These are the values of taste and good taste, imagination, and creativity that go through Italian cultural history and from this they pass to cuisine, wines, design, artifacts, social relationships, and quality of life. In the past centuries, foreigners who chose to study Italian (cultivated people, nobles, prelates, traders) constituted a higher percentage than those who could use Italian as a native, as their own L1. This has produced a sense of linguistic "ownership" of the foreigner that we do not want to interpret in terms of absolutism or prevaricating will, but as a condition of the one who had the opportunity to create and build a language from what were then his interests, his motivations for learning and use. Today we believe that this sense of belonging still remains, although changed from the past, because the conditions of the global Italian language space have changed, and are an important manifestation of the exemplifications of Italianisms and pseudo-Italianisms that distinguish the cities of the world, as the attention of the foreign public precisely to the semiotic prerogatives of our language.

To these elements is added the plan of the visibility of words in urban panoramas. Visibility is neither random, nor obvious: visibility is a consequence that is placed on the level of the choices that foreign public people make, for example, to use (and prefer) Italian (or pseudo-Italian) words to "make their business speak," to give a name to their stores, to give a linguistic face to the environment, streets, and places of meeting, contact, and social exchange of the cities of the world. A plan linked to economic and commercial dynamics, in the first instance, but which allows to embrace consideration of a more generally semiotic style, inherent in the value scope that through linguistic use is meant to evoke. In this sense, we believe that the analysis of Italianisms and pseudo-Italianisms can refer to the theoretical model of semiotic creativity: a creative use that is such that it is capable of innovating and finding new solutions, sometimes, to overcome the "normal" language while remaining within the possibilities offered by the system. In line with this assumption, the hypothesis we propose looks at Italianisms and pseudo-Italianisms as two different outcomes; the first are incalculable and the second are creative. Consider how the reference to the forms of semiotic creativity seems to guarantee the possibilities of communication and understanding because it grants the possibility of choice, sometimes making a slalom, to arrive at new expressive skills able to tend to the communicative end.

Italianisms and Pseudo-Italianisms: A Reflection on the Greater Toronto Area (GTA)

The phenomenon of Italianisms and pseudo-Italianisms is a worldwide phenomenon: for example, we refer to Barni, Extra and Bagna (2008); Shohami, Ben-Rafael and Barni (2010); Vedovelli (2005); Vedovelli and Casini (2013); Turchetta and Vedovelli (2018). The reflections that we make with the relevant examples, although they can be extended to the global world in quantitative terms, propose an analysis essentially related to the Greater Toronto Area (GTA)[10] with a body of data collected since 2015.[11] The choice of Toronto and Ontario is not random: The GTA represents the paradigm of mobility and the presence of Italian/Italian speakers both for emigration reasons related to the past (we will return to this aspect considering Italiese) and for neo-emigration (RIM 2019). But Toronto is also one of the most important metropolises in North America. It is the largest urban, cultural, and economic space in Ontario and one of the most important in Canada. Therefore, the semiotic phenomena that take place in Toronto can be considered emblematic and significant for the global world (Turchetta and Vedovelli 2018).

Historically, the statistics of Italian emigration to Canada are summarized here using the research by Sanzone (2012–2015). There were 1,035 Italians in Canada in 1871; by 1901 there were 10,000; and 7 years later, there were 50,000. This migration was part of a massive diaspora that saw 7 million people leaving Italy to countries in Europe, the Americas, and elsewhere for 30 years after World War II. According to the 2016 Census of Canada, 1,587,970 Canadians (5.1% of the total population) consider themselves to be of Italian origin. Up until the 1990s, Italy was among the top 10 countries with the highest number of immigrants in Canada, but in the following years the number decreased dramatically. Every year, hundreds of Italians are given temporary study permits and thousands decide to work in Canada. According to Statistics Canada, Italian is the third most common language spoken in Canada (Sanzone 2012–2015; Statistics Canada 2011, 2016). In Canada, the total Italian population by mother tongue is 455,040: the total by Italian "spoken most often at home" is 170,330; by Italian "spoken on a regular basis at home" is 130,070; and at work is 3,895.

The corpus consists of 682 photos comprising a total of 1,029 occurrences, collected in different areas of the GTA. The research was carried out in different areas of the GTA, ranging by geographical location, residential type, and consequently semiotic: *Yorkville Ave* (area between Avenue Rd. and Yonge St. and Bloor St.); the traditional *Little Italy* (area between Spadina Avenue and College Street up to the intersection with Bathurst St.); *St. Clair*—Corso *Italia*; *Vaughan* (particularly the residential-commercial area of Woodbridge); *Mississauga* (commercial area).

The analysis conducted allows us to propose some results in terms of visibility and linguistic use of Italian and pseudo-Italian forms. The semantic fields of reference link 426 units to the food and catering sector, to which more than 270 occurrences are linked to the dimensions of both the varied world of coffee and different alcoholic or non-alcoholic drinks.

This is followed by the fields of *fashion* and *design* (154 occurrences) and *health* and *diaspora* (110 occurrences). The remaining occurrences look at multiple areas on which it is difficult to propose a unitary reference. The units that we present, unless otherwise noticeable, are attested with a frequency value of two or greater, in order to provide a photograph of the urban landscape that avoids the hapax nature of the occurrence. The overall corpus is composed in the first instance of Italian words used to indicate realia otherwise non-speakable. More than 40 percent of the corpus consists

Figure 5.1 Map of the Detection Areas. *Source:* Dati mappa © 2019 Google Termini

of units related to the kitchen and catering sector: examples of these are *spaghetti, espresso, cappuccino* (with the *capuccino* or *capuccinno* variant), *crostini* (which is also attested as *crustini*), *pizza* (with *pizzetta* and *pizzette* variant), *gelato, piadina, pane, cannoli* (used only with plural morpheme *-i*), *pasta, spaghetti, salumi, ristorante* (with the variant *restorante*), *trattoria, osteria, forno, gelato* (*realia* different than *ice cream*; so different, in fact, that restaurant menus included both forms of vanilla *gelato* and vanilla *ice cream*), *focaccia, mozzarella, ricotta, latte* (other than *milk*), and *piadina.* Included in this first group, we attest the forms of *panino* (in addition to the second standard variant also in the variant *pannino*), we find the unit *panini*, with the plural grammatical morpheme *-i*, used in singular function, *paninis* with the English grammatical morpheme *-s* for the plural and *panouzzo*. The same phenomenon is attested with the Italianism *zucchini* used as a singular to which the English morpheme *-s* is associated, while a kind of phenomenon of hyper-correction can be found in the case of *baresa* (in place of *barese*) associated with a name with female morphology such as *trattoria*. Add to that *buon appetito, dolcini, cibo, gelato, cucina,* and *mercato* (respectively, with the *cucinetta* and *mercatto* variants).

Widespread in a homogeneous way within the corpus is the link with the Italian tradition, marked through the use of nonverbal elements, such as symbols of Italian art or the use of the colors of the Italian flag to which, in the prevailing cases of catering, the expression *proprietario* is associated in addition to a name of a person, also linked to the traditional Italian name. Other cases of Italianisms not related to the field of catering are found in the use of *borgo, salone, sartoria, specchio, donna, oggi salon,* and the use of expressions such as *dall'Italia* or *dell'Italia*—sometimes also in English, *of Italy.*

Even the adjective dimension seems to be used with equal symbolic intent: the cases of *grande, famoso, bravo, arte, italiano* (sometimes in association with the adverb *semplicemente* or "simply"), *antico, sportivo, creativo, squisito,* and *tradizionale.* The positive connotation of Italicity is also highlighted by the adjectives *amabile, bravo, buono, familiare, grande, luminoso, nuovo, pronto, vero, giusto,* and *elegante* (sometimes also used as a noun function with the definite article as in the case of *l'elegante*). The use of Italianisms is also accompanied by a regional characterization, whereby the adjectives identifying specific Italian regions (associated with the areas of origin of emigration): *Siciliano* (or *Siciliana* associated with cooking), *Calabrese, Abruzzese,* and so on. Of interest, in that line, is the expression, found on Bloor St., *L'eleganza della moda italiana,* without any translation in English or other references except linguistic and contextual (the expression is placed in the window inside a luxury clothing store).

Figure 5.2 Italianisms in Toronto. *Source:* Created by the author.

Figure 5.3 Italianisms in Toronto. *Source:* Created by the author.

Figure 5.4 Italianisms in Toronto. *Source:* Created by the author.

Figure 5.5 Italianisms in Toronto. *Source:* Created by the author.

The cases presented show that both the units detected are built mainly according to a regular creativity on the level of *langue*. In the cases of *baresa, zucchini, panini,* and *paninis,* creativity extends to forms of violation of the Italian linguistic rule to embrace phenomena of assonance (*baresa*) or morphological rules of the English language. In our opinion, these are not "simple" cases of Italian-English interference: the contact has no systematic value and therefore is not constantly found in all the forms detected. For example, with the *panini* and *paninis* units, the morphological dimension of Italian-English contact also extends to the semantic level, not "wrong translations" of the English *sandwich,* but signs that identify different referents. To these are added classic examples of Italian contact: *capuccino*; *lemoncello* (with clear influence of *lemon*); and *crustini,* in which a tension of the Italian morphological rules toward forms that declare them simply "errors" does not account for their semiotic function. There is no doubt that they are linguistic errors, if by mistake we mean any attempt of failure to adapt to an established model. The question, however, moves to a semiotic level, because of the objectives with which these words are used, the non-compliance with the norm, and the possible lack of competence in the Italian language which, in fact, determines the error of not doubling the *p* in *capuccino*, and the replacement of the voiced *u* compared to *o* in *crustini*; these are not factors that affect language use, nor do they limit the possibility of the message going into the communication of semiotic value.

As we have considered, the most used restaurant words we find are *pizza, spaghetti* and *gelato*: what interests us most is the form of morphological suffixation, in *-eria* that produces the cases of *pizzeria, spaghetteria*, and *gelateria*. These examples recall what Vedovelli (2005) has already pointed out for the case of *freddoccino*, that is, to consider the mechanism by which Italian is not only a source of loan of lexical elements already constituted, but is a source of models of words or morphological mechanisms that create new words.[12] Other forms of the Italian suffixation model can be found in the cases of *whitissimo* (figure 5.6), used either as a name of a cosmetic product or *caldina* and *decoretta*[13] (figure 5.7) as names of a car and a bicycle.

Also, within the context of suffixation, another interesting case is the derivation *-ini* in *panini*. If *panini* and *paninis* have a very high diffusion, compared to the much less visible unit *pane* from which *panini* and *paninis* should derive, this suggests that the less scrutinized forms are, rather, morphological derivational elements. In the urban landscapes we also find *piattini*, in which the Italian suffix *-ini* does not represent a true diminutive: *piattini* (not attested *piattino*) is not proposed as an alternative of *piatto* or

Figure 5.6 Italianisms in Tokyo. Also examined in Vedovelli, Casini (2013). *Source:* Created by the author.

Figure 5.7 Italianisms in Tokyo. Also examined in Vedovelli, Casini (2013). *Source:* Created by the author.

piattone, but as an alternative of *insalata* and *antipasto*. If *piattini* opposes *insalata* and *antipasto*, the suffix *-ini* does not recall the smallness of one thing compared to another larger thing.[14]

A further case of morphological derivation is represented by the suffix *-issimo*, which creates *grandissimo* and *altissimo*, but also the pseudo-Italianism *berrissimo* and *blendissimo* (the latter are cold drinks). As in the case of *piattini*, again the suffix *-issimo* does not recall the degree of quality or quantity (e.g., *grandissimo* corresponds to the largest measure of product that a consumer can request). In the cases of *berrissimo* and *blendissimo*, one loses the quantitative value of the quantity of the product, since both drinks are served in containers of non-variable size, not even corresponding to the largest in use for other products even within the same store. Built through the same model we find *mozzarellissima*, *cherrissimo*, or *tippissimo* that demonstrate the great morphological productivity of the suffix *-issimo*. If we consider the constituent characteristics of the Italian lexicon (De Mauro 2005b), more than 90,000 terms are derived. Among these, suffixes are on average twice as productive as prefixes: among the most productive suffixes in the Italian language are found (in alphabetical order[15]): *-ano* (1107), *-ato* (1304), *-bile* (1466), *-eria* (652), *-ese* (6944), *-ezza* (691), *-ico* (4598), *-ina* (1233), *-ino* (1738), *-ismo* (2291), *-ista* (1977), *-istico* (827), *-ità* (2233), *-mento* (3644), *-one* (877), *-tore* (2714), *-tura* (2009), and *-zione* (1909). Considering the examples of our corpus, we add the previous suffixes *-issima* and *-issimo* with fifteen derivatives. The reference to the mechanisms of morphological derivation of the Italian lexicon demonstrate that the cases of Italianisms and pseudo-Italianisms detected in urban panoramas can be traced back to forms of creativity of *langue* according to the formal mechanisms of the language;

however, for the advanced considerations of semantical and pragmatical productivity of Italian suffixes, it appears to be in crisis in the case of Italianisms, since lexical units are mainly blocks that cannot be analyzed as derivative signs, but can be analyzed as stand-alone units. This is also only noted by the lack in the corpus of the starting lexical element to which the suffix is associated for the creation of the derivative. Interesting cases of Italianisms are the expressions that cover the semantic field of coffee. The word coffee is attested in *caffè*, *caffé*, and *caffe*. In addition to the claims of *caffè*, there is *latte*, attested both in the regular form and *latté*. *Latte* and *caffè* (in the different variants) then give rise to *caffè corretto* (attested to both in the regular form and in the variant of contact (*caffe correct*), *caffellatte* (also in variants *caffè latte*, *caffe latte*, *caffé latté*), *caffe moka* (also *caffe mocha*), and *caffè lungo* (also *caffe luongo*).[16] Within the same semantic sphere we find the pseudo-Italianisms *iperespresso*, *dolcespresso*, and *italatte*. The term *latte* often identifies new referents with respect to the Italian use, that is, *realia* of hot drinks based on milk with the addition of a little coffee, enjoyed generally during breakfast. With clear creative intent one may build the expression of gratitude (toward someone or something) *Thanks a latte!* (Figure 5.8), in which *latte* is not a drink, but an innovative and creative form with which to recall the English *a lot*.

In the same way, Italianisms and pseudo-Italianisms in urban landscapes represent cases where forms of *rule-governed creativity* and forms of *rule-changing creativity* are seen on the morphological level as well as the semantic/pragmatic level.[17] As already mentioned, the quantitative analysis of the corpus of Italianisms and pseudo-Italianisms in the urban linguistic panoramas of the global world is not unique to the Toronto context and, although the downtown of the capital of Ontario can be a privileged context for its

Figure 5.8 Italianisms in North America. *Source:* Created by the author.

conformation to the multicultural metropolis, what is highlighted in terms of results allows us to propose the idea for which the situation of the Italianisms in Toronto is not much different from what is detected in other areas of the world.

Toronto is not Tokyo. Toronto is not Paris. Toronto is not Miami.[18] Or maybe it is.

It is not from a historical and social point of view, because since World War II the quantitative flow of Italian immigrants to Canada, and Toronto in particular has grown to such an extent that in a short time, Italians have outnumbered migrants of Anglo-Saxon origin through mass mobility, favored by the need for labor and also the result of Canadian migration policies being less restrictive than those of other countries. Traditional emigration therefore leads to the creation of ethnic neighborhoods such as the first College Street West in which craftsmanship flourishes, all managed by Italians and representing more than 80 percent of the local economy (Paina 2006). Then, from the 1970s to the 1980s, the movements towards the northern direction of the city, with the population achieving an economic and social status of undoubted improvement over that of arrival, led to the birth of other ethnic realities, respectively, on St. Clair and Woodbridge (the latter located outside the confines of Downtown Toronto and north of the GTA). We refer to Ramirez (1989) and Zucchi (1992) for a general consideration on Italian emigration but, starting from a linguistic analysis, we verify that in Toronto, even in the areas that have been most characterized by Italy, today there are symbolic uses of the Italian language far beyond its referential value. That is, the value for which the link with Italy, although declared linguistically, is not found in the facts because, for example, the commercial exercise is not Italian, it does not sell Italian products, or is not managed by Italians or Italians of origin. This is a case of the manifestation of creativity that may not even directly invest the morphological or syntactic dimension but considers semantics and pragmatics. This represents one of the outcomes of semiotic creativity, one of the forms through which it, as the property of the code, is determined by its use through semantic enlargements or the construction of different senses from the social norm, since there are no formal restrictions on creativity resulting from a radically arbitrary system (both in expression and content). One fact appears significant: between 5 and 10 percent of Italianisms detected in the different areas are built on semiotic models in which there is no adherence of meaning in use with the Italian language standard. Moreover, these signs are used not for a direct reference to the Italian tradition (culinary, fashion, artistic, etc.), but because they are able to evoke an artificially constructed (or to be constructed) imaginary. But this is not necessarily bad. It is artificial because it is wanted, because it is required, and because it is chosen, as best, compared to other economic systems and symbols in the global language market.

These are the cases in which Italian is used not with an ostentatious reference and therefore linked to a semiotic form that is communication and information, but by value and symbolic scope generally linked to the idea of Italy and Italian. The values of taste and good taste, of creativity and elegance that characterized Italian in Tokyo (Vedovelli and Casini 2013) characterize today the group of Italianisms in Toronto, even in traditionally Italian areas, such as College Street, St. Clair Avenue, and Woodbridge. In the College Street West area, the percentage of semantic creativity of the Italianisms found reached 24 percent, making it the third area in quantitative order to be most characterized by the phenomenon, followed by Little Italy and Woodbridge in which the percentage settled at 20 percent.[19] They are obvious examples of forms of semantic creativity. For instance, *a cappella* detected at St. Clair and *motoretta* detected within the College Street area. *A cappella* is a sign in the center of St. Clair which one would assume to be a musical instrument shop run by Italians of origin in the heart of a historically Italian area. The reality, however, is completely different: it is a clothing store run by Canadians, without any connection to Italy, who have arbitrarily chosen the name *a cappella* only for a general interest in Italian opera, so as to assign an Italian name to a store that has no reference with Italy and music. The same goes for the *motoretta* sign: this second sign is located at the center of College Street and is the name of a shop with a *Guzzi* motorcycle on display (it is a brand), a symbol of Italian style.

Again, forms of semantic violation through creativity are evident being a non-Italian clothing store, but predominantly American and Canadian, managed historically by American owners who do not have a traditional link with Italy and, in this case, demonstrate a slight symbolic link with Italy and the world of engines or fashion. The reasons for this choice are to be considered linked to a kind of history of the place: wanting to look Italian in a place that in the past was Italian, and now, despite changed circumstances, not interested in changing the name because it does not give value (semiotic) to the choice made. The cases presented, although examples, show how both College Street and St. Clair represent areas that are merely artificially Italian and how, in some cases, Italianness is sought through names, now devoid of an actual link and tradition with the Italian linguistic and cultural space.

In terms of semantic creativity, the urban area in which this phenomenon is most found is Yorkville central; this is not unusual, being the area of Toronto's downtown more open to the social colors of international commerce and luxury, among the most significant tourist destinations of the city. However, the cases of College Street and Woodbridge are, in our opinion, significant, especially if we compare the former with what was attested just over thirty years ago in which more than 80 percent of shops were Italian, and Italian (rather, the Italian language space) was undoubtedly the L1 of this area. And the second, Woodbridge, which had a similar situation in the early years of the millennium but today no longer appears to be a modern Little Italy.[20] What are the consequences in semiotic terms? What are the direct social and linguistic implications evident: Italians are no longer the most important component of the reality of Toronto, and for the young and very young generations of Italian descendants, Italian assumes those positive values sought as L2, beyond ethnic neighborhoods that no longer represent a source of identity.[21] On a strictly linguistic level, Italianism is not synonymous with linguistic competence and/or evidence of immigrant groups, recalling in this sense the sociolinguistic characterization of immigrant language as a code capable of addressing communities who can express themselves and understand it (in its normal meaning). Italianism in Toronto, therefore, communicates (increasingly) symbolic value in the contact between different forms and codes and different loads of meaning. What are the consequences in terms of semiotics and identities? What are the conditions in terms of language and education? These questions propose a reflection in sync and above all in diachrony, perhaps questions that, at the moment, are devoid of a definitive answer, but only of a movement, between weights and counterweights, by hypothesis. Of course, we record the data and we sense the consequences, at least as far as the idea of the presence in Toronto of an Italian community (defined according to the traditional models to which we were accustomed). If we consider the language (its use and its competence) as an effective parameter to define a community that in this language is recognized, on the basis of the results of the project, we are today led to support a hypothesis already put forward by Corrado Paina (2006) for which today it is no longer possible to speak of an Italian community in Toronto because its identifying characteristics of cohesion, self-referentiality, autonomy and identity appear increasingly blurred and not able to recall the original principles. The issues we are facing, however, do not overlook the formulation only of nuanced hypotheses, and not certainties: it is perhaps too clear today to argue that there is no Italian community in Toronto, that it does not have a social and identity role and that there are no references and links for the new generations. Of course, it is that social change that has taken place, and this, in our opinion, has also led to a change in perception and identity perception of what Italy and Italian means.

In terms of creativity, however, it is clear that this is a confirmation of what we had recorded in previous research on contact territories in Italy (Casini 2012, 2019b): in the areas of College, St. Clair, and Woodbridge (as well as in Yorkville) there is the greatest concentration of semantic creativity. We do not have reliable historical data on Yorkville, being a relatively recent neighborhood and built from scratch in the 1970s and 1980s. But College Street, St. Clair, and Woodbridge can suggest a reflection: at the moment when these areas began to lose their ethnic dimension—undergoing a process of social and urban transformation from mainly Italian areas to multilingual and multicultural areas—the process of semiotic creativity on an urban level bore fruit, hypothesized precisely as the contact between languages, cultures, and forms of life. Basically, in the areas where there is more contact, including Yorkville, creativity takes on higher quality and quantity levels than what happens (and happened) in the more monolingual areas. This is evident in the linguistic panoramas of Toronto and was also evident in the urban area of Esquilino in Rome, the most multiethnic area of the Italian capital. In research carried out in 2012 in Esquilino, the sign of a repair shop for shoes and purses included the expression *Vendita Al Minuto* (figure 5.8). The expression *Vendita Al Minuto* from the morphological point of view is an expression of the Italian language with the meaning of retail and not wholesale. However, if we consider the plan of use, meaning, and pragmatics, the expression appears to take on a different value: a value linked to the more common meaning of the individual words that make up the expression. Specifically, the word Minuto (minute) becomes a sign for the time unit: the chronological minute. It is significant in this sense that the sign appears over a shop that deals with rapid repairs, almost instantaneous, for which it takes just a minute. The senses arising from the live use somehow exceed the linguistic norm by redefining the semantic field of the expression: very rapid repairs, repairs "in a minute" resulting in the sale of the repair and the repaired object in just one minute.

During research, the shopkeeper was interviewed and asked for a reason behind the use of the expression *Vendita Al Minuto*, to which the shopkeeper confirmed that he had used it because he wanted to indicate rapid sales of his products.

Another recorded case is given by the expression *Al Modina* (written in capital letters) (figure 5.9), detected as a clothing store sign, which sells garments, accessories and fashionable (*alla moda,* in Italian) clothing. The expression *AL MODINA* refers to the name of the city Medina in Saudi Arabia, which is the second holy city of Islam after Mecca. The shopkeepers were Muslim and, during the survey and interview, referred several times to the city of Medina. At the same time, however, the shopkeepers confirmed that they used the expression *AL MODINA* as both a reference to the city Medina and because the store sells fashionable (*alla moda*) clothing and therefore: *modina*. The expression *alla modina* is not lemmatized in the *Grande dizionario dell'uso della lingua italiana*: however, although in a limited number of occurrences, it is found online, on social media (Facebook and Instagram) associated with posts related to the fashion industry (figure 5.10).

The examples proposed do not suggest that the Italian language is changing: they simply suggest that the seed of variation, which is given by creativity, is born and developed mainly from contexts where linguistic and cultural contacts between people (which are relationships of forms of virtue) are

Figure 5.9 Expression detected in the Esquilino district of Rome in 2012. *Source:* Created by the author.

Figure 5.10 Expression detected in the Esquilino district of Rome in 2012. *Source:* Created by the author.

greater. From these arises the attempt to violate and change the norm. From these contexts comes the *rule-changing* creativity that will then be the actual social use to declare if and how, in fact, the variations born in contact will manage to change the language and its norm.

ITALIESE: A CREATIVE LANGUAGE

Semiotic creativity represents an interpretive paradigm of a further linguistic (and cultural) phenomenon that has been created in the contact between the Italian and English linguistic spaces. This language was defined by Clivio (1976) as Italiese (from Italiano + Inglese), a language of survival; that is, a language other than Italian, dialect and English that allowed thousands of Italian emigrants to have their own linguistic identity and to be more autonomous in the social life of the new country despite the lack of competence in both L1 (Italian) and L2 languages of the country of arrival.

We consider Italiese not because our research adds data to the well-established literature.[22] We do not even study linguistic phenomena that may be different in respects to previous years: the goal is to consider how Italiese can also represent an area in which creativity is an interpretive model: in its creation through loans, calques, phonetic interferences, morphology, and syntax. Italiese represented a language that, born for concrete needs of communication and wanted by its users, was in fact a laboratory of creativity. What is Italiese? It is the language created and used by Italian immigrants in English-speaking countries. Canada is by no means the only country where Italiese can be heard, even though it takes a different name: in the United States it is called Broccolino (Prifti 2013, 2014); in Australia, Italo-Australian (Bettoni 1986, 1987a,b); in Buenos Aires, Lunfardo and Cocoliche (Cancellier 2001); and in Brazil, Portoliano. It can also be found in countries such as the United Kingdom and South Africa.[23] Italiese is a language that was developed out of necessity by immigrants when they needed to interact in their foreign countries of adoption. According to Clivio and Danesi, Italiese is a hybrid language which assumes the guise of an "external dialect" of the Italian language. In other terms, Italiese does not have the properties to be considered a pidgin or an auxiliary language, but rather it is a result of Italian and Italian dialects in contact with English in Anglophone countries (Iuele-Colilli 2018). Italiese has been developed and used by Italian Immigrants of the post–World War II immigration wave to Canada. As analyzed by Iuele-Colilli (2018: 56) "the linguistic profile of an average Italian Immigrant to Canada was someone who arrived with a regional identity, expressed in terms of the dialect of place of origin." In a general sense, Italian (if they spoke it) would have been their second language, and English and French would have been their third and the fourth languages, respectively. However, the Italian immigrants did not immediately become fluent in English or French, and many of them struggled with Italian in any event. This means that the default language would have been their dialect. Italiese is indeed a language of survival and success because the dialect speaker, in order to communicate with Italians from other regions and with Canadians, would develop a mode of speaking that combines his/her dialect with standard Italian and with English (or French). This would allow them to communicate with other Italians (who come from different regions of Italy and speak different dialects) with their own children and with other Canadians.

As for the emigration history of Italians in Canada (and their relationship with the Italian language space) we can distinguish three generations of Italian immigrants: first-generation immigrants, most of whom arrived from Italy in the period from the mid-1950s to the mid-1970s; second-generation Italian Canadians or the Canadian-born children of Italian immigrants; and third-generation Italian Canadians. Pietropaolo (2010, 120) argues that

> these three components of the community are considerably different, since the members of the second and third generation are more highly educated and integrated in the larger community, in which many of them occupy positions of considerable authority in various fields, including politics, law, industry, the arts and education. Unlike their ageing parents . . . they have no need to rely on Italiese for effective communication other than in contexts that involve the older members themselves.

The distinctive features of the Italiese of the first generation could be summarized by the reflection of Pietropaolo:

> The distinctive features of the Italiese of the first generation are (i) that it is based on a sizeable and frequently used corpus, (ii) that it is entirely oral, (iii) that it serves cognitive and communicative needs that transcended the obligations of solidarity, and (iv) that it is acquired horizontally, in direct conversation with linguistically comparable members of the same community.

It would be important from a scientific and linguistic point of view to consider the evolutions, changes, and uses of Italiese in the younger generations of Italian descendants because, with quantitatively limited data, but capable of signaling trends, it is evident that Italiese has a future for the new generations (e.g., through social media). Research being published (Casini in press) also shows how the younger generations of Italian descendants feel it is the language "of the family" as part of their personal linguistic space, in a continuum ranging from English, to Italian (if studied for example in school or university), to dialects, to any other L2, up until Italiese.

In the late 1970s and the 1980s research about Italiese, predominantly from the University of Toronto (by Clivio 1985, 1986; Danesi 1982, 1985; Pietropaolo 1974, 2010), appeared, delineating the phonological, morphological, syntactic, and lexical structure of the true Italiese of Toronto. The research on the linguistic structure of Italiese conducted by Danesi and Pietropaolo, and more recently by Scarola (2007), pay specific attention to the lexical dimension which predominantly refers to the pragmatic and functional nature of the language. To date, indispensable tools for the analysis of Italiese are *The G.P. Clivio Online Dictionary of Italiese* (Italian-Italiese-English) by Pietropaolo and Bancheri (2007), and the dictionary created and directed by Iuele-Colilli. The first tool created in 2007 was designed to be expandable, giving the community of users the possibility to add more words. Iuele-Colilli's dictionary covers 5,000 words/phrases and has a consolidated base of over 20 years of work. Both works represent an essential database for any further research on Italiese.

As anticipated, the objective with which this paper addresses Italiese is to consider how typical phenomenon of Italiese such as loanwords (of luxury and necessity),[24] semantic calques, and Italian-English interferences are semiotic phenomena that go beyond the contact between languages and can be interpreted and justified by referring to semiotic creativity.[25]

Within general *rule-changing* creativity, we see some forms of Italiese used and with an extension of meaning in relation to Italian: for example, the word *classe* which takes on the meaning of a school or university course (English "class") compared to the Italian, in which "class" stands at 16 meanings, none of which include the meaning of an academic course.[26] The Italiese *carro* (from the English "car") takes on the meaning of an automobile, and *sciabola* (from the English "shovel") represents a shovel, a tool for digging, lifting, and moving bulk materials. The *morgheggio* (from the English "mortgage") is the mortgage, an agreement by which a bank or other creditor lends money at interest. *Acconto* (from the English "account") loses the Italian meaning of sum of money paid in advance to assume the meaning of bank account. The same phenomenon appears in *basamento,* that is not the backbone of a building, but is a basement (English "basement"). *Costruzione* (from the English "construction") is not the result of the act of building a work but acquires the sense of the precise construction.[27] *Farma* (from the English "farm") takes on the meaning of farm, just as *fattoria* represents a factory. The Italiese *compostiscene* (from the English "compensation board") takes on the meaning of workplace injury compensation but also the entity that manages the compensation, while *smescio* (from the English "to smash") represents an accident.

If we assume the perspective of creativity, both that of *langue* and that of *language,* we can give a theoretical and semiotic justification on some linguistic phenomena that occur constantly in contact situations. What Danesi has highlighted (1985) about *paradigmatic principle* and *phonological synchronization principle* is part of the cases where the language code uses its own resources, creating different expressive possibilities allowed by the system but not in line with the norm (especially morphologically). While on the semantic level the contact sometimes leads to a narrowing of meaning, sometimes an extension of meaning, sometimes a slippage of meaning that, in the cases examined, is the result of interference between languages. These are the languages of life forms and therefore forms of identity, so the interference is between identity, symbolic, and cultural systems.

ITALIESE AND ITALIANISMS: ISSUES OF CREATIVITY WITH DIFFERENT GRADIENTS

From the contexts examined both abroad and in Italy, hypotheses emerge that different levels of creativity are identifiable. Different types of creativity, sometimes not perfectly identifiable with those already present in literature, demonstrate how language is perhaps the symbolic system most open to welcome creativity as an integral part of its functioning. The hypotheses we propose are part of a level of *rule-changing creativity*, whereby the rules of the language system are so tense as to force the linguistic norm, to hypothesize a change, without, however, leaving the system of communication possibilities. However, there are some basic questions to answer before understanding the levels of creativity in contact languages: first, what and how many are the communicative possibilities of a semiotic system? Also, are what and how many the communicative potentials of languages? Tarski (1936), Hjelmslev ([1961] 1963) wrote that a language can be defined as a paradigmatic system, whose paradigms (i.e. the fundamental elements of the system) can be expanded indefinitely. In practice, each language is a semiotic in which every other semiotics, that is, every other language and any other conceivable semiotic structure, can be translated and realized, according to the principle of semantic omniformativity.[28] To assert that with linguistic signs it is always possible to convey any meaning, means to challenge the perception that other iconic expressive means, movies, music, dance, and so on manage to give life to experiences or manage to animate experiences that verbal language can approximately yield. For this reason, instead of stating with confidence that all the senses are speakable with the signs of a language, it is more correct and certain to say that, unlike other semiological codes, language is the code in which, much better than in other codes, you can determine endless plans of the content. Language is multilevel (has multiple levels) (De Mauro 2019). Language is therefore a weak multilevel, because it is the place where the levels of the contents of many other semiological codes are established. But language is multi-level (and much more) in a strong sense, because it does not seem possible to indicate *a priori* which content and experience can be included in a given sign, and on the contrary, which type of content and experience are excluded from that same sign.

The indeterminacy of linguistic meanings and signs (as well as the indeterminacy of the number of linguistic signs and the possibility that these can grow more and more numerous) is configured exactly like the impossibility of defining *a priori* the limits of the speakable and some consider the very possibility of thinking what cannot be said. In terms of philosophy and linguistics, this thesis recalls Humboldt's concept of language then developed in the North American context by Sapir and Whorf known as the *Sapir-Whorf Hypothesis* (Whorf 1956). It is a controversial issue to interpret the *WH Hypothesis (Whorfian Hypothesis)* because in its strongest conception this hypothesis comes to the radical conclusion that without language there is no thought. In a less radical, but certainly interesting conception which we believe it is appropriate to confront, an equally controversial but permissible issue is to understand to what extent the perception of experience (of the things of the world) is addressed or not addressed by the presence or absence of a word in our language. It is certain that the presence or absence of a word orients the articulated awareness of our experience. Articulate awareness means the ability that an experience can be classified, repeated, and therefore semiotically known.

The perception of experience alone is not in itself knowledge. Knowledge is possible through a semiotic operation that passes from codes and then from languages. If we take this perspective of linguistic relativism, albeit weak, what is the role of creativity, in the concrete facts of the world and in the languages in contact? This is the question from which we started and which we have not yet answered. We respond in a nutshell: it is a creativity in the creation of new words that takes up the general processes of word creation even within the same language, taking advantage of the expressive potential of the system. But even more so, it is a creativity of concept and of survival, for which not only is a word created, but also a semiotic world to which the word is associated and that before (before the creation of the word) there would not have been. This is a semiotic world, a cultural world, an identity world. To introduce a first exemplification, we proceed in order, through a proposal to articulate creativity to different gradients.

In Casini (2012) and Vedovelli and Casini (2013) we had suggested the hypothesis that creativity could have a graphic representation in the shape of a sine. We had proposed the hypothesis that creativity fluctuated in the territory and in the communicative space as a sinusoid from levels of minimum to maximum: the latter represented by the contexts of linguistic contact in which the interaction between languages and cultures explodes the quantitative dynamics of creativity. They are complemented by levels of creativity at a minimum degree, that is, those linguistic and semiotic cases in which creativity exists, but is predominantly part of the forms of creativity of the *parole* and *rule-governed creativity* that comprehend the constant functioning of the language and the perennial innovation of the individual. We deal with the moments when the sinusoid has a higher height than a hypothetical axis and when the creativity appears identifiable within a continuum that defines different degrees. These degrees are the results of semiotic parameters that refer to the speaker's awareness of being creative and innovating, his linguistic proficiency and his explicit desire to create new forms. We summarize the degrees of creativity in a syntactic framework, and then propose examples and explanations:

 i) Degree 1 creativity or *skill creativity*
 ii) Degree 2 creativity or *standard creativity*
 iii) Degree 3 creativity or *return creativity*
 iv) Degree 4 creativity or *crystallized creativity*
 v) Degree 5 creativity or *advertising creativity*
 vi) Zero-Degree creativity or *survival creativity*

Degree 1, which we call "skill creativity," is found in the cases of the Italianisms *crustini* or *capuccino* or in the Italiese *amm* (ham) and *aronkè/adonkè* (I don't care) or *aronò/arenò* (I don't know) in which the new word is the result of lack of linguistic proficiency of the reference language (Italian for Italianisms and English for Italiese) and sometimes, especially for Italiese, by the need to reproduce sounds heard (but not included) in L2. It is certainly an Italian (or an English) contact, whose creativity is an unintentional violation of the rule, but violation caused by a kind of basic linguistic awareness, the result of the lack of competency. It is a case of creativity that is not so much in the intentions of the speaker who did not intend to be creative, but one of external and contingent factors.

In the cases of *paninis*, *baresa*, and *zucchini* but also in *Vendita Al Minuto*, creativity is still unintentional, but it is placed on a different degree than the previous one. It is a creativity that we define as Degree 2: it is a creativity that is unaware, but that cannot be defined only as a linguistic error. This is "standard creativity" for example due to the addition of the English morpheme -*s* to make a plural on an already plural name (such as *panini* or *zucchini*). The phenomenon of associating *baresa* with a feminine Italian name (trattoria) is the same "standard creativity" as extending the expression *al minuto* to the most common (and therefore normal) temporal value in *Vendita Al Minuto*. The creative intent, the awareness of the speaker, is not obvious: certainly, the linguistic construction requires a higher level of competence (in L1 and L2) than in the previous case and thus allows us to profile a second degree of creativity.

Degree 3 of creativity is in the case of an awareness of language violation, however realized, despite the knowledge of the rule, because it is in line with common uses. This is the case of some expressions of Italiese such as *cugi* or *cugis* (Italian cousin and cousins) by third- and fourth-generation Italian descendants, whose linguistic level in Italian L2, although not high, would still allow them to produce the correct expression. This creativity is intended, especially in the use of social media, where there are many similar examples in which the use of expressions of contact, with a reference to the Italian origin of the family (and partly also to their identity) allows to create new linguistic forms. It is a "return creativity" used, in the case of Italiese, by the younger generations of Italian descendants to imitate or recover, using precisely the expressions or formulas of parents or grandparents, and recall a little of that world that never belonged entirely to young people but in which young people were immersed through the family.

An additional degree of creativity (creativity Degree 4) is defined in cases of morphological derivation in *-issimo*, *-ino*, and *-etta*, in which creativity is intentional, but to some extent "crystalized." In these cases, the use of derivational suffixes is not transparent. That is, its meaning is not transparent and its construction, desired for nonlinguistic purposes, is essentially semiotic-cultural. That is, the new word is created through Italian linguistic elements to recall the Italian language and culture and its current value in the field of fashion or catering. This category includes all cases of semantic creativity detected in urban landscapes, where the reference to the referent gives way to the semiotic identity. Also, part of this Degree 4 of creativity are the *a cappella, nervosa,* or *motoretta* units with which two clothing stores and a restaurant are named.

In most cases of Italiese, creativity is intermediate, a degree ranging from 2 to 3: *classe* (and many other examples attested by literature) are cases built on morphological and phonetic interference between the Italian and English linguistic space. However, if the creativity at Degree 2 still maintains an unawareness of creative use, in Degree 3 the awareness is manifested. And therefore, the cases of *cracca* (a crack), *ceramica* (ceramic), *desco* (desk), *iarda* (yard), and *moneta* (money) are references to the fact that for example the *y* is not a phoneme with which the words begin (the same *yogurt* has

Turkish etymology) and, always in general, the Italian words end with a vowel (such as *ceramica* and *desco*). In this case, awareness is a kind of adaptation to an Italian standard to be sought (and created) through a phonological and morphological adjustment to a hypothetical standard.

An additional degree of creativity, a Degree 5, can be seen in cases of *AL MODINA* or *thanks a latte!*: it is a "marketing" or "commercial" creativity whose innovative element is wanted and sought for essentially commercial reasons. For example, the use of *latte* for *a lot* has a commercial purpose, so much so that many brands of international cafés offer gadgets with the expression *thanks a latte!* In *AL MODINA* the creative intent was confirmed by the managers of the clothing store in the centre of Rome who played with the Italian expression *alla moda* (fashionable) to also recall both the holy city of Islam, Medina, and, in fact, a pseudo-Italian expression linked to their business. We do not find examples of creativity Degree 5 in Italiese; this is because Italiese (the one attested by the literature to which we refer) is a language of survival, a language of necessity, and therefore, this does not include a creative advertising or commercial purpose.

But Italiese deserves a consideration in its own right: the 5 degrees of creativity we have identified do not appear completely relevant to consider this particular language of contact. And this is because Italiese is not simply a linguistic phenomenon that can be interpreted with the categories of contact. It is much more than that. It is a language born for semiotic and identity purposes. It is a language that arises from the *creativity of psychopedagogists* (De Mauro 1982) so that the users of the code are able to remove themselves from the established rules of the game and change the data of the problem in order to solve it. It is a close relative of *Humboldtian* creativity or *language* that allows us to find creative solutions to express previously unexpressed or inexpressible concepts and principles.

This is, for us, a Zero-Degree of creativity. A creativity "of necessity": words of Italiese such as *morgheggio, carro, sciabola, fattoria, farma, compostiscene,* or *smescio* are not able to be analyzed semiotically, but only as a semantic and/or morphological interference between the Italian and English linguistic space: these words represent a life status to be achieved, a goal that first-generation emigrants had to seek in their new homeland and which they did not have in the one left behind. *Morgheggio* is not a loan between private individuals or compatriots but has institutional value that in Canada evokes a feeling not present in the agricultural Italy of the mid-twentieth century from which the emigrants came. The same value is achieved with *carro*, which is not simply a machine, but represents a status of economic well-being sought and sometimes obtained by the sacrifice of work. This is therefore a creativity of necessity. This creativity has allowed the first emigrants to create, along with a language, a conceptual and life identity framework: we assume that the general (communicative and instrumental) meaning of the Italian words and expressions such as *mutuo ipotecario, macchina* (as *automobile*), *pala, fattoria, fabbrica, indennità per infortunio sul lavoro, incidente automobilistico,* although known by Italian emigrants, were not part of their identity life experience because they were linked to a social world unknown to them. Therefore, Italian emigrants were only able to live the meaning of these terms through Italiese. For them, Italiese was the (semiotic) form of their new life (the reference to the concept of Wittgenstein's *(PU) form of life - lebensform*- is evident). *Mutuo ipotecario* is not *morgheggio*; *macchina* is not *carro*; *pala* is not *sciabola*; *Indennità* does not mean *compostiscene*; *incidente automobilistico* is not equivalent to *smescio*. Linguistically, Italian and Italiese words cover (or can cover) the same semantic field, but what changes is their semiotic value, that is, the identity value that these words have for first-generation Italian/Canadian emigrants.

In Italiese the words *carro, sciabola, stretto* and *fabbrica* are not calques of the corresponding Italian words. The relation between English, Italian and Italiese is very complex, as illustrated in the following few examples. The English word "car" (Italian macchina, automobile) in Italiese becomes *carro*, which in Italian is a cart. "Shovel" becomes *sciabola* (English: saber, Italian: pala). "Street" (strada, via) in Italiese could be rendered with *stretto*, which in Italian means strict, tight, narrow. "Factory" (Italian fabbrica) becomes *fattoria*, in Italian farm. The English "farm" in Italiese is *farma* (this word does not exist in Italian). Furthermore, the English word "fabric" (tessuto, stoffa) in Italiese becomes *fabbrica* (even though not very common).

The Zero-Degree of creativity is perhaps the most difficult creativity to realize and research. Where zero is not the quantitative level, but is, *in nuce*, the nucleus, the core from which the creative principle is born. A creativity of intellect, perhaps unconscious for the user, that has allowed in history the achievement of important communication and social results for those who have left Italy to open themselves in life to the new world. By studying Italiese through the principle of maximum creativity, we do not exclude the other forms of creativity that also characterize it in some lexical elements through processes of code mixing, calques, and loans. What we propose has linguistic evidence, but results in a generally semiotic and semantic plan. From this perspective the question is no longer regarding how Italiese was born from the contact between English and Italian linguistic space but, if anything, it becomes why the Italiese was born and what were the consequences that its birth has determined for the community of speakers. This is why we do not consider it possible to interpret Italiese only as a contact language. No one doubts that it is also a language of contact, but not to consider its value in the Italian Canadian identity means not fully understanding its semiotic and creative value. It means, at the same time, going back to the old Chomskyan school for which creativity was simply to make endless use of finite linguistic means. Instead, by assuming the prospect of maximum creativity for Italiese, it is well understood how this language is the mother tongue of an entire community of speakers.[29]

Italiese is not a mother tongue for chronological factor, because it is not the first language learned by the first generation of Italian Canadians. It could be the mother tongue for the next generation, as long as one defines what mother tongue means and what is meant by generation of emigrants. It is true, however, that we can count at least two generations with sociolinguistic profiles that highlight the predominant use of Italiese in the family and in work.[30] In this context, however, it is not interesting to know whether Italiese was the most used language by the community in different communication contexts, given the massive pressure of English, Italian, and dialects, with inevitable differences between generations. And if even Italiese had been at some point, for a certain generation of emigrants,[31] the most used language, the quantitative factor would have little consequences for the semiotic reflection and framing that we propose.

Italiese is the mother tongue of emigration because it created the Italian Canadian community. It is the mother tongue because it has given the community the linguistic and communicative tools, but even more symbolic, semiotic, and identifying, to become a united community, to equip itself with a political statute (in an ethological sense) that, in another case, the community would not have had. Italiese is a language of power: power to create a group of people who have emigrated from an essentially agricultural and backward Italy, a community recognized, cohesive, determined, and strong in the new migratory reality (Casini and Bancheri in press). However, the maximum creativity of Italiese is also manifested in another aspect: Italiese is the language of emigration that reflects the feeling of the *nostos*. From this perspective, Bancheri (2020) analyzed the literature of a Sicilian poet, Lina Riccobene, who recounted the life of her city, Delia,[32] through poems and comedies written in dialect and in Italiese. Riccobene could not make a different semiotic choice: Italian emigrants to Canada spoke Italiese, and the emigrants who returned from Canada to Italy continued to speak Italiese.[33]

We want to change our perspective: we do not make the mistake made in the past (even in the recent past) or give a value judgment to this language, initially perceived by the community itself with a negative meaning. In the past, Italiese has been considered an "inferior" language, a language to be ashamed of and not to make "public" use of because it was linked to a social condition (at least perceived) of inferiority and not adequacy to the new world. This superficial general attitude of Italiese has also found the shore in Italian linguistic research, as well pointed out by Haller (1993). Moreover, where Italiese had not come to be the language of ignorance and hatred to which to pour attitudes of racism aimed at the Italian immigrated community, it was nevertheless relegated to the language of irony and sneering: a language perceived as ridiculous, on which one could only laugh from a position of superiority. Italiese was the language that reflected the lack of skills in English and Italian and this was reason to create the conditions of irony, play, fun, teasing, and laughter, always with a negative profile (Iuele-Colilli in press). Regarding Italiese, an attitude of irony and comedy has developed, but without reaching the *humor* of Pirandello, that is, to the awareness of its semiotic and creative value. Even recently the comic conception of Italiese has been only the dark face of the moon: the lack of institutional support, added to a perception of inferiority, has formed the prerequisites to exclude most of the young generations of Italian descendants from the Italian language space, which has produced significant damage to the future of the Italian language abroad (Casini and Bancheri 2019).

This writing wants to discover the other side of the moon, through a model analogous to Pirandello's *humor*, that gives new light, new emphasis, and new identity to Italiese, through the lens of creativity. We therefore want to semiotically rehabilitate this language, giving it the place it deserves in the landscape of contact linguistics. Creativity, *nostos*, and the identity of thousands of people, are well-expressed feelings by the words in Sicilian, of which we report translation in English, by Lina Riccobene, who in this unpublished poem from 2020 gave the semiotic sense to the facts described by us.

Cch'è simpaticu 'stu 'taliese[34]
N'ammancàva lu 'talièse
e ora l'avièmmu midè.
Nun ni sèrvi cchiù lu 'nglese! Ora basta! *Azzocchè*?

A l'America tutti lu sànnu,
lu pàrlanu li 'ranni e li carùsi
e si sbàgli . . . nun fa' dànnu,
nun fa' bùca né pirtùsi.

Lu 'taliese jè lingua nòva
ca a l'America arrivà.
La Sicilia. . .cuòmu l'òva. . .
'ntra 'n panàru ci lu purtà.

'Nsignà a tutti l'americani
ca nun sèrvi arti di pìnna
ppi 'ncucchiàri 'taliàni

e cannatìsi ccu' la Lingua.

Lu 'talièse 'ncùcchia a tutti:
nichi, 'rànni, dotti e scecchi.
Lu 'talièse lu pàrlanu tutti
quannu jè festa e ccu' li *chècchi*

càntanu, sònanu e . . .*azzocchè*!
siddru dumàni ccu l' *aijuè,*
ccu' lu *carru* e ccu' lu *tròccu,*
vannu tutti a lu *stòru*

e s'è chiùsu per . . . chicchesia,
no problem. . . ca vicìnu c'è 'na *bekerìa.*
Gud moning a tutti dici.
Pìgli, paghi e ti ni va.'

Poi guìdi e va' a *Wubrigi* e. . .
stu 'talièse cchi fìni fa?
Parli arrièri siciliànu
siddru ìntra c'è ta' muglièri

ma si c'è lu picciliddru. . .
. . .lu 'taliese! Cuòmu ajèri!

As we have highlighted precisely thanks to the Italiese, semiotic creativity has worked within the community through a process that in this paper we have repeatedly recalled, and which outlines the final and deepest meaning: the emigrants of Italian origin were creative because they found a solution to a problem. They had a linguistic problem, communicative, identity and social problem to which they created a solution, shifting the terms of the matter: in this way, they invented a new language. Whatever its formal, semiotic, and linguistic definition, the term *creativity* implies the ability to evoke something new and valuable in people's minds and behaviors. Among its manifestations, there is the ability to make analogies, establish associations, connect elements of experience to each other, to make inferences and express or produce something that embodies intellectual, social, and aesthetic values.

In line with this consideration, let us remember the story as told by Hans Christian Andersen, whereby in the story *Clumsy Hans* reflects on the importance of putting oneself out of the scheme and finding creative solutions to a problem that go beyond the imagined or the predictable. In the same way that Clumsy Hans managed to marry the king's daughter in Andersen's fable, the

Italian emigrants were able to create a language, their own life, and their own identity in the larger world.

Andersen's fable features the prototype of a creative individual. Clumsy Hans was deemed stupid by family members. He was considered stupid by a brother who knew all the Latin vocabulary by heart, and another brother who knew all the *Codex Iustiniane*. The brother who knew the vocabulary by heart had a typical imitative creativity, while his "jurist" brother had a typical combinatorial intelligence, and therefore was creative in the Chomskian sense. Clumsy Hans was deemed a fool for his ways of dealing with things and situations. When the daughter of the king announces a competition to find a husband among those who will best answer her questions, the two good brothers present themselves to the challenge and, much to everyone's surprise, Clumsy Hans attempts the challenge as well. The latter, mocked by his brothers while walking on the street stops to collect a dead crow, an old broken hoof, and a handful of mud: these things would be his salvation. Long story short, in an unforeseen situation, in front of bizarre phrases proposed by the king's daughter, the imitative brother and the combinatorial brother fail to say another word other than "Well. . . ." Clumsy Hans, on the other hand, does it perfectly, because he creatively uses the objects he had collected on the street, becoming king, finding a bride and the crown. *Clumsy Hans* is, in this sense, the fable of creativity.

Every fable, since the Greek and Latin tradition has a pedagogical and ethical value. It has a lesson that applies to common morality, but it also applies because it wants to be a model for the future, to guide future behaviors of others in similar situations. For this reason, fables and fairy tales are not the same textual genre, they are not the same thing, although sometimes, mistakenly, the two terms are used synonymously. Andersen didn't write fairy tales, but he wrote fables. The behavior of Clumsy Hans, in changing the rules of the game and finding a creative solution to the problem, is the teaching to follow for the future and represents the pedagogical value of the stressful fable. In the case that we have dealt with for a long time, we find some similarities which we propose as a conclusion.

Our real "fable" is called Italiese: it is a real thing because it is an integral part of the Canadian migration reality since the seventies and even today moves within the streets and places of the Italian community in Toronto where one reads and hears Italiese. But Italiese is also a fable, because it taught something: it taught linguistic and semiotic creativity to linguists, Canadians, and Italians. For this reason, Italiese is the language of creativity; at the same time, it anticipated—as is the case of fables—a linguistic and semiotic process involving Italian and English, but in reverse parts. Reading Italian newspapers today and listening to television debates, interviews by Italian politicians and economists, means immersing yourself in a linguistic world not totally Italian. We follow when De Mauro (2016a) highlights the weight of the Greek-Latin base for English, and therefore we do not venture any kind of prediction or bad future for Italian due to its contact with English. From the reflections we have made within the book, our consideration toward a supposedly perfect language and a supposed linguistic purity is clear. There is neither linguistic purity nor linguistic perfection, because every language is a language of contact.

What we still want to focus on in this process is what Italiese (and in general the languages in contact) has brought to light, through its being in some way a language imperfect with respect to the Italian norm, and imperfect with respect to the English norm. We do not see significant differences from what is happening today when we consider the widespread presence of anglicisms in Italian public and media communication. Without wanting to touch the phonetic field, which highlights pronunciations of English words that closely follow the Italian pronunciation, we refer to the widespread cases of semantic creativity, of the use of English words in Italian that in English would not have the same meaning. In addition, in the predilection, in the fields of medicine, biology, computer science, economics, and English words instead of Italian words (however present and worthy of use).

What does this process represent? Why does this happen?

We respond briefly and propose a gamble: this process is *in nuce* semiotic creativity, and it happens because if Italiese was a language of necessity (of social, identifying and semiotic necessity), today anglicisms in Italian are, *mutatis mutandis*, the evidence of a language, of the need for economic and scientific power.

NOTES

1. Gauls are separated into three parts, one of which is inhabited by the Belgae, another by the Aquitani, and those who in their own language are called Celts, in ours Gauls, inhabit the third. All these are different from each other in language, customs, and rules. The river Garonne divides the Gauls from the Aquitani; the Marne and the Seine isolate them from the Belgae—Julius Caesar *The Gallic Wars* (our translation).

2. And as is necessary, in order to prevent this evil, to accord valid and logical (not hurried and illegitimate, miss-judged and chaotic) citizenship to foreign words, too, if they are required, so is it much more important to search with care, and to welcome, once found, with good grace, and to allow into the treasury of good, writable, rightful speech, both stem from good and already established roots and those roots which, being as yet unestablished, go wandering through the usage of the nation, without being studied or analyzed by those who might halt them, solicit them, call them, invite them, bring them in to join the group of established words or expressions, and have a share in the honors owed to the citizens of good language (our translation).

3. In De Mauro (1994, 80): "la variazione non è un qualcosa che colpisca le lingue dall'esterno: essa invece si insedia in ogni punto della realtà di una lingua come necessaria conseguenza della sua semantica e pragmatica che, a loro volta, traggono necessariamente i caratteri di estensibilità e flessibilità dalle esigenze funzionali di ciascuna lingua in se stessa. Ogni parlante di ogni lingua ha in se stesso, nell'uso effettivo che fa di una lingua, il principio e i semi della variazione. . . . forze e fattori esterni obbligano al coagulo, alla stabilizzazione e nel caso del tempo, alla morte, insomma limitano e non già favoriscono o determinano la potenziale illimitata differenziazione delle lingue. In sé e per sé le lingue sono inevitabilmente innumerevoli perché l'unica universale *faculté du language* deve rispondere ai requisiti semantico-pragmatici *che soddisfino i bisogni comunicativi degli esseri umani* e da essi discende la continua variabilità dei repertori di lingua in cui il linguaggio si realizza."

4. The phenomenon of Italianisms, which we consider in particular in the North American and Canadian context of Ontario, is a model of contemporary contact, the study of which has been accentuated in more recent years also as a result of the *Linguistic Landscape* (Casini 2018; 2019c).

5. Further insights into Italiese and creativity, as its paradigm of interpretation, will be provided in paragraphs 3 and 4 of this chapter.

6. In De Mauro (1981, 87): "con *plurilinguismo* intendiamo qui anzitutto la compresenza sia di tipi diversi di semiosi, sia di idiomi diversi, sia di diverse norme di realizzazione di un unico idioma. Esso pare una condizione permanente della specie umana e, quindi, di ogni società umana. . . . In Italia i fenomeni sono intensi e contraddittori. Per peculiari vicende storiche, il Paese è, come pochi, idiomaticamente eterogeneo."

7. Preface in Weinreich ([1963] 2008).

8. In reference to the notion of language contact, we refer to Nelde (1998, 287–288) that *contact linguistics* can be defined as "an interdisciplinary branch of multilingual research, . . . triad of the following standpoints: language, language user, and language sphere. Research in contact linguistics incorporates linguistic levels like phonology, syntax, and lexicon as well as discourse analysis, stylistics and pragmatics. In addition, there are external factors such as nation, language community, language boundaries, migration, and many others." And again, Thomason (2001, 1) points out how "in the simplest definition, language contact is the use of more than one language in the same place at the same time . . . . The problem is that the boundary between two dialects of a single language and two different languages is fuzzy."

9. For further insight on Weinreich's interactive model, refer to Thomason, Kaufman (1988).

10. The GTA consists of the central city, Toronto, along with 25 surrounding suburbs, distributed among four regional municipalities: Durham, Halton, Peel, and York.

11. The survey involved more than one researcher, both from Italian and Canadian origins. Much data is taken from Turchetta and Vedovelli 2018. The corpus data is updated from a research project composed by a group of undergraduate students from the University of Toronto Mississauga in May 2019 within a research project titled *Scholar in Residence, University of Toronto and Jackman Humanities Institute*. This

undergraduate research group was composed by Michelle Galati, Olivia Didoné, Tatiana Fimognari, Isabel Bonacci, and Hanna Green under the scientific supervision of the writer.

12. A similar case had been considered by Serianni (2002) for the semantic field of fashion: remaining in the morphological derivation mechanism, we report the case of Japanese, *shiroganēze*, an adjective taken from the name *Shirogane*, a Tokyo fashion district. The case can be a testament to the Italian prestige in the field of fashion so the suffixation, in the case, *-ese (-ēze)* of *shiroganēze* is conformed to the model *milanese*, right from Milan, the Italian capital of national and international fashion.

13. Detected in Japanese and non-North American context.

14. Another case with an apparent *-ini* suffix is represented by *Rotini*, that is, a particular type of pasta sold by an Italian multinational company, essentially for the North American market.

15. In parentheses we indicate the number of derivatives in the Italian lexicon according to the *Grande dizionario dell'uso*.

16. These are in addition to the case of *cappuccino* (with variants) that we have already discussed. We also detect expressions such as *il vero caffè all'italiana*, *l'espresso del bar*, *un caffè per amico*, and *caffè e tentazioni*.

17. Refer to Casini's contributions 2017, 2018, 2019c; Galati *et al.* (in press); and Turchetta and Vedovelli 2018 for a detailed analysis of Italianisms and pseudo-Italianisms in Toronto.

18. Tokyo, Paris, and Miami are paradigmatically considered to be realities in which the historical and social weight of Italian emigration has not reached any level comparable to those in Canada and Toronto but, however, where linguistic and semiotic facts are recorded similar to what is happening in Toronto.

19. In quantitative terms, the uses of semantic creativity of the Italianisms detected are found, in addition to the cases indicated, in the Mississauga city area (15%) and St. Clair (19%).

20. In the proposed analysis, we deliberately did not take into account the menus of the restaurants, which would inevitably have affected the data both in quantitative terms and in reference to semantic creativity.

21. Some of the data was discussed in Casini (2019c).

22. The linguistic and sociolinguistic literature on Italiese is extensive: important theoretical and methodical points of reference, that study the nature of Italiese as a contact language, can be found in Bancheri (2003, 2007); Clivio (1985, 1986); Clivio and Danesi (2000); Colilli and Iuele-Colilli (2017); Danesi (1982, 1985); Haller (1993); Iuele-Colilli (1993, 2018); Pietropaolo (1974, 2010); Pivato (2014); Scarola (2007); Tosi (1991); and Vizmuller-Zocco (1995, 1998, 2007). The Digital Archives of the Frank Iacobucci Centre for Italian Canadian Studies (Bancheri 2007–) are an important starting point of reference for this material.

Danesi (1982, 1985), Haller (1993), Pivato (2014), and Scarola (2007) have linked the Italiese language to identity issues of the Italian community in Canada by reflecting on the reasons for the birth and the use of the language in specific contexts. Colilli and Iuele-Colilli (2017) and Iuele-Colilli (1993, 2018) address Italiese at a pedagogical level, often linked to theatrical use.

23. Consider also the work on Camfranglais by Siebetcheu and Machetti (2019).

24. Clivio (1985) points out that in the case of Italiese loans of necessity correspond to more technical words such as the words related to the field of industry or the car. But also, for construction, there are a number of needs, not because they lack the terms in Italian, but because the first generations of emigrants were mainly employed in agriculture and for them construction was a new and unfamiliar industry of work.

25. For the analysis of contact at the phonetic, morphological, and syntactic levels, we refer to the existing literature, in particular Clivio (1985), Danesi (1985), and Pietropaolo (1974, 2010).

26. For the analysis of the meaning, we use as a lexicographic tool the online dictionary of Tullio De Mauro (dizionario.internazionale.it).

27. For a complete list of lexical phenomena, we refer to the works of Clivio, Danesi, Pietropaolo, and Scarola indicated in the bibliography.

28. Even in the languages of Lecce, Sicily, Bari, and Siena, one can translate Kant or speak about the moon landing (Bernardini and De Mauro 2003).

29. This perspective could be applied to Italianisms and pseudo-Italianisms, when the word detected in urban landscapes has no referential value, but semiotic and identity value. What drives us to consider the ultimate creativity of Italiese is related to the fact that Italianisms and pseudo-Italianisms are isolated lexical elements, possibly present in the same text along with other nonverbal languages, while Italiese is configured as a language in its own right in its lexical and communicative structures.

30. The issue is complex, in terms of migration, in the definition of the generations of emigrants, in the linguistic level and in the definition of mother tongue. We do not add to this discussion and use these terms broadly.

31. We refer to the communicative contexts of family, friends, and work. At least in the first generations, work was carried out within the community and did not foresee a particular differentiation by sociolinguistic profile.

32. Delia is a small town in Sicily (Italy) in the province of Caltanissetta. Many of its inhabitants have emigrated to Canada and North America.

33. Consider also the case of the Italiesco on which Bancheri (2009) and Vilardo (1975) have reflected.

34. We did not have Italiese / And now we have it. / We don't need English anymore / Now enough! *Azzocchè* (that's ok)? // In America, everyone knows how to speak it / it is spoken by big and small / and if you make an error . . . there is no damage / You will not make holes or cracks. // Italiese is the new language / that has arrived in America. / The Sicilians . . . as with eggs . . . / brought it with a basket. // (Italiese) It taught Americans that one does not need the art of a pen / to gather and unite Italians / and Canadians with the use of their language. // Italiese unites everyone: / Small, large, educated and stupid. / Italiese is spoken by everyone / when it's a celebration and with *chècchi* (cakes) // you sing, you play and . . . "*Azzocchè* (it doesn't matter)" / if tomorrow they will be on the *aijuè* (highway) / in the car or by the *tròccu* (truck) / to reach the *stòru* (store) that // if closed for a reason / *no problem*, one goes to the *bekerìa* (bakery). / *A gud moning* (good morning) everyone." / Pay and leave. // Go back to driving and go to *Wubrigi* (Woodbridge) / and . . . Italiese (at home) what does it do? / One goes back to speaking Sicilian / if your wife is home // but if there is your child / . . . you speak Italiese! Like yesterday!

Conclusion

Sed quia unamquanque doctrinam oportet non probare, sed suum aperire subiectum, ut sciatur quid sit super quod illa versatur dicimus, celeriter actendentes, quod vulgarem locutionem appellamus eam qua infantes assuefiunt ab assistentibus cum primitus distinguere voces incipiunt; vel, quod brevius dici potest, vulgarem locutionem asserimus quam sine omni regula nutricem imitantes accipimus. Est et inde alia locutio secundaria nobis, quam Romani gramaticam vocaverunt . . . . Harum quoque duarum nobilior est vulgaris: tum quia prima fuit humano generi usitata; tum quia totus orbis ipsa perfruitur, licet in diversas prolationes et vocabula sit divisa; tum quia naturalis est nobis, cum illa potius artificialis existat.

Et de hac nobiliori, nostra est intentio pertractare. . . .

Itaque, adepti quod querebamus, dicimus illustre, cardinale, aulicum et curiale vulgare in Latio quod omnis latie civitatis est et nullius esse videtur, et quo municipalia vulgaria omnia Latinorum mensurantur et ponderantur et comparantur.[1]

Dante Alighieri, *De vulgari eloquentia*

An old Neapolitan expression states the following: "*'e pparole 'e ssape, ma nun 'e ssape accucchià.*" In English, it means that a person knows the words of a language (an L1 or an L2) but does not use them appropriately (De Mauro 2001). It's as if he knows the rules of a system and its elements, but can't manage the two things together, and so he can't effectively use that system.

We conclude our reflection on creativity, recalling precisely that Neapolitan expression which semi critically reflects the dichotomy between knowledge and use, between proper use and misuse, between freedom and rules.

Constraints and freedom. However defined, creativity implies the ability to evoke something new and precious within a code: language, music, mathematics, etc. Among its manifestations there is the ability to make analogies, establish associations, connect elements of experience with each other, to make inferences, intuitions, in order to express or produce something that has value, intellectual, social, and aesthetic. Creativity manifests itself in specific ways in all areas of human activity, from poetry to scientific theories and technological innovations. All that can be said, in a very general but understandable way, is that creativity is a universal mental faculty that allows us to realize something that was not there before, at least not in the same way or form. This implies that it is part of the human brain, either as a specific area within it or, more likely, spread in various modules of the brain.

From Plato and Aristotle to Chomsky, a creative conception of the language conceived through an innatist perspective has been carried out that implies the presence of a linguistic organ in the speaker's mind. The social and cultural environment in which the speaker is immersed provides only a stimulus, that is, it provides the conditions to activate a device through which the speaker can build the language-specific grammar. The innate linguistic faculty, Chomsky argued, is characterized by universal grammar which is the general model on which all specific linguistic grammars are built. The presence of a universal grammar in every person's brain from birth would therefore explain why children learn to speak so naturally without any concrete education and would explain why both the child and the adult manage to produce a potentially infinite number of words. Universal grammar is not a grammar in the generic sense, but it is a set of principles that govern the rules that are available to all, so it defines a universal conception of language that goes beyond individual cultures, history, social and semiotic traditions. So when the child learns a fact about a language in a certain context, the child can easily infer other facts without having to learn them one by one. In this theoretical framework, creativity implies the ability to infer the rules of a linguistic grammar on the basis of the principles of universal grammar. Although this is, of course, a reductive synthesis of the theory of universal grammar, there is a fact that seems not to be accepted by such a fascinating, yet narrow and rigid mechanism: alongside the constraints and universal rules, there is individual freedom, there is the possibility of unpredictable change of the behavior of the individual that can be a variation of the rules and/or change of the rules themselves. Change, which gives freedom of use, is not a limit to rigor, nor does it imply the failure of the code, it is indeed the guarantee of the response of the code (and the subject) to the social, cultural, historical, and semiotic environments. Chomsky had also pointed out that constraints and freedom coexist and highlights that in a language regular creativity (essentially syntactic) and free creativity (that exceeds the rules) work together. Even if the American linguist dealt essentially with what in languages is reducible to natural and universal rules.

Constraints and freedom. If we were to use two words to describe language from the perspective of creativity, constraints and freedom could provide the conceptual frameworks that *in nuce* can portray what an idiom is, how it works, and what are its relations with the general faculty of semiotic management. Constraints and freedom. Thus, a language is presented to the specialist but also to the common speaker, provided the latter to accept that language is both something regular and something that can be innovated in terms of signifiers and meanings. Constraints and freedom, free creativity and regulated creativity, so they live together. They live in a relationship with each other. If we then think of multilingualism as an undeniable fact in the world, then the question moves from the issue of a single language, to the issue of contact languages and linguistic variety. In the world there are different languages (as there are different people, different histories, different identities) and languages are not merely a material instrument consisting of phonemes, morphemes, and syntagmas (they are, but in a very marginal way). Languages are, much more radically, a principle of history and culture. Languages are a paradigm of identity.

But are the languages of the world all the same or are they different? Are some languages better than others? What relationships exist between them? Languages are (or can be) profoundly different from each other in signifiers and meanings, in grammar and syntax, in phonetics and morphology. Or languages are (or can be) all the same: equal (and therefore universal) for their deep structure, and differences only in marginal elements, which do not affect their ability to create meaning, communicate, and see the world. Solving this knot is a complex and important philosophical problem. A solution to the universalist issue, from Aristotle to Chomsky, argues that there is a universal language and through this universal idea lies the explanation of how different people, with different languages, eventually manage to understand and communicate with each other. At the same time, this solution fails to explain why human beings, possessing a language on which to rely with deep semantic structures, have in fact had (or wanted) to resort to the birth of many different languages.

The second solution, from Humboldt to Sapir-Whorf, enhances the infinite variety of languages, which is also an infinite variety of morphological, syntactic, semantic, and pragmatic structures. However, this solution clashes with the fact that, in the end, people understand each other (or can understand each other) and languages can be translated into each other: unlike other semiotics, the meanings of the signs of a language can be translated into the meanings of the signs of another language through the difficult task of translation: *This is not something to be treated lightly—/ to describe the bottom of the universe—/ nor for a tongue that cries Mama and Papa*[2] (Inf. XXXII: 9).

The reflection that we conducted on linguistic creativity, starting from an essentially theoretical framework, had in nuce a goal: to develop theoretical frameworks, with some practical application, and some analysis of concrete facts, which interpret the semiotic phenomena of language as creative phenomena. The phrases and texts that we produce or listen to in L1, where all the elements fall within the grammatical rules often without errors or misunderstandings, are creative. The phrases and texts we produce or listen to in L2 are creative, where sometimes some syntactic uncertainty, or the semantic extension of a sign, make it clear to the interlocutor that we are learning a language; after all, the same linguistic anomalies are also carried out by the native in his/her L1. Italiese is creative, because the contact between Italiano and Inglese created new words, cultural and conceptual models, and semiotic frameworks that were not present in the languages of first-generation emigrants (dialects or Italian). And then Italianisms and pseudo-Italianisms are creative because, thanks to them, from below, in an unforeseeable way, the urban landscapes of the cities are carpeted with Italian language, and these Italian words, even where they do not directly innovate a linguistic form (its signifier), are loaded with senses very different from those of the Italian norm. Finally, language education is creative (or should be) as a non-linear learning process that does not aim at acquiring a grammatical rule, a formal style, or a written register. Language education is creative because it supports an adjustment from time to time, *upon the field*, of the phrase or text spoken or written to a concrete situation, to a contrast and to a communicative domain, in which the compass to follow is only that of communicative functionality.

In language there are constraints and freedoms: in one word, there is creativity. We do not believe that there is a contradiction between constraints and freedom. The assumptions previously recalled about the universality of languages, or their relativism, essentially have the same idea: that a language is a static instrument, given once and for all, in a rigid relationship with the cultural world which is also conceived as static, firm, also given once and for all (De Mauro 1982). But that is not the case. Languages are codes that cannot be fully calculated; they are creative codes, and on the semantic side this entails a perennial possibility of extending meanings to the new senses that allow languages to constantly adapt to the social and communicative needs of human beings.

The engine of *rule-changing* creativity allows you to assert with plausible certainty how languages are vague codes. Vagueness is not bad, but it is the result of a generally creative process that allows languages not to put limits on the field of speakable and thinkable things. Not only poetry, or the abstract themes of love, freedom, or democracy, rests on semiotic creativity in order to be expressed; even the most rigorous and scientific uses of languages are based on the creative aspects that are not previously regular. These can be called sectoral languages, or rather, sectoral uses of language; for example, legal, scientific, medical, or logical-mathematical uses of the language could not function if they did not rely on semiotic creativity.[3] Creativity, at the same time, does not act alone on languages: articulation, globality, historicity, naturality, *rule-governed* creativity, and *rule-changing* creativity coexist and merge into every sentence and text. And in this sense, the Greek *logos*, which embraces the faculty of reasoning, measuring, counting, and even speaking, collects the plurality of properties, which often also oppose, live, and interact in every language.

Languages have a cultural and identity dimension. Languages are a form of life, said in the words of Ludwig Wittgenstein. Linguistic plurality rests on this identity and cultural dimension. Languages are different because they are constantly diversifying in their grammar and in relation to culture. And thanks to creativity, which is the antidote to linguistic approval and political subdivision (in the etymological sense of *polis*), languages respond with multilingualism to nuclear needs of reflection and communication beyond an insignificant temptation to monolingualism and universalis[4] (Campa 2019). Therefore, there is no problem in accepting the evidence of creativity and diversity, and at the same time, the possibility of mutual understanding among people of different languages.

The analysis of creativity has an important theoretical apparatus; however, we have tried, from the outset, to open the theory to the concrete fact. This is for a scientific intent, because we believe that in science, theory and practice are different sides of the same coin, and that theory without practice is incomplete and practice without theory is useless and wrong. But also, because in the practical dimension, a work on creativity can find new openings and new developments. What can be the prospects for linguistic and semiotic creativity? What can be the fields of interest?

We answer these questions with the belief that language contact is really the paradigm in which creativity takes on the most challenging levels, and therefore future research perspectives can still investigate the field of contact language. In works dated a few years ago, we had guessed and hypothesized a kind of sinusoid model for semiotic creativity. In our hypothesis, a multilingual context, such as an ethnic district of our cities, would have been the highest point of the sinusoid, while a district with fewer languages in contact would have been the lowest point of the sinusoid. The hypothesis requires a linguistic and semiotic test, which puts the Italian language space at the center of the contact space and compares the semiotic processes that take place in Italy with those that can be accessed abroad. The aim will be to semiotically consider an urban and social space through a unitary model of study and an analysis of creativity. A linguistic, but generally semiotic, analysis involves linguistic visibility as a system of power and semiotic affirmation on the territory; and by virtue of the social need, the semiotic territory can be a laboratory of creativity (Shohamy and Gorter 2009, De Fina *et al.* 2017).

Further development of research may be linked to renewed interest in Italiese: the current literature has quantitative and qualitative data related to the first generation of emigrants. Today, the presence of the third and fourth generations of Italian descendants allows us to glimpse a significant linguistic vitality of Italiese (Casini 2020) which, we hypothesize, will be a language inevitably different from the first Italiese created in the 1970s. The diverse linguistic and social conditions of Italian descendants and new emigrants have introduced, into a traditional territory of contact, further uses and linguistic forms to analyze in terms of creativity. What Italiese is today—its linguistic characteristics, its semiotic characteristics, the degree to which these characteristics can be influenced by social media and by a communication essentially different from the past, but freer and with degrees still different in creativity—represents a challenge and a new frontier for linguistic creativity.

The web, however, is not only a context of linguistic contact: the internet and social media are the places of an apparent global expressive freedom that sometimes results in phenomena that are not ethically uplifting, but of certain semiotic interest. One case is *hate speech*. Literature tells us what *hate speech* is (De Mauro 2016b, Petrilli 2020) and semiotics and linguistics are called to interpret the phenomena that characterize it. The phenomenon of *hate speech* has taken on particular importance in a communication space different from the traditional one, in which the relationships between orality/writing, synchronicity/diachrony, and *absentita/praesentia* seem to crumble toward different dynamics, in which we label a space of action for creativity. Is it a form of negative creativity? Do ethical questions about creativity require consideration? Can there be an ethical limit to creativity? Can we discuss a new semantic creativity in the case of neutral words that can prove to be "words to hurt" in a significant part of their uses? These are questions to which at this time we cannot give a single answer supported by scientific data, but which allow us de facto to confirm that, *sic stantibus rebus*, creativity can be an engine (the most powerful engine) to consider language as a semiotic code, made to relate, and conceive its use as *lebensform* within society.

"A *property* that studies the life of signs within society is conceivable; . . . I shall call it *creativity*" (CLG: 16—our italics). The phrase is known and is the theoretical basis of CGL. From the original Saussurian version, we replaced the word *science* with *property* and *semiology* with *creativity*, to show how, from our perspective, creativity is the very foundation of a science that wants to study the language. Or rather, to show that creativity is the foundation of a science that wants to study the language with its speakers. Such clarification is not superfluous or redundant; it is simply a reminder that without the experiences of the speakers, there would be no language and creativity. It is not through the study or the consultation of a dictionary, but through real experiences and through the life within society that we are able to expand the meaning of the words we know, to learn new words, to create new meanings and to create new words that are functional to our experiences, our life contexts, and our social contexts.

The consequences of this fact on schools, the university, and education in general are obvious. There is no education in the linguistic uses of a society that is not at the same time education in cultural and social customs. This is the principle of language education which schools, universities, and each individual teacher must be aware of in their role. The task of the language teacher is institutional, social, and cultural as much as it is linguistic; it is education in the uses of languages, their varieties, their registers, the different meanings, the grammar, the rules, and also their variation: it is, in essence, education of creativity.

Gianni Rodari wrote in the 1970s a grammar of creativity titled *The Grammar of Fantasy: An Introduction to the Art of Inventing Stories*,[5] a set of principles for a creative approach to the issues of education, having well understood that the intellectual development of the child (and the adult) cannot be separated from creativity. *The Grammar of Fantasy*, in the words of Rodari himself (1996: 113), "is not a theory of the child's imagination . . ., nor a collection of recipes, nor a textbook of stories but, I believe, a proposal to be placed on all the other books that seek to enrich the environment in which the child grows up (at home as well at school) by providing certain stimuli." What is fantasy for Rodari? What is creativity for Rodari? A unified answer is not possible, but "it is necessary to know more about this 'creativity'":

> "Creativity" is a synonymous with "divergent thought," that is, thinking that is capable of continually breaking the schemes of experience. A mind that is always at work is creative, a mind that always asks questions, discovers problems where others find satisfactory answers. It is a mind that prefers fluid situations where others only sense danger, a mind that is capable of making autonomous and independent judgments (also independent from the father, the professor and the society), that rejects everything that is codified, reshapes objects and concepts without letting itself be hindered by conformist attitudes. All these qualities are manifested in the creative process. And this process—it should be stressed—has a playful character. Always. Even when we are dealing with "strict mathematics." (Rodari 1996, 114)

The words closely recall many considerations that we have put forward in this writing. It originates in a more general perspective than ours, involving the child's mind and its development, and arrives at conclusions very much in line with our own. What is divergent thinking if not creativity that breaks the rules? What is divergent thinking if not the ability of first-generation emigrants to create a new language, overcoming the language barrier, and achieving the communicative end?

All this has a profound educational and linguistic implication. Gianni Rodari (1996: 116) clearly writes this when he senses that education, even the most rigorous, logical, and abstract, must not sacrifice creativity; on the contrary, for education to be rigorous, logical, and abstract, it must rest on creativity. This is a first principle of *rule-changing* creativity:

> Creativity is the number one spot. And the teacher?
>
> The teacher... is transformed into an "animator." Into a promoter of creativity. The teacher no longer transmits beautiful, prepackaged knowledge, a snack a day. The teacher is no longer a circus trainer of ponies and seals. The teacher is an adult who is with the children to express the best in himself or herself, to develop his or her own creative inclination, imagination, and constructive commitment as well, in a series of activities that receive equal consideration. Emotional and moral qualities (the values and norms of leaving together) are elicited in works of painting, theater, sculpture, and music; one's cognitive ability (natural science, linguistics, sociology) and constructive technology are elicited in games. None of these activities should be treated as mere entertainment or pastimes, in contrast to others that are considered more serious.
>
> There is no hierarchy of field whatsoever. Basically, there is only one field—real life, encountered from all points of view, beginning with the reality of the school community, togetherness, the ways we live and work together. In a school of this kind, the child is no longer a consumer of culture and values, but a creator and producer of values and culture.

Gianni Rodari flies high. Tullio De Mauro and democratic language education fly high.

In daily teaching, which is not theory but is practical in the classroom, which confronts the needs of students with models, techniques, behaviors, exercises, and activities, creativity is neither a limit to the educational plan, nor a result now achieved and therefore stored. Creativity is not even an empty word which everyone uses, but that few consider and fewer really tend. Creativity is still a game to play and, above all, a challenge to be won. The (educational) challenge of creativity shifts the terms of the issue from the education level, to the civil society level: the issues at stake are not "simply" passing a test or exam, nor the search for the best method of teaching, not even the search for the best teaching tool and the best teachers; in other words, what to teach and how to teach it. The issues at stake are quite different and involve the social and civil dignity of an entire class of students (and not only). Doing language education today is a difficult undertaking, because the audience to which language education is addressed is complex and complex is the subject. To think that teaching a language can still be done, as sometimes happens, from an essentially formal perspective, is frustrating for students and defies the lines of language policy (as well as having little sense in itself). Doing this is simply wrong under a theoretical and conceptual plan. It is wrong because it is contrary to the minimum principles of semiotic functioning of the language code. Just as theoretically wrong it is not to invest in language education. It is wrong not to consider (or marginally consider) the dimension of research, of the specialization that creates teachers of L2, of evaluation, of supporting the expressive needs of the learners, based on linguistic uses in different contexts. In addition, the cultural industry can revolve around language education in which educational materials and new technologies interacting with what is already in use represent a future that the world's education systems cannot escape. Not to consider all this means to bend to the false opinion in which teaching a language is a recipe that everyone knows, or simply because you have seen it done, or simply because you are a native speaker and therefore you know the language to teach. Doing language education is, on the other hand, a very complex process, a creative process in its highest conception, plural and *rule-changing*. To be carried away by illusory convictions, then, means, even more seriously, to deprive students of real work and the professional expendability of the title of Master or PhD that they have achieved after years of study. Today's international labor market is more significantly geared toward teaching, tourism, business, and the web rather than just academic and literary research alone.

In the global linguistic landscape, Italian occupies a special place. From the public, political level of national institutions, to the private level of the individual teacher, Italian is a "language of culture"; this expression, often abused, is a justification for language policy and behavior in the classroom.[6] The expression "language of culture," sometimes used with instrumental value to suppose the cultural and intellectual superiority of Italian over other languages, is resurfacing in modern times, in Italy and abroad, to stave off the process of renewal and openness of the Italian language to different cultural forms than its own literary and intellectual tradition.

This means that, today as yesterday, the use of the Italian language as a language of culture is made to reject the possibility of a reworking of the symbolic values with which the Italian language space relates to other languages in the global world. Again, as always, those who work with Italian in the world are divided into two parties. There are the innovators who consider the positivity of the relationship between intellectual and traditional heritage and its new elaborations. Then there is the party of conservatives who see only the prevalence of intellectual tradition and who place the linguistic dimension of learning and teaching Italian in the appropriate forms to meet the needs of the new public in a marginal position, subordinate to that supposed central attributed to intellectual culture (Vedovelli 2019).

It is, however, a conflict that is devoid of theoretical sense and linguistic policy. This contrast risks weakening, especially numerically, the position of those who see Italian as a language of only intellectual tradition. From a political consideration, therefore, comes an educational consideration that reflects on the model of language teaching in which the premise and purpose cannot be essentially formal and functional to access the literature. To have language teaching guided by a grammatical purpose, and to ensure that grammar is the basis of the language assessment (so as to garner the student's greatest attention), in the hope of one day reaching the speaker's native competence is a method and merit error that today cannot continue to be supported. Just as it is not possible to ensure that this dedication on grammar will one day be useful, in the case of language use (or attempted use), in fact, such a model is pragmatically non-functional (it hardly reaches the desired results) and theoretically wrong, as it contradicts the semiotic principles of creativity.

This does not mean that the semiotic code is not also a code made by rules (and therefore grammar). Constraints and freedom. Rules and the ability to deviate from these same rules and create new ones. The grammatical dimension of the language plays a fundamental role, but it is defined only if it becomes a tool with which to direct words, and oral and written phrases towards communicative functionality in the contexts of social life. In this way only, grammar serves and makes sense and teaching becomes creative language education.

Giacomo Leopardi was right when copying and commenting upon, in the *Zibaldone*, an old letter dedicated to the climate change of his time compared to his past. Here he argues that the older people (who metaphorically are even the old methods, the old models, the old perspectives) are self-centered.[7] We must look to the future with optimism so that language education and creativity can exist. And if creative language education exists and is carried out in the schools of the world, then the child, like the adult, at last, *'e pparole 'e ssape, ~~ma nun~~ e 'e ssape accucchià*.[8]

NOTES

1. Since it is a requirement of any theoretical treatment that it not leave its concept implied, but state it openly, so that it may be clear with what its argument is

concerned, I say, urging to face the question, that I call vernacular language that which children acquire from speakers around them when they first begin to ascertain sounds; or, to put it more clearly, I state that vernacular language is what we learn without any formal instruction, by imitating our enviroment. There also exists a different kind of language, one removed from us, which the Romans called *grammatica*. . . . Of these two kinds of language, the more important is the vernacular: first, because it is the language originally used by the human race; secondly, because the whole world uses it, though with different pronunciations and using different terms; and thirdly, because it is natural to us, while the other is, in contrast, unnatural. And this more important type of language is what I plan to discuss. . . . So we have found what we were searching for: we can describe the illustrious, cardinal, aulic, and curial vernacular in Italy as that which pertains to every Italian city yet seems to belong to no one, and against which the vernaculars of all the cities of the Italians can be calculated, weighed, and compared (our translation).

2. "Ché non è impresa da pigliare a gabbo / discriver fondo a tutto l'universo, / né da lingua che chiami mamma o babbo" (*Inf.* XXXII: 9).

3. Consider for example, a doctor-patient dialogue, that is, between a connoisseur (also linguist) of medicine and an ordinary person, who in describing his symptoms in order to recieve a diagnosis and a cure, often resorts (unconsciously) to semantic creativity in expressing symptoms of health. The doctor, likewise, uses the semantic creativity of the signs heard to identify (or attempt to identify) and provide a diagnosis and to find a cure. We can talk of different levels of creativity between common uses and the sectoral uses of language.

4. The ontological need for communication and understanding among human beings is a kind of survival instinct implemented through linguistic plurality that overcomes the defence of linguistic forms that are only an expression of the relationship with the particular external environment. As Campa (2019, 31–32) argues, "il plurilinguismo risponde a esigenze nucleari di riflessione e di comunicazione. In ogni ambito comunitario è presente un condotto espressivo che appaga le esigenze e le aspettative conoscitive e relazionali dei suoi componenti. La ricerca di connotazioni espressive testimonia l'affidabilità con la quale la lingua detiene il rapporto con l'ambiente nel quale si esplica. Se l'uniformità linguistica, continuamente riproposta alla temperie solidaristica del genere umano, fosse ritenuta provvidenziale, il suo raccordo con la pratica attuazione si sarebbe verificato nelle stagioni più propizie per la pacifica convivenza dei popoli e delle nazioni. Il potere politico, invece, rinviene nella lingua il suo condotto d'interazione e d'interdizione di vigenza universale. . . . La prerogativa dell'intesa tra i popoli derubrica la primigenia incontinenza nel fortilizio conoscitivo a preminenza decisionale."

5. The Italian writer Gianni Rodari was the author of many beloved children's books, for which he was awarded the prestigious Andersen Prize. He was also an educator and activist who truly understood the power of the imaginative life. In this delightful classic, Rodari presents numerous and wonderful techniques for creating stories. He discusses these specific techniques in the context of the imagination, fairy tales, folk tales, children's stories, cognitive development, and compassionate education. The original work was titled *La grammatica della Fantasia*.

It is no coincidence that Rodari's reflection was born in the same year the foundations of Tullio De Mauro's democratic language education were formed, which are, we have considered, an educational manifesto of creativity.

6. Consider Riccardo Campa's reflections (2019) in *Convivio linguistico* in which the need to redefine the concept of Italian language of culture through theoretical, philosophical, and linguistic frameworks is answered.

7. "The old man, *laudator temporis acti se puero* [eulogizer of the past times when he was a boy], unhappy with human affairs, wants even natural things to have been better in his childhood and youth later. The reason is clear: that is, that that is how they seemed to him at the time; the cold annoyed him and made itself felt infinitely less, etc. etc." (Giacomo Leopardi *Zibaldone*: 4242).

8. The child, as the adult, knows the words and knows how to use them appropriately.

Afterword

Frank Nuessel

Dr. Simone Casini, a professor of Italian at the University of Toronto Mississauga, has already distinguished himself through his outstanding research with one book published, more than two dozen articles in important academic journals, and a half dozen more in press, thirty presentations at major national and international conferences on various aspects of Italian studies, and seventeen invited lectures at major international conferences. Moreover, Dr. Casini has also taught graduate and undergraduate courses at the University of Toronto Mississauga, the Università della Tuscia (Viterbo), and other universities. He has supervised a doctoral dissertation and other graduate and undergraduate students in various research projects. Based on his previous scholarly research in Italian language pedagogy and applied linguistics, Dr. Casini possesses the academic credentials and experience to write a reasoned, innovative, and informative monograph on the subject of linguistic creativity.

It must be noted that Dr. Casini's research on creativity has contributed significantly to the graduate courses that he teaches at the University of Toronto. These courses join theory and practice with the essential theoretical linguistic and semiotic foundational notions such as code, sign, signal, arbitrariness of language, and metalanguage for a course in educational linguistics. With this significant theoretical background, students learn to apply a practical methodological approach to teaching Italian in a global context. This unification of theory and practice, a hallmark of all of Dr. Casini's graduate classes, is the most effective way to instill in students a lasting knowledge of the basic tenets of linguistics and semiotics so that they can practice the science and art of teaching Italian.

Linguistic Creativity: A Semiotic Perspective is an especially important contribution to the topic of linguistic creativity because it builds on the

Chomskyan perspective that language is a species-specific faculty that possesses the unique capacity to utilize a finite set of grammatical rules to generate an infinite number of exceptional and inimitable utterances. This special ability explains why humans are able to generate novel ideas and concepts that cause people to marvel at this inimitable linguistic property to resolve problems, to provide ever-new perspectives on human activity by maintaining a delicate balance and tension between a set of finite rules and their capacity to provide new ways of perceiving the reality that surrounds us. The literary genius of Dante (1265–1321) whose *opus magnum La Divina Commedia* is a verbal and cultural masterpiece, the problem-solving approaches of the mathematician Carl Friedrich Gauss (1777–1855) who revolutionized number theory through his clear and precise use of the language of mathematics with its succinct and symbolic syntax, and the introspective capacity of a theoretical physicist such as Albert Einstein (1879–1955) who reconceptualized the notions of space and time are all manifestations of this creativity. All three of these scholars demonstrate the rule-governed and rule-changing nature of creativity. They are individuals who have taken the grammatical rules of their respective disciplines and have changed how we view the world.

Dr. Casini's book contains two parts. The first addresses a theory of creativity within the framework of linguistics and semiotics in which he employs Ferdinand de Saussure's (1857–1913) dyadic approach to language, namely, the signifier and the signified. In his second chapter, Dr. Casini considers language and games as creative activities. The third chapter explicates the give-and-take of rule government and rule change to achieve creativity. The second part of this volume considers the concrete manifestations of linguistic creativity in education. Likewise, Dr. Casini employs linguistic landscape theory to demonstrate the evolving linguistic creativity in Toronto's multilingual and multicultural society. Furthermore, he discusses *italiese*, the fusion of the two Italian words *italiano* and *inglese*, or code-switching between the two languages, in Toronto, as a perfect exemplar of linguistic creativity in which there is a continuous interplay between a rule-governed and rule-changing grammar.

This is a must-read book because of the insights and innovations about creativity that it provides for the teacher, scholar, and the general public. In it, Dr. Casini demonstrates his profound knowledge of the linguistic, semiotic, psychological, social, and anthropological dimensions of language and how all of these academic domains play a vital and essential role in the multidisciplinary notion of creativity.

References

Aarsleff, Hans. 1982. *From Locke to Saussure: Essays on the Study of Language and Intellectual History*. Minneapolis: University of Minnesota Press.

ACTFL (American Council on the Teaching of Foreign Languages). 2015. *World Readiness Standards for Learning Languages*. Alexandria: ACTFL.

Andersen, Hans Christian. *Clumsy Hans*. Accessed March 13, 2020. https://literature.fandom.com/wiki/Clumsy_Hans.

Aristotle. 1964. *On the Soul*. Cambridge: Harvard University Press (consulted edition)

Aristotle. 2003. *Ethics*. London: Folio Society (consulted edition).

Aristotle. 2009. *Politics*. Oxford: Oxford University press (consulted edition).

Avalle, D'Arco Silvio. 1973. *L'ontologia del segno in Saussure*. Torino: Giappichelli.

Badiou, Alain. 2011. *Wittgenstein's Antiphilosophy*. London/New York: Verso.

Baker, Gordon P., and Peter M. S. Hacker. 2009. *Wittgenstein: Rules, Grammar and Necessity*. Hoboken: Wiley Blackwell.

Bancheri, Salvatore. 2003. "Siciliano e Italiese nelle opere di Lina Riccobene." *Italian Canadiana* 17: 47–66.

Bancheri, Salvatore. 2007a. "Riccobene's *Nun mi maritu ppi procura*: The Italian Canadian linguistic pastiches in a comedy of errors." In *Patois and Linguistic Pastiche in Modern Literature,* edited by Giovanna Summerfield, pp. 47–75. Newcastle: Cambridge Scholars Publishing.

Bancheri, Salvatore. 2007b. *Digital Archives of the Frank Iacobucci Centre for Italian Canadian Studies*. Accessed March 13, 2020. https://bancheri.utm.utoronto.ca/iacobucci/

Bancheri, Salvatore. 2009. "Italiese and Italiesco: Two different faces for the otherness of emigration in the work of Riccobene and Vilardo." In *Diversity, Otherness, and Pluralism in Italian Literature, Cinema, language, and Pedagogy. Yesterday, Today, and Tomorrow*, edited by F. Calabrese, L. Ghezzi. T. Lobalsamo, W. Schrobilgen, pp. 263–280. Ottawa: Legas.

Bancheri, Salvatore. 2020. In "Un viaggio nel mio nostos. La comunità siciliana globale di Delia tra tradizione, teatro, dialetto ed *Italiese*." *Nostos in Italian Canadian*

Literature and Other Media, edited by G. Niccoli. A special issue of *Italian Canadiana* 35 (2021): 129–151.
Barni, Monica, and Guus Extra, eds. 2008. *Mapping Linguistic Diversity in Multicultural Contexts*. Berlin/New York: Mouton de Gruyter.
Barry, Donald. K. 1996. *Forms of Life and Following Rules*. Leiden, New York: Brill.
Bassetti, Pietro. 2015. *Svegliamoci Italici! Manifesto per un futuro glocal*. Venezia: Marsilio.
Bernardini, Carlo, Tullio De Mauro. 2003. *Contare e raccontare. Dialogo sulle culture*. Roma/Bari: Laterza.
Berretta, Monica. 1978. *Linguistica ed educazione linguistica. Guida all'insegnamento dell'italiano*. Torino: Einaudi.
Berruto, Gaetano, ed. 1977. *Scienze del linguaggio ed educazione linguistica*. Torino: Stampatori didattica.
Berruto, Gaetano. 1987. *Sociolinguistica dell'italiano contemporaneo* Roma: Carocci.
Berruto, Gaetano. 2018. "Tullio De Mauro e la sociolinguistica." In *Sull'attualità di Tullio De Mauro*, edited by Ugo Cardinale, pp. 101–119. Bologna: il Mulino.
Berwick, Robert, Angela D. Friederici, Noam Chomsky and Johan J. Bolhuis. 2013. "Evolution, Brain, and the Nature of Language." *Trends in Cognitive Science* 17(2): 89–98.
Bettoni, Camilla. 1986. *Altro Polo: Italian Abroad*. Sidney: University of Sidney Press.
Bettoni, Camilla, ed. 1987. *Italian in Australia: Applied Linguistics*. Special issue of *Australian Review of Applied Linguistics* 4.
Bettoni, Camilla. 1987. "L'Austraitaliano: un'ispirazione o una realtà?" *Il Veltro* 31(1–2): 97–110.
Blommaert, Jan. 2010. *The Sociolinguistics of Globalization*. Cambridge: Cambridge University Press.
Bruni, Francesco. 1984. *L'italiano. Elementi di storia della lingua e della cultura*. Torino: UTET.
Burns, Linda Claire. 1991. *Vagueness: An Investigation into Natural Languages and the Sorites Paradox*. Boston: Kluwer Academic Publishers.
Caesar, Julius. 1819. *Opera omnia*. London: Valpy. (consulted edition)
Calvet, Jean-Louis. 2002. *Le marché aux langues: essai de politologie linguistique sur la mondialisation*. Paris: Plon.
Campa, Riccardo. 2019. *Il convivio linguistico. Riflessioni sul ruolo dell'italiano nel mondo contemporaneo*. Roma: Carocci.
Cancellier, Antonella. 2001. "Italiano e spagnolo a contatto nel Rio de la Plata. I fenomeni del 'cocoliche' e del 'lunfardo.'" In *Italiano e spagnolo in contatto*, edited by Antonella Cancellier and Renata Londero, pp. 69–84. Padova: Unipress.
Casini, Simone. 2012. "La creatività linguistica: un modello interpretativo dei fenomeni semiotici nei contesti di super contatto." *SILTA – Studi italiani di Linguistica teorica e applicata* 41(1): 175–195.

Casini, Simone. 2017. "Italianismi e pseudoitalianismi a Toronto: una ricerca tra gli studenti di italiano del St. George Campus della University of Toronto." *Italica* 94(1): 153–176.

Casini, Simone. 2018. "Italianismi e pseudoitalianismi: uno sguardo semiotico sull'italiano a Toronto." *Italian Canadiana* 32: 15–30.

Casini, Simone. 2019a. "In Principio erat verbum? Tullio De Mauro e le riflessioni americane di educazione linguistica democratica." *Italica* 96(1): 94–126.

Casini, Simone. 2019b. "Questioni di teoria linguistica: per un paradigma teorico della creatività semiotica." *Forum Italicum* 53(1): 69–89.

Casini, Simone. 2019c. "Questioni identitarie per l'italiano a Toronto: uno studio sui panorami linguistici urbani." In *Plurilinguismo migratorio. Voci italiane, italiche e regionali*, edited by Raffaella Bombi, and Francesco Costantini, pp. 77–92. Udine: Forum.

Casini, Simone. 2020. "L'italiano all'estero: riflessioni linguistico-semiotiche tra Italia e Canada." *A Journey through Knowledge: A Festschrift in Memory of Paul. A. Colilli (1952–2018)*, edited by Simone Casini, Christine Sansalone, Salvatore Bancheri and Michael Lettieri (in Press). Florence: Cesati.

Casini, Simone and Salvatore Bancheri. 2019. "'Stanno tutti bene'. Una ricognizione sugli studi di italianistica nel Nord America." In *Il mondo dell'Italiano: L'Italiano nel mondo*, edited by Carla Bagna and Laura Ricci, pp. 213–239. Ospedaletto (PI): Pacini.

Casini, Simone and Salvatore Bancheri. 2021. *Italiese: the Language of Power. A New Perspective on the Language of Italian-Canadians*. Toronto: Toronto University Press. In press.

Census 2011. *Statistics Canada*. Accessed September 3, 2019. https://www12.statcan.gc.ca/census-recensement/2011/dp-pd/index-eng.cfm.

Census 2016. *Statistics Canada*. Accessed September 3, 2019. https://www12.statcan.gc.ca/census-recensement/2016/dp-pd/index-eng.cfm.

Chomsky, Noam, Marc D. Hauser, and W. Tecumseh Fitch. 2002. "The Faculty of Language: What Is It, Who Has It, and How Did It Evolve?" *Science* 22(298): 1569–1579.

Chomsky, Noam. 1964. *Current Issues in Linguistic Theory*. London: Mouton.

Chomsky, Noam. 1965. *Aspects of the Theory of Syntax*. Cambridge: Massachusetts Institute of Technology Press.

Chomsky, Noam. 1966. *Cartesian Linguistics. A Chapter in the History of Rationalist Thought*. New York/London: Harper&Row.

Chomsky, Noam. 1980. *Rules and Representations*. New York: Columbia University Press.

Chomsky, Noam. 1981. *Lectures on Government and Binding: The PISA Lectures*. Dordrecht: Foris Publications.

Chomsky, Noam. 2015. *The Minimalist Program*. Cambridge: Massachusetts Institute of Technology Press.

Cicero, Marcus Tullius. 1617. *Opera omnia*. Coloniae Allobrogum: P. & I. Chouet (consulted edition).

Cimatti, Felice. 2018. "Lingua e creatività. Il soggetto parlante per De Mauro e Chomsky." *Bollettino di italianistica. Rivista di critica, storia letteraria, filologia e linguistica* 15(2): 57–68.
Cimatti, Felice. 2002. *Mente e linguaggio negli animali. Introduzione alla zoosemiotica.* Roma: Carocci.
Clivio, Gianrenzo P. 1976. "The Assimilation of English Loanwords in Italo-Canadian." In *The Second LACUS Forum*, edited by Peter A. Reich, pp. 584–589. Columbia: Hornbeam.
Clivio, Gianrenzo P. 1985. "Su alcune caratteristiche dell'italocanadese di Toronto." *Il Veltro* 29: 483–491.
Clivio, Gianrenzo P. 1986. "Competing Loanwords and Loanshifts in Toronto's Italiese." In *Altro Polo. Italian Abroad*, edited by Camilla Bettoni, pp. 129–146. Sydney: Frederick May Foundation.
Clivio, Gianrenzo P., and Marcel Danesi. 2000. *The Sounds, Forms, and Uses of Italian. An Introduction to Italian Linguistics.* Toronto/Buffalo/London: University of Toronto Press.
Colilli, Paul, Diana Iuele-Colilli, and Christine Sansalone. 2017. *La sala verde/ Divorzio alla canadese.* Ottawa/New York/Toronto: Legas.
Collins–Cobuild. 2019. *English Language Dictionary.* Glasgow: Collins.
Conway, John H., and Derek A. Smith. 2003. *On Quaternions and Octonions. Their Geometry, Arithmetic, and Symmetry.* Natick: AK Peters.
Coseriu, Eugenio. 1958. *Sincronía, diacronía e historia. El problema del cambio lingüístico.* Montevideo: Facultad de Humanidades y Ciencias.
Coseriu, Eugenio. 1962. *Teoría del lenguaje y lingüística general.* Madrid: Editorial Gredos.
Coseriu, Eugenio. 1977. *El Hombre y su lenguaje. E studios de teoría y metodología lingüística.* Madrid: Editorial grados.
Council of Europe. 2001. *Common European Framework of Reference for Languages: Learning, Teaching, Assessment.* Cambridge: Cambridge University Press.
Council of Europe. 2018. *Common European Framework of Reference for Languages: Learning, Teaching, Assessment. Companion Volume with New Descriptors.* Accessed March 17, 2020. https://rm.coe.int/cefr-companion-volume-with-new-descriptors-2018/1680787989.
Croce, Benedetto. 1912. *Estetica, come scienza dell'espressione e linguistica generale, teoria e storia.* Bari: Laterza.
Danesi, Marcel. 1982. "L'interferenza lessicale nell'italiano parlato in Canada (Toronto)." *Les langues néo-latines* 241: 163–167.
Danesi, Marcel. 1985. "Ethnic Language and Acculturation: The Case of Italo-Canadians," *Canadian Ethnic Studies* 17(1): 98–103.
Danesi, Marcel. 2000. *Semiotics in Language Education.* New York: Mouton de Gruyter, 2000.
Danesi, Marcel. 2002. *Semiotics in Education.* Dresden: Thelem.
Danesi, Marcel. 2004. *Messages, Signs, and Meanings: A Basic Textbook in Semiotics and Communication.* Toronto: Canadian Scholars's Press.
Danesi, Marcel. 2008. *Problem-solving in Mathematics: A Semiotic Perspective for Educators and Teachers.* New York: Peter Lang.

Danesi, Marcel. 2016. *Language and Mathematics: An Interdisciplinary Guide*. Boston/Berlin: Mouton de Gruyter.

De Fina, Anna, Didem Ikizoglu, and Jeremy Wewgner. 2017. *Diversity and Super-diversity: Sociocultural Linguistics Perspectives*. Washington: Georgetown University Press.

De Mauro, Tullio. 1963. *Storia linguistica dell'Italia unita*. Roma/Bari: Laterza.

De Mauro, Tullio. 1965. *Introduzione alla semantica*. Roma/Bari: Laterza.

De Mauro, Tullio. 1967. "Introduzione." In *Corso di linguistica generale di F. de Saussure. Introduzione, traduzione e commento*, v-xxxix. Roma/Bari: Laterza.

De Mauro, Tullio. 1971a. *Pedagogia della creatività linguistica*. Guida: Napoli.

De Mauro, Tullio. 1971b. *Senso e significato. Studi di semantica teorica e storica*. Bari: Adriatica Editrice.

De Mauro, Tullio. 1974. "Fantasia della grammatica." In *La comunicazione non-verbale*, edited by Robert A. Hinde, v-xxxi. Roma/Bari: Laterza.

De Mauro, Tullio. 1980. *Guida all'uso delle parole*. Roma: Editori Riuniti.

De Mauro, Tullio. 1981. *Scuola e linguaggio. Questioni di educazione linguistica*. Roma: Editori Riuniti.

De Mauro, Tullio. 1982. *Minisemantica dei linguaggi non verbali e delle lingue*. Roma/Bari: Laterza.

De Mauro, Tullio. 1984. *Ai margini del linguaggio*. Roma: Editori Riuniti.

De Mauro, Tullio. 1987. *L'Italia delle Italie*. Roma: Editori Riuniti.

De Mauro, Tullio. 1994. *Capire le parole*. Roma/Bari: Laterza.

De Mauro, Tullio and Sara Fortuna. 1995. "Eticità e linguaggio." In *Senso e storia dell'estetica. Studi offerti a Emilio Garroni per il suo settantesimo compleanno*, edited by Pietro Montani, pp. 488–510. Parma: Pratiche.

De Mauro, Tullio. 2001. *Minima scholaria*. Roma/Bari: Laterza.

De Mauro, Tullio. 2002. *Prima lezione sul linguaggio*. Roma-Bari: Laterza.

De Mauro, Tullio. 2000-2003. *Grande dizionario italiano dell'uso*. Torino: UTET.

De Mauro, Tullio. 2005a. "Introduzione, traduzione e commento." *Scritti inediti di linguistica generale*. Ferdinand de Saussure, edited by VII-XXVI. Roma/Bari: Laterza.

De Mauro, Tullio. 2005b. *La fabbrica delle parole: il lessico e problemi di lessicologia*. Milano: UTET.

De Mauro, Tullio. 2006a. "Crisi del monolitismo linguistico e lingue meno diffuse." *LIDI. Lingue e idiomi di Italia* 1(1): 11–37.

De Mauro, Tullio. 2006b. "Educazione linguistica oggi." In *Linguaggio, mente, parole. Dall'infanzia alla adolescenza. Atti del XIII convegno del GISCEL (Lecce, 22-25 aprile 2004)*, edited by Immacolata Tempesta, Maria Maggio, pp. 19–25. Milano: FrancoAngeli.

De Mauro, Tullio. 2008. *Lezioni di linguistica teorica*. Roma/Bari: Laterza.

De Mauro, Tullio. 2009. "A che serve la grammatica?" In *Perché la grammatica?*, edited by Giuliana Fiorentino, pp. 12–22. Roma: Carocci.

De Mauro, Tullio. 2012. "Linguistica educativa: ragioni e prospettive." *Linguistica educativa. Atti del XLIV Congresso internazionale di studi della Società di Linguistica Italiana (SLI). Viterbo, 27-29 settembre 2010*, edited by Silvana Ferreri, pp. 3–22. Roma: Bulzoni.

De Mauro, Tullio. 2014. *Storia linguistica dell'Italia repubblicana*. Roma/Bari: Laterza.
De Mauro, Tullio. 2016a. "Antiquam exquirite matrem (Virgilio Aen. III 96.)" In *Lingue in contatto/Contact Linguistics*, edited by Raffaella Bombi and Vincenzo Orioles, pp. 19–26. Roma: Bulzoni.
De Mauro, Tullio. 2016b. *Le parole per ferire*. Accessed May 21, 2020. https://www.internazionale.it/opinione/tullio-de-mauro/2016/09/27/razzismo-parole-ferire
De Mauro, Tullio. 2018. *Educazione linguistica democratica,* edited by Silvana Loiero and Maria Antonietta Marchese. Bari: Laterza, 2018.
De Mauro, Tullio. 2019. *Il valore delle parole*. Roma: Treccani.
De Mauro, Tullio, Massimo Vedovelli, Monica Barni, and Lorenzo Miraglia. 2002. *Italiano 2000. I pubblici e le motivazioni dell'italiano diffuso fra stranieri*. Roma: Bulzoni.
De Mauro, Tullio, and Silvana Ferreri. 2005. "Glottodidattica come linguistica educativa." In *E.L.I.C.A. (Educazione linguistica e conoscenze per l'accesso)*, edited by Miriam Voghera, Grazia Basile, and Anna R. Guerriero, pp. 17–28. Perugia: Guerra.
Den Ouden, Bernard D. 1975. *Language and Creativity. An Interdisciplinary Essay in Chomskyan Humanism*. Lisse/Netherlands: The Peter De Ridder Press.
De Palo, Marina. 2016. *Saussure e gli strutturalismi. Il soggetto parlante nel pensiero linguistico del Novecento*. Roma: Carocci.
De Palo, Marina, and Stefano Gensini, eds. 2018. *Saussure e la scuola linguistica romana. Da Antonino Pagliaro a Tullio De Mauro*. Roma: Carocci.
Descartes, René. 1956. *Discourse on Method*. New York: Liberal Arts Press (consulted edition).
Descartes, René. 1972. *L'Homme. Treatise of man. Cambridge*: Harvard University Press (consulted edition).
Di Cesare, Donatella. 1987. "Aristotele e Humboldt e la concezione dinamica della lingua come enérgeia." *Paradigmi* 5(13): 65–86.
Di Cesare, Donatella. 1997. "Humboldt, Saussure e l'arbitraire du signe." In *Ai limiti del linguaggio*, edited by Federico Albano Leoni, Daniele Gambarara, Stefano Gensini, Franco Lo Piparo and Raffaele Simone, pp. 179–210. Roma/Bari: Laterza.
Di Cesare, Donatella. 2005. "Introduzione." In *La Diversità delle lingue,* by Wilhelm von Humboldt, xv-civ. Roma/Bari: Laterza.
Eco, Umberto. 1976. *A Theory of Semiotics*. Bloomington: Indiana University Press.
Eco, Umberto. 1979. *The Role of the Reader: Explorations in the Semiotics of Texts*. Bloomington: Indiana University Press.
Eco, Umberto. 1984. *Semiotics and Philosophy of Language*. Bloomington: Indiana University Press.
Eco, Umberto. 1990. *The Limits of Interpretation*. Bloomington: Indiana University Press.
Eco, Umberto. 1995. *The Search for the Perfect Language*. Cambridge: Blackwell.
Eco, Umberto. 2004. *La combinatoria della creatività*. Accessed January, 9 2020. http://www.umbertoeco.it/CV/Combinatoria%20della%20creativita.pdf.

Ferreri, Silvana. 2002. "Educazione linguistica: L1." In *La linguistica italiana alle soglie del 2000 (1987-1997)*, edited by Cristina Lavinio, pp. 213–252. Roma: Bulzoni.

Ferreri, Silvana. 2005a. "Le dimensioni dell'educazione linguistica." *Bollettino di italianistica. Rivista di critica, storia letteraria, filologia e linguistica* 2: 119–142.

Ferreri, Silvana. 2005b. *L'alfabetizzazione lessicale*. Roma: Aracne.

Ferreri, Silvana. 2012. "Linguistica educativa: tema antico e campo nuovo." In *Linguistica educativa. Atti del XLIV Congresso internazionale di studi della Società di linguistica italiana (SLI). Viterbo, 27-29 settembre 2010*, edited by Silvana Ferreri, pp. ix–xvii. Roma: Bulzoni.

Ferreri, Silvana. 2013. "Educazione linguistica: L1." In *La linguistica italiana all'alba del terzo millennio (1997-2010)*, edited by Gabriele Iannaccaro, pp. 207–242. Roma: Bulzoni.

Fiorentino, Giuliana, ed. 2009. *Perché la grammatica?* Roma: Carocci.

Fondazione Migrantes. 2019. *Rapporto Italiani nel Mondo 2019*. Todi: Editrice Tau.

Formigari, Lia. 1977a. *La linguistica romantica*. Torino: Loescher.

Formigari, Lia. 1977b. *La logica del pensiero vivente*. Roma/Bari: Laterza.

Frascolla, Pasquale. 2000. "Wittgenstein su regole e dimostrazioni." In *La regola linguistica, Atti del VI congresso di studi della società di filosofia del linguaggio Bagheria (Palermo) 14-16 ottobre 1999*, edited by Marco Carapezza and Franco Lo Piparo, pp. 229–238. Palermo: Novecento.

Galati, Michelle, and Olivia Didoné. 2020. "Sociolinguistics on the Road. Italian Linguistic Landscape in the GTA." *A Journey through Knowledge: A Festschrift in Memory of Paul. A. Colilli (1952–2018)*, edited by Simone Casini, Christine Sansalone, Salvatore Bancheri and Michael Lettieri (in press). Florence: Cesati.

Gambarara, Daniele, ed. 1999. *Semantica. Teorie, tendenze e problemi contemporanei*. Roma: Carocci.

Gargani, David. 2018. "Creatività e origini del linguaggio in Tullio De Mauro." *Bollettino di italianistica. Rivista di critica, storia letteraria, filologia e linguistica* 15(2): 110–118.

Garroni, Emilio. 1976. *Estetica e epistemologia: riflessioni sulla "Critica del giudizio."* Roma: Bulzoni.

Garroni, Emilio. 1977. *Ricognizione della semiotica*. Roma: Officina.

Garroni, Emilio. [1978] 2010. *Creatività*. Macerata: Quodlibet.

Gensini, Stefano, and Fusco Maria, eds. 2010. *Animal loquens. Linguaggio e conoscenza negli animali non umani da Aristotele a Chomsky*. Roma: Carocci.

Gilmore, Richard A. 1999. *Philosophical Health: Wittgenstein's Method in Philosophical Investigations*. Lanham: Lexington.

GISCEL (Gruppo di Intervento e Studio nel Campo dell'Educazione Linguistica). 1975. Dieci Tesi per l'educazione linguistica democratica (everything italics). Accessed September 13, 2020. https://giscel.it/.

Givone, Sergio. 2010. "L'idea di creazione tra metafisica ed estetica." In *Storia naturale della creatività*, edited by Salvatore Califano, and Ernesto Carafoli, pp. 27–38. Roma: Scienze e lettere editore commerciale.

Hacker, Peter M. S. 2001. *Wittgenstein: Connections and Controversies*. Oxford: Oxford University Press.

Hacker, Peter M. S. 2019. *Wittgenstein: Meaning and Mind*. Hoboken: Wiley Blackwell.
Haller, Hermann W. 1993. *Una lingua perduta e ritrovata: l'italiano degli italo-americani*. Firenze: La Nuova Italia.
Hjelmslev, Louis. [1961] 1963. *Prolegomena to a Theory of Language*. Madison: The University of Wisconsin Press.
Hjelmslev, Louis. 1971. *Essais linguistiques*. Paris: éditions de minuit.
Hjelmslev, Louis. [1959] 1981. *Saggi di linguistica generale*, edited by Massimo Prampolini. Parma: Pratiche editrice.
Horace. 1867. *Opera omnia*. Lipsia: Teubner (consulted edition).
Horrocks, Geoffrey. 2016. *Generative Grammar*. Georgetown: Routledge.
Humboldt von, Wilhelm. [1836] 1988. *On Language. The Diversity of Human Language-Structure and Its Influence on the Mental Development of Mankind*. Cambridge: Cambridge University Press.
Iuele-Colilli, Diana. 1993. "Materials for a Linguistic Atlas of the Canadian Italian Spoken in Ontario." *Italian Canadiana* 7: 59–74.
Iuele-Colilli, Diana. 2018. "Documenting Italiese. Necessity or Luxury." *Italian Canadiana* 32: 55–68.
Iuele-Colilli, Diana. 2020. "Italiese nel mondo: Creation, Dissemination and Gradual Disappearence." In *A Journey through Knowledge: A Festschrift in Memory of Paul. A. Colilli (1952–2018)*, edited by Simone Casini, Christine Sansalone, Salvatore Bancheri and Michael Lettieri (in press). Florence: Cesati.
Karlin, Anna R., and Yuval Peres. 2016. *Game Theory, Alive*. Providence, Rhode Island: American Mathematical Society.
Kripke, Saul A. 1982. *Wittgenstein on Rules and Private Language. An Elementary Exposition*. Oxford: Basil Blackwell.
Ladusaw, William. 1983. "Logical Forms and Conditions on Grammatically." *Linguistics and Philosophy* I, 39(6): 373–392.
La Fauci, Nunzio. 2011. *Relazioni e differenze. Questioni di linguistica razionale*. Palermo: Sellerio.
Lamb, Sydney. 1966. *Outline of Stratificational Grammar*. Washington: Georgetown University Press.
Lenneberg, Eric. 1971. "Of Language Knowledge, Aspes, and Brains." *Journal of Psycholinguistic Research* I: 1–29.
Leopardi, Giacomo. 1900. *Zibaldone*. Firenze: Le Monnier (consulted edition).
Leroi-Gourhan, André. 1993. *Gesture and Speech*. Cambridge: Massachusetts Institute of Technology Press (consulted edition).
Lieberman, Philiph. 1991. *Uniquely Human: the Evolution of Speech, Thought, and Selfless Behavior*. Cambridge: Harvard University Press.
Lo Piparo, Franco. 2003. *Aristotele e il linguaggio: cosa fa di una lingua una lingua*. Roma/Bari: Laterza.
Lucretius, Titus Carus. 1896–1898. *De rerum natura*. Torino: Loescher (consulted edition).
Machetti, Sabrina. 2006. *Uscire dal vago. Analisi linguistica della vaghezza del linguaggio*. Roma/Bari: Laterza.

Manzoni, Alessandro. 1923. *Sentir messa. Libro della lingua d'Italia contemporaneo dei* Promessi Sposi. Milano: Bottega di Poesia (consulted edition).
Marconi, Diego. 1997. "Transizione." In *Guida a Wittgenstein*, edited by Diego Marconi, pp. 59–102. Roma/Bari: Laterza.
Marconi, Diego. 1999. *La filosofia del linguaggio. Da Frege ai giorni nostri.* Torino: UTET.
Martinet, André. 1964. *Éléments de linguistique générale.* Paris: Colin.
Martinet, André. 1967. "Preface." In *Languages in Contact*, edited by Uriel Weinreich. London/Paris: Mouton (consulted edition)
Messeri, Marco. 1997. "Seguire la regola." In *Guida a Wittgenstein*, edited by Diego Marconi, pp. 150–191. Roma/Bari: Laterza.
Nelde, Peter H. 1998. "Language Conflict." In *The Handbook of Sociolinguistics*, edited by Florian Coulmas, pp. 285–300. Oxford: Blackwell.
Neumann von, John, and Oksar Morgenstern. 1953. *Theory of Games and Economic Behavior.* Princeton: Princeton University Press.
Nuessel, Frank. 2000. *Linguistic Approach to Hispanic literature.* New York/Ottawa: Legas.
Nuessel, Frank. 2010. *The Esperanto Language.* New York/Ottawa: Legas.
Nuessel, Frank. 2016. "The Consequences and Effects of Language Transformations in Legal Discourse." *Semiotica* 209: 125–148.
Nuessel, Frank. 2017. "The Traffic Sign as a Sign: Silent Speech Acts." *International Journal of Semiotics and Visual Rhetoric* 1: 1–10.
Pagliaro, Antonino. 1952. *Il segno vivente. Saggi sulla lingua e altri simboli.* Napoli: Edizioni scientifiche italiane.
Pagliaro, Antonino, and Tullio De Mauro. 1973. *La forma linguistica.* Milano: Rizzoli.
Paina, Corrado. 2006. *College Street, Little Italy: Toronto Renaissance Strip.* Toronto: Mansfield.
Palermo, Massimo. 2013. *Linguistica italiana.* Bologna: il Mulino.
Peirce, Sanders S. 1958-60. *Collected Papers.* Cambridge: Belknap Press of Harvard University Press.
Petrilli, Raffaella. 2020. *Hate speech. L'odio nel discorso pubblico. Politica, media, società.* Roma: Round Robin Editrice.
Petrilli, Susan, and Augusto Ponzio. 2007. *Semiotics Today: from Global Semiotics to Semioethics, a Dialogic Response.* Toronto: University of Toronto Press.
Pierno, Franco. 2017. "Gli italianismi nell'inglese di Toronto e nel francese di Montreal. Stato delle ricerche e del progetto sugli italianismi in Canada." In *Osservatorio degli italianismi nel mondo. Punti di partenza e nuovi orizzonti. Atti dell'incontro OIM, Firenze, Villa Medicea di Castello, 20 giugno 2014*, edited by Matthias Heinz, pp. 111–133. Firenze: Accademia della Crusca.
Pietropaolo, Domenico. 1974. "Aspects of English Interference on the Italian Language in Toronto." *Canadian Modern Language Review* 30(3): 234–241.
Pietropaolo, Domenico. 2010. "Language Loyalty and the Culture of Immigration in Early Canadian Italiese." In *Into and out of Italy: Lingua e cultura della migrazione italiana*, edited by Adam Ledgeway, Anna Laura Lepschy, pp. 119–127. Perugia: Guerra.

Pivato, Joseph. 2014. "1978: Language Escapes: Italian-Canadian Authors Write in an Official and Not in Italiese." In *Translating Effects: The Shaping of Modern Canadian Culture*, edited by Kathy Mezei, Von Flotow Luisea, and Simon Sherry, pp. 197–207. Montreal: McGill-Queen's University Press.

Prampolini, Massimo. 1997. "Il concetto di vaghezza." In *Ai limiti del linguaggio*, edited by Feredico Albano Leoni, Daniele Gambarara, Stefano Gensini, Franco Lo Piparo and Raffaele Simone, pp. 97–109. Roma/Bari: Laterza.

Prampolini, Massimo. 1981. *Traduzione e commento ai Saggi di linguistica generale di Luis Hjelmeslv*. Parma: Pratiche editrice.

Prampolini, Massimo. 2001. "La creatività nella filosofia di L. Wittgenstein." *Il Cannocchiale. Rivista di studi filosofici* 3: 133–171.

Prieto, Luis J. 1976. *Pertinenza e Pratica. Saggio di semiotica*. Milano: Feltrinelli.

Prieto, Luis J. 1995. *Saggi di semiotica. III Sul significato*. Parma: Pratiche Editrice.

Prifti, Elton. 2013. *Italoamericano. Italiano e inglese in contatto negli USA. Analisi diacronica variazionale e migrazionale*. Boston/Berlin: de Gruiter.

Prifti, Elton. 2014. "Enérgeia in trasformazione. Elementi analitici di linguistica migrazionale." *Zeitschrift für romanische Philologie* 130(1): 1–22.

Purpura, James E. 1999. *Learner Strategy Use and Performance on Language Tests: A Structural Equation Modeling Approach*. Cambridge: Cambridge University Press.

Purpura, James E. 2004. *Assessing Grammar*. Cambridge, New York: Cambridge University Press.

Ramirez, Bruno. 1989. *The Italians in Canada*. Ottawa: Canadian Historical Association

Rasmussen, Eric. 2001. *Games and Information. An Introduction to Game Theory*. Malden: Blackwell.

Rasmussen, Michael. 1993. *Louis Hjelmslev et la sémiotique contemporaine*. Copenhague: Cercle linguistique de Copenhague.

Ricento, Thomas, ed. 2015. *Language Policy and Political Economy*. Oxford: Oxford University Press.

Rodari, Gianni. [1973] 1996. *The Grammar of Fantasy. An Introduction to the Art of Inventing Stories*. New York: Teachers & Writers Collaborative.

Sanzone, Daniela. 2012–2015. "From Mass immigration to Professional Workers. A Portrait of the Present Italian 'Comunità' in Ontario, Canada." *Italian Canadiana* 26–29: 31–52.

Saussure, Ferdinand de. [1922] 1959. *Course in General Linguistics*. New York: McGraw-Hill.

Saussure, Ferdinand de. 1997. *Second Course of Lectures on General Linguistics (1908-1909)*. New York: Pergamon (consulted edition).

Saussure, Ferdinand de. [2002] 2006. *Writing in General Linguistics*. New York: Oxford University Press.

Scarola, Giovanni. 2007. *L'italiese in Canada: Considerazioni sul lessico*. Vaughan: Graphics.

Scuola di Barbiana. 1996. *Lettera a una professoressa*. Firenze: Libreria editrice fiorentina.

Serianni, Luca. 2002. "L'italiano e le altre lingue." In *La lingua nella storia d'Italia*, edited by Luca Serianni, pp. 579–642. Società Dante Alighieri. Roma: Libri Scheiwiller.

Serianni, Luca. 2006. *Prima lezione di grammatica italiana*. Roma/Bari: Laterza.
Serianni, Luca. 2012. *Italiani scritti*. *Bologna*: il Mulino.
Serianni, Luca and Giuseppe Antonelli. 2017. *Manuale di linguistica italiana*. Milano: Mondadori.
Shohamy, Elana, and Durk Gorter, eds. 2009. *Linguistic Landscape: Expanding the Scenery*. New York: Routledge.
Shohamy, Elana, Eliezer Ben-Rafael, and Monica Barni, eds. 2010. *Linguistic Landscape in the City*. Bristol/Buffalo: Multilingua Matters.
Siebetcheu, Raymond and Sabrina Machetti. 2019. *Le camfranglais dans le monde global. Contextes migratoires et perspectives sociolinguistique*. Paris: L'Harmattan.
Simone, Raffaele. 1970. *Introduzione al secondo corso di linguistica generale (1908-1909)*. Roma: Ubaldini.
Simone, Raffaele. 1976. "L'educazione linguistica dalla lingua al linguaggio." *Scuola e città* 8–9: 319–340.
Spolsky, Bernard. 1978. *Educational Linguistics: An Introduction*. Rowley, Mass: Newbury House Publishers.
Spolsky, Bernard, Francis M. Hult, eds. 2008. *The Handbook of Educational Linguistics*. Oxford: Blackwell.
Stenius, Erik. 1960. *Wittgenstein's Tractatus: A Critical Exposition of Its Main Lines of Thought*. Oxford: Blackwell.
Stern, David G. 2004. *Wittgenstein's Philosophical Investigations. An Introduction*. Cambridge: Cambridge University Press.
Sullivan, Peter, and Michael Potter. 2013. *Wittgenstein's Tractatus: History and Interpretation*. Oxford: Oxford University Press.
Tarski, Alfred. 1936. "Der Wahrheitsbegriff in den formalisierten Sprachen." *Studia philosophica* I: 261–405.
Thomason, Sarah G. 2001. *Language Contact: An Introduction*. Washington: Georgetown University Press.
Thomason, Sarah G., and Terrence Kaufman. 1988. *Language Contact, Creolization, and Genetic Linguistics*. Berkley: University of California Press.
Thrane, Torben (ed.). 1980. *Typology and Genetics of Language: Proceedings of the Rask-Hjelmslev Symposium Held at the University of Copenhagen 3rd–5th September 1979*. Copenhagen: Linguistic Circle of Copenhagen.
Tosi, Arturo. 1991. *L'italiano d'oltremare. la lingua delle comunità italiane nei paesi anglofoni*. Firenze: Giunti.
Turchetta, Barbara, and Massimo Vedovelli. 2018. *Lo spazio linguistico italiano globale: il caso dell'Ontario*. Pisa: Pacini Editore.
Vedovelli, Massimo. 2003. "Note sulla glottodidattica italiana oggi: problemi e prospettive." *SILTA: Studi italiani di Linguistica teorica e applicata* 32(2): 17–23.
Vedovelli, Massimo. 2005. "L'italiano nel mondo da lingua straniera a lingua identitaria: il caso freddoccino." *SILTA – Studi italiani di linguistica teorica e applicata* 34(3): 585–609.
Vedovelli, Massimo. 2010. *Guida all'italiano per stranieri. Dal quadro comune europeo per le lingue alla sfida salutare*. Roma: Carocci.
Vedovelli, Massimo, ed. 2011. *Storia linguistica dell'emigrazione italiana nel mondo*. Roma: Carocci.

Vedovelli, Massimo. 2017. "Tullio De Mauro e gli studi linguistici e linguistico-educativi in Italia." *Italica* 94(1): 5–30.

Vedovelli, Massimo. 2018. "L'italiano come L2 e la linguistica migratoria." In *Tullio De Mauro. Un intellettuale italiano*, edited by Stefano Gensini, Maria Emanuela Piemontese, and Giovanni Solimine, pp. 135–149. Roma: Casa Editrice Università La Sapienza.

Vedovelli, Massimo. 2019. "Prefazione." In *Il convivio linguistico. Riflessioni sul ruolo dell'italiano nel mondo contemporaneo*, by Riccardo Campa, pp. 11–27. Roma: Carocci.

Vedovelli, Massimo, and Simone Casini. 2013. "Italianismi e pseudoitalianismi in Giappone: le radici profonde di una consonanza culturale in un mondo globale." In *La lingua italiana in Giappone 2*, edited by Maria Katie Gessato, and Patrizia Peruzzi, pp. 34–106. Tokyo: Istituto Italiano di Cultura.

Vedovelli, Massimo, and Simone Casini. 2016. *Che cosa è la linguistica educativa*. Roma: Carocci.

Vertovec, Steven. 2007. "Super-diversity and Its Implications." *Ethnic and Racial Studies* 30(6): 1024–1054.

Vilardo, Stefano. 1975. *Tutti dicono Germania Germania*, con introduzione di Leonardo Sciascia. Milano: Garzanti.

Vizmuller-Zocco, Jana. 1995. "The Languages of Italian Canadians." *Italica* 72: 512–529.

Vizmuller-Zocco, Jana. 1998. "L'italiano in Canada: ai margini o al centro del cambiamento linguistico?" In *Atti del XXI Congresso Internazionale di linguistica e Filologia Romanza*, edited by Giovanni Ruffino, pp. 731–739. Tubingen: Niemeyer.

Vizmuller-Zocco, Jana. 2007. "Language, Ethnicity, Post-Modernity: The Italian Canadian Case." *Studi Emigrazione* 166: 355–368.

Voltolini, Alberto. 1998. *Guida alla lettura delle ricerche filosofiche di Wittgenstein*. Roma-Bari: Laterza.

Vygotsky, Lev S. 1962. *Thought and Language*. Cambridge: Massachusetts Institute of Technology Press.

Weinreich, Uriel. [1963] 1967. *Languages in Contact: Findings and Problems*. London/Paris: Mouton.

Weinreich, Uriel. [1963] 2008. *Languages in Contact*, edited by Vincenzo Orioles, introduction of Giorgio Raimondo Cardona. Torino: UTET.

Whorf, Benjamin L. 1956. *Language, Though and Reality*. Cambridge: Massachusetts Institute of Technology Press.

Wittgenstein, Ludwig. [1953] 1972. *Philosophical Investigations (PU)*. Oxford: Basil Blackwell (consulted edition).

Wittgenstein, Ludwig. 2005. *The Big Typescript TS 213*. Oxford: Blackwell Publishing (consulted edition).

Wittgenstein, Ludwig. [1964] 2014. *Tractatus Logico-Philosophicus*. Peterborough: Broadview. (consulted edition)

Zingarelli, Nicola. 2019. *Lo Zingarelli: vocabolario della lingua italiana*. Bologna: Zanichelli.

Zucchi, John. 1988. *Italians in Toronto: Development of a National Identity, 1875-1935*. Montreal: McGill-Queens University Press.

Index

Aarsleff, Hans, 50
abstraction and concreteness dichotomy, 57–62
ACTFL (*American Council on the Teaching of Foreign Languages*), 78–80
Alighieri, Dante, 123, 136
American Council on the Teaching of Foreign Languages (ACTFL), 78–80
ancient world, 25, 29, 85. *See also* Aristotle
Andersen, Hans Christian, 116–17
arbitrariness of language, 16, 21, 27n5, 66
Aristotle, 7, 8–9, 10, 25, 52–53, 69, 125
Ars poetica (Flaccus), 29
articulate awareness, 109
articulation of language signs, 69–70
Aspects of the Theory of Syntax (Chomsky), 48–49, 54–57

Bancheri, Salvatore, 80, 107, 114
Barni, Monica, 92
Ben-Rafael, Eliezer, 92
Berretta, Monica, 74
Berruto, Gaetano, 74
biblical tradition, 86–87
bilingualism, 54, 86, 88–90
broad language faculty (FLB), 13n4

Caesar, Julius, 85, 118n1
Canadian emigration from Italy, 93. *See also* Italianisms and Pseudo-Italianisms; Italiese
Cartesian Linguistics (Chomsky), 10, 48–50
Casini, Simone, 76, 78, 92, 110
Cch'è simpaticu 'stu 'taliese (Riccobene), 115–16
CEFRL (*Common European Framework of Reference for Languages*), 78
CGL. See Course in General Linguistics (Saussure)
chess game, 20, 25, 29–30
Chomsky, Noam, 3–4, 10, 48–53, 72, 124, 125
Cicero, Marcus Tullius, 15, 65
classification of semiotic codes, 68–73, 81–82n5
Clivio, Gianrenzo P., 88, 105
Clumsy Hans, 116–17
comic conception of Italiese, 115
"commercial" creativity, 112
Common European Framework of Reference for Languages (CEFRL), 78
communication as survival instinct, 133n4
concreteness and abstraction dichotomy, 57–62

consistent rules, 34
constraints in language, 124–26, 132
contact language, 127–28
Coseriu, Eugenio, 18, 50, 52–53, 58–59, 60, 89
Course in General Linguistics (Saussure), 5, 13n2, 16, 18, 22, 23, 29–30, 32–33, 72, 128–29
creative rules, 34, 40–45
creativity: as calculation, 83n15; classification of codes, 71–73; defined, 1–2, 5–7; examples in fable, 117; as foundation of language, 8; gradients of, 108–18; innovation and, 11, 89; intentional, 111; intermediate, 111–12; of *langage*, 72; as language, 15–17; of *langue*, 72; necessity of, 112, 121n24; negative creativity, 128; of *parole*, 72; of psychologists, 73; of psychopedagogists, 112; regularity and, 34; standard, 110–11; syntactic framework, 110–13; unintentional, 110–11; universal mental faculty for, 124. See also game and language; Italianisms and Pseudo-Italianisms; Italiese; rule-changing creativity; rule-governed creativity
Croce, Benedetto, 60, 72, 82n11
Current Issues of Linguistic Theory (Chomsky), 56

Danesi, Marcel, ix–xv, 88, 105, 107, 108
Dante, 123, 136
De Bello Gallico (Caesar), 85
De Mauro, Tullio, 4, 7–8, 17, 23, 24, 25, 57, 62, 66–73, 74–76, 80–81, 81–82n5, 83–84n20, 88, 90, 118, 130
De Palo, Marina, 29
Descartes, René, 9, 10, 48, 50
De vulgari eloquentia (Dante), 123
dialects of Italian, 105–6. See also Italiese
dialogue and semantic creativity, 133n3

Di Cesare, Donatella, 49, 50
dictionaries, 6, 55, 107, 120n26, 129
Dieci Tesi Giscel, 76–78, 83–84n20
Discourse on Method (Descartes), 9–10
diversity and creativity, 127
doctor-patient dialogue, 133n3

educational linguistics: classification of semiotic codes, 68–73, 81–82n5; exams, 84n22; issues of creative education, 73–81. See also language education
Educational Linguistics (Spolsky), 74
Einstein, Albert, 136
Éléments de linguistique générale (Martinet), 69–70
enérgeia (activity), 7, 17, 49–53, 72
ergon (product), 17, 49–52
erzeugen ("generate"), 50
European Framework, 78
exams, 84n22
expressive creativity, 82n12
Extra, Guus, 92

fable on creativity, 117
Ferreri, Silvana, 74–75
Filosofia della Romantik (Formigari), 54
Flaccus, Quintus Horatius, 29
FLB (broad language faculty), 13n4
FORM, 23–26, 28n13
formal semiotic arbitrariness, 66
form and substance dichotomy, 33
form of language, 49–51
free creativity, 124–25
freedom in language, 124–26, 132
future research perspectives, 127–28

game and language: *jeu de signes appelé langue*, 34–37; linguistic rule, 37–41; playing with creativity, 130; semiotic analogies, 29–34
Garroni, Emilio, 16, 39–40, 48, 55
Gauss, Carl Friedrich, 136
generative grammar, 49–54

Genesis, 86–87
Gensini, Stefano, 29
The G.P. Clivio Online Dictionary of Italiese (Italian-Italiese-English), 107
gradients of creativity, 108–18
GRADIT (Dictionary of the Use of the Italian Language), 6
gramatica, 132–33n1
grammar, 39–41, 54–56, 132; communal nature of, 46n4; of creativity, 129–30; generative, 49–54; non-restrictive concept of, 44; traditional language education and, 77. *See also* rules
The Grammar of Fantasy (Rodari), 129–30

habla, 58–62
Hacker, Peter M. S., 36
Haller, Hermann W., 114
hate speech, 128
historical perspective, 86–87
Hjelmslev, Louis, 8, 17–18, 27n4, 34, 58, 108
humanity and animality, 9–10
Humboldt, Wilhelm von, 7, 10, 17, 49–54, 55–56, 60, 125
Humboldtian creativity, 112

ideal speaker-listener, 54
infinity of code signs, 70
innate linguistic faculty, 124
innovation, 89
intentional creativity, 111
interference, mechanisms of, 89–90
intermediate creativity, 111–12
Italianisms and Pseudo-Italianisms: about, 88; artificially constructed Italian in, 100–105, *104*; Canadian emigration from Italy, 93; community setting in Canada for, 93, *94*, 100–102, 119n10; creativity of, 126; examples of use of, 93–105, *95–99*; model of contemporary contact, 119n4; rule-governed and rule-changing creativity, 99–100; sociolinguistic framework, 90–92; syntactic framework, 110–13; as worldwide phenomenon, 92–93
Italian suffixation model, 97–99
Italiese: about, 88, 105–7, 117–18; creativity of, 90, 126; as fable, 117–18; generations of Italian Canadians using, 114; as language in its own right, 121n29; as mother tongue and language of necessity, 114–18; vitality of, 128
Iuele-Colilli, Diana, 105–6, 107

jeu de signes appelé langue, 34–37

Karlin, Ann R., 31
"knowing," 2
Kripke, Saul A., 42–43

language: awareness of violations in, 111–12; creativity of, 15–23, 67–68; of culture, 131–32; game, economics and, 31–32; as mathematical operation, 55–57, 70–71, 73, 127, 129; as non-non-creative semiotics, 67–68; as system of united signs, 19–23; universalist issue, 125–26
language, creativity of, 72
language education, 129–32. *See also* educational linguistics
language policy, 74, 131
Languages in Contact (Martinet), 87
langue, 57–62, 72, 96–99
Leopardi, Giacomo, 47, 85, 132
L'Estetica (Croce), 72
Lettera a una professoressa, 84n22
L'Homme (Descartes), 9
linguistic diversity, 86–88
linguistic errors, 96–97

man and animals, 9–10
Marconi, Diego, 36
"marketing" creativity, 112

Martinet, André, 69–70, 87
masse parlante, behavior of, 41–45, 86
mathematical theory and games, 31–32
meaning, 3–5, 20–21, 27n6, 39
merge concept, 56–57
Milani, Don Lorenzo, 84n22
The Minimalist Program (Chomsky), 56–57
Minisemantica (De Mauro), 68–73, 81–82n5
Morgenstern, Oksar, 31
multilingualism, 86–90, 119n8, 125
mutton versus sheep (signs and values), 22

necessity, creativity of, 112, 121n24
negative creativity, 128
Neopolitan expression, 123–24
Neumann, John von, 31
non-creativity, 67
non-non-creative semiotics, 67–68
norma, 58–62, 64n16
normal rule, 34
not-not-creativity, 72–73
Nuessel, Frank, 135–36

object of linguistics, 5; Saussure's, 32
On Interpretation (Aristotle), 69
On Language (Humboldt), 10
Orioles, Vincenzo, 89

Pagliaro, Antonio, 34
Paina, Corrado, 102
painting analogy, 60
parole, 57–62, 72
Peres, Yuval, 31
Performance Descriptors for Language Learners, 78–80
performance *versus* proficiency, 78–80
Philosophical Investigations (Wittgenstein), 11, 26, 34–42, 44, 47–48
Pierno, Franco, 91
Pietropaolo, Domenico, 88, 106, 107
play and language analogy, 20

playfulness of creativity, 129. *See also* game and language
Politics (Aristotle), 8–9, 10
Porphyrian tree, 69
Prampolini, Massimo, 31, 44–45, 45–46n4, 47
Proficiency Guidelines, 78
proficiency *versus* performance, 78–80
Prolegomena (Hjelmslev), 17–18
psychologists, creativity of, 73
psychopedagogists, creativity of, 112
PU. *See Philosophical Investigations* (Wittgenstein)

quaternion, 23–25, 28n11

Rasmussen, Eric, 31
Rasmussen, Michael, 58
regularity and creativity, 34
"return creativity," 111–12
Riccobene, Lina, 114, 115–16
Rodari, Gianni, 129–30, 133–34n5
Romanticism, 1
rule-changing creativity, 54–57, 60, 62, 65–66, 72, 99–100, 107–8, 126–27, 130–32
rule-governed creativity, 48–54, 60, 62, 65–66, 72, 99–100, 110, 127
rules: communal aspect of, 42–45; creative rules and *masse parlante*, 41–45; grammar of a language, 39–41; of language-game, 34–37; linguistic rule in the *PU*, 39–41. *See also* grammar

Sanzone, Daniela, 93
Sapir, Edward, 109, 125
Sapir-Whorf Hypothesis, 109
Saussure, Ferdinand de, 5, 7, 8, 13n2, 18–26, 54, 66, 72, 136
Scarola, Giovanni, 107
scientific approach to creativity. *See* rule-changing creativity; rule-governed creativity; rules
Second Course of Lectures on General Linguistics (Saussure), 21, 29

sectoral uses of language, 127
semiotic analogies between language and game, 29–34
semiotic codes, 15–17
serré system, 23, 24–25, 37
Shohami, Elana, 92
signals in games, 33
sinusoid model for semiotic creativity, 127–28
sistema, norma, and habla, 57–62
skill creativity, 110
social sharing of rules, 41–45
societal multilingualism, 86–88
society, life within, 128–29
sounds and concepts, 21
Spolsky, Bernard, 74
standard creativity, 110–11
Stenius, Erik, 36
Storia linguistica dell'Italia unita (De Mauro), 66
Sullivan, Peter, 36
survival instinct, 133n4
synonym calculability, 71
synonyms, 70–71
syntactic framework of creativity, 110–13
syntax, 67, 71, 84

Tarski, Alfred, 108
teachers as animators, 130
termini technici, 32–33
theoretical and educational linguistic link, 73–81
Theory of Games and Economic Behavior (Neumann and Morgenstern), 31–33

Toronto's multilingual society. *See* Italianisms and Pseudo-Italianisms; Italiese
Tractatus (Wittgenstein), 25, 36–37, 43–44, 47
traditional language education, 77
translations, 22, 26n1, 125–26
Turchetta, Barbara, 92

unintentional creativity, 110–11
universal grammar, 55, 124
universal language, 125–26

vagueness of signs, 57, 126–27
value, system of, 19–23, 27n8, 30–32, 66
Vedovelli, Massimo, 76, 92, 97, 110
vernacular language, 132–33n1
Voltolini, Alberto, 36

Weinreich, Uriel, 54, 88–89
Whorf, Benjamin Lee, 109, 125
Wittgenstein, Ludwig, 11, 25, 34–45, 47–48, 127
Wittgenstein on Rules and Private Language (Kripke), 42–43
Writings in General Linguistics (Saussure), 23–26, 29

X principle of *Dieci Tesi*, 76

Zero-Degree of creativity, 112–14
Zibaldone di pensieri (Leopardi), 85
Zingarelli (dictionary), 6

About the Author

Simone Casini holds a PhD in semiotics and Italian language teaching and learning from the University for Foreigners in Siena. He is assistant professor of semiotics and Italian linguistics at the University of Toronto Mississauga and until 2017 he was professor of educational linguistics at Tuscia University of Viterbo. His studies focus on the science of language, with emphasis on the field of educational linguistics and semiotics. His research concentrates on the analysis of the Italian linguistic space inside and outside national borders. His scholarly publications include *Per uno spazio linguistico personale* (globale): considerazioni tra Italia e Canada (2020) *In principio erat verbum? Tullio De Mauro e le lezioni americane di educazione linguistica democratica* (2019); *Italianismi e pseudoitalianismi: uno sguardo semiotico sull'italiano all'estero* (2018); *Che cosa è la Linguistica educativa* (2016, with M. Vedovelli). In 2019 he was the supervisor of the research project "Sociolinguistics on the Road: Italian Linguistic Landscape" in the GTA funded by the Jackman Humanities Institute, University of Toronto.

www.ingramcontent.com/pod-product-compliance
Lightning Source LLC
Chambersburg PA
CBHW032150010526
44111CB00035B/1436